Donald R. Shaffer

# After the Glory

*The Struggles of*
*Black Civil War Veterans*

University Press of Kansas

Published by the University Press of Kansas (Lawrence, Kansas 66049),
which was organized by the Kansas Board of Regents and is operated and
funded by Emporia State University, Fort Hays State University, Kansas
State University, Pittsburg State University, the University of Kansas, and
Wichita State University

Library of Congress Cataloging-in-Publication Data
Shaffer, Donald Robert.
  After the glory: the struggles of Black Civil War veterans / Donald R.
Shaffer.
    p.   cm. — (Modern war studies)
Includes bibliographical references (p.   ) and index.
    ISBN 0-7006-1328-5 (cloth : alk. paper)
  1. United States—History—Civil War, 1861–1865—Participation,
African American.   2. United States—History—Civil War,
1861–1865—Veterans.   3. African American veterans—History—19th
century.   4. African Americans—History—1863–1877.   I. Title.   II.
Series.
E585.A35S53   2004
305.896'073'008697—dc22                                    2003023965

British Library Cataloguing in Publication Data is available.

Printed in the United States of America

10 9 8 7 6 5 4 3 2 1

# Contents

*A photo section appears after page 96.*

# Acknowledgments

**M**ANY PERSONS ASSISTED ME during the dissertation phase of this project, as well as during the process of turning it into a book for a wider audience. Foremost among them was my doctoral adviser Ira Berlin, who no matter how busy always found the time to offer perceptive criticism and wise advice. The other members of my dissertation committee also provided invaluable assistance. Edward C. Papenfuse, Maryland state archivist, employed me for two summers to study that state's Civil War veterans, providing priceless practical experience with the sources and issues at the heart of this study. Leslie Rowland generously gave of her time to offer constructive criticism of my writing and to share her encyclopedic knowledge of relevant historical literature and primary source materials. David Segal freely shared his knowledge of pertinent scholarly writing outside of history, especially military sociology. Alfred Moss provided friendship and encouragement and helped in countless other ways both large and small. Special thanks are due to the following individuals, who read the manuscript in its various incarnations and offered valuable advice: Gary Gallagher, Deborah Gershenowitz, Louis S. Gerteis, Herman Hattaway, Larry Logue, Stuart McConnell, Ted Ownby, and Elizabeth Regosin. The following people also provided support along the way, and although space prevents me from describing their contributions individually, their assistance helped this project reach its final form. They are (in alphabetical order) Richard Bensel, David W. Blight, Maxwell Bloomfield, Paul Cimbala, Catherine Clinton, Marshall Clough, Pauline Dambournet, Eric T. Dean, Lawrence B. de Graaf, Gaines Foster, Jennifer Frost, Barbara Gannon, Joseph T. Glatthaar, Patrick J. Kelley, Barry LaPoint, Gordon B. McKinney, Margaret Merrick, Randall M. Miller, Robert and Stephanie Morrow, Earl Mulderink, Michael P. Musick, James C. Riley, Nick Salvatore, Michael Siedenhaus, Richard J. Sommers, Paul Taillon, Larry Wimmer, and Janet Worrall.

# Abbreviations

| | |
|---|---|
| AME | African Methodist Episcopal |
| FSSP | Freedom and Southern Society Project, University of Maryland, College Park |
| GAR | Grand Army of the Republic |
| GPO | Government Printing Office |
| NAACP | National Association for the Advancement of Colored People |
| NHDVS | National Home for Disabled Volunteer Soldiers |
| RG | Record Group |
| USCC | United States Colored Cavalry |
| USCHA | United States Colored Heavy Artillery |
| USCI | United States Colored Infantry |
| USCLA | United States Colored Light Artillery |
| USCT | United States Colored Troops |
| VA | Veterans Administration |
| WPA | Works Progress Administration |

# Introduction

I N JUNE 1864, James Monroe Trotter wrote a letter to Edward W. Kinsley, a well-connected Bostonian and strong supporter of the African-American troops in the Union army. Then a sergeant in the all-black 55th Massachusetts Infantry, Trotter (see fig. 11) proved to be an ambitious man with wide-ranging interests in politics, business, and the arts after the war.[1] (His son, William Monroe Trotter, would become a prominent civil rights activist and editor of the *Boston Guardian.*) The letter was the second of nine such missives from Trotter that would survive among Kinsley's papers. In these letters, Trotter already showed the determination he would exhibit in his postwar activities. He passionately informed Kinsley of the situation of the men in his regiment—their anger at being paid less than white soldiers and other discrimination they faced, as well as the aspiration of Trotter and other leading African-American soldiers in the 55th to receive commissions as officers. Most important, Trotter also communicated the essence of what black soldiers were fighting for in the Civil War. "It is a great Principle," Trotter wrote to Kinsley, "that for the attainment of which we gladly peril our lives—Manhood & Equality."[2]

Like their white counterparts, Northern and Southern, Trotter and other African-American soldiers believed they were fighting for a cause. Rather than Southern independence, states' rights, or preservation of the Union, they fought for freedom and the occasion to actualize that freedom by gaining for black men the same opportunities, rights, and status enjoyed by white men. It was no mistake that James Monroe Trotter used the term *manhood.* As Trotter's word choice and the nature of his complaints to Kinsley suggest, black soldiers reckoned their position in gendered terms. Theirs was a battle not for freedom in the abstract but for the visible trappings of nineteenth-century manhood. They wanted to demonstrate their manly status tangibly.

African-American soldiers[3] in the Civil War were certainly not alone in this aspiration. After initial skepticism, historians since World War II have come to recognize the quest of black men for manhood as a significant theme in the study of African Americans in the nineteenth century. The priority of scholars in the 1950s and early 1960s, such as Kenneth Stampp and Stanley

Elkins, was discrediting the notion of planter benevolence by emphasizing
the oppression of American slavery. They could hardly credit the existence
of significant manhood among male slaves, given what they saw as the overwhelming and malevolent power of slaveholders.[4] Beginning in the late 1960s,
however, other authors described male slaves exhibiting manly prerogatives
even within the oppressive restrictions of chattel bondage. John Blassingame
contended that slaveholders generally found it beneficial to interfere as little
as possible in the internal family matters of their slaves, giving black men some
leeway to exercise male authority. Male slaves were able to bolster their status
further by acquiring extra food, making furniture, or in other ways providing
independently for their families.[5] Eugene Genovese agreed with Blassingame's
assessment and went even further by claiming that the presence of male slaves
on the plantation limited the sexual exploitation of black women by white men.[6]
It was Herbert Gutman, however, in his analysis of slave naming practices, who
most strongly defended the manhood of male slaves. Gutman believed that the
common practice of naming children for their fathers was potent evidence of
men's high standing in the slave community. He stated, "It strongly disputes
frequent assertions that assign a negligible role to slave fathers and insist that
'patriarchal' status came only after black men 'acquired property' or assimi-
lated 'American attitudes and patterns of behavior' following emancipation and
the 'breaking down of social isolation.'"[7]

More recent scholarship has explored the limits of male power among
African Americans in the nineteenth century. Both Deborah Gray White and
James Oliver Horton have emphasized that for black men, slave and free, their
relative lack of access to economic resources compared with white men limited their power over black women. "In almost all societies where men consistently dominate women, their control is based on male ownership and
distribution of property and/or control of certain culturally valued subsis-
tence goods," stated White.[8] With weaker access to such economic power,
African-American men before and after emancipation were forced to find
alternative ways to bolster their manhood. Prince Hall Masonry, the Masonic
tradition for African-American men (since they were denied admission to
white lodges), provided one such avenue. Maurice Wallace wrote, "Through
their Masonic affiliation, well-known ex-slaves and free black men . . . were
helped, as it were, 'along the road to self-hood.'"[9] According to Michelle
Mitchell, African Americans' activity in Africa during the nineteenth century
provided another path to strengthen manhood. "Africa appeared to be one

of the few fields where black Americans could flex muscle, build nations, and demonstrate virility by fending off white-skinned intruders," she stated.[10]

Despite these creative approaches described by Mitchell and Wallace, racism placed considerable limits on black men in the exercise of their manhood, especially as the nineteenth century drew to a close. Numerous scholars have attempted to define the position of American men at the turn of the century, particularly among the articulate middle and upper classes. They have debated whether these men were in a crisis of manhood during this period.[11] In an influential study, Gail Bederman denied the existence of such a crisis but asserted that middle-class men did find their superior position in American society threatened at the end of the nineteenth century. Economic change, Bederman claimed, was denying more and more men access to the resources that underlay their relatively exalted status, and they faced competition from working-class and immigrant men for power in politics, as well as women's demands for suffrage. One way these men reacted, according to Bederman, was increasingly to buttress manly prerogatives with white supremacy. She stated, "Middle-class white Americans [starting in the 1880s] were discovering an extraordinary variety of ways to link male power to race."[12] Yet by tying their manly superiority to race, they undercut manhood for nonwhites, especially African Americans. Such was the situation faced by black men in American society by the late nineteenth century.

Yet as previous scholarship demonstrates, the reaction of black men in the nineteenth century to attempts to deny them their manhood was anything but passive. Although white racism certainly circumscribed their privileges as men, it could not eliminate them entirely—not for the least reason that at midcentury, African Americans experienced a revolution in their lives due to the Civil War and emancipation. It is unquestionable that the Civil War was a seminal moment in the history of black men in the nineteenth century. It opened up new opportunities for African Americans in the exercise of manhood that heretofore had been closed, often to free black men as well as to slaves. The advent of suffrage and full citizenship during Reconstruction finally put African-American men on equal footing with their white counterparts, at least in theory, in terms of manhood rights under the U.S. Constitution. The question became whether such theoretical gains could be translated into real and permanent improvements.

Hence, the story of black manhood in the nineteenth century is dominated not only by shifting and intensifying white racism but also by emancipation and how that seismic event played out in ordinary lives. Perhaps no group is better suited to an examination of this phenomenon than African-American veterans of the Civil War. They are well documented as a group, and their experience helps clarify the outer boundaries of black manhood for the Civil War generation. Black soldiers in the Union army went almost overnight from the abject subjugation of slaves to the exercise of manly power as soldiers. But as spectacular as the effect of military service in the Civil War was on the manhood of African-American troops, their battle for manhood after the Civil War was much more profound, if less dramatic. In one sense, their postwar fight is merely emblematic of the larger battle of all African Americans to maintain their gains as a result of the Civil War and Reconstruction. Black men and women from many walks of life, not just veterans, fought against the counterrevolution of Jim Crow and disfranchisement that came to the United States at the end of the nineteenth century. Yet in another sense, former soldiers are a particularly important group to study because they enjoyed certain advantages compared with nonveterans in confronting the resurgence of racism and discrimination after the end of Reconstruction. If any group in African-American society could have preserved its gains from the Civil War and Reconstruction, it was veterans. That they were at least partly successful demonstrates how the legacy of their service, and other advantages they enjoyed, could help mitigate the indignities of black life during the last decades of the nineteenth century and the first decades of the twentieth. Still, at best, black veterans achieved a partial victory, preserving some but not all of the manhood they had won.

So what did manhood mean for African-American veterans following the Civil War? First, it is necessary to emphasize that its meaning was dynamic and contingent. As Bederman asserted, manhood is "an ongoing ideological process, [which] implies constant contradiction, change, and renegotiation."[13] Black ex-soldiers, like other groups of men, redefined the meaning of manhood over time. For example, in the immediate aftermath of the war, with the future state of Southern society in flux, assertiveness was much more of a manly ideal than it would be later on. Second, place as well as time helped shape the meaning of manhood for African-American veterans.[14] Although veterans from the South, particularly former slaves, were much more likely to be assertive immediately after the war, over the course of the entire postwar period, Northern veterans exhibited this quality more consistently, as they were freer from white repression, especially violent repression. Third, the prewar backgrounds of veterans made a difference. Former soldiers who had been free before the Civil War were likely to react more quickly and vociferously throughout the postwar period to perceived assaults on their manhood. Besides being more likely to respond to racist affronts, they also tended to counter them in an organized fashion.

In other words, manhood could mean many things for African-American veterans—including, but not limited to, money, power, pride, dignity, respect, self-control, citizenship, autonomy, bravery, physical prowess, fraternal solidarity, and patriarchal authority—but its exact character depended on when, where, and who, as well as on what. That is, the character of manhood was also contingent on the arena of battle, or what was being fought over. The struggle of black Union veterans for manhood appears to have encompassed six discernible areas: politics, veteran-government relations, economics, family and marital life, interracial and intraracial veteran relations, and historical memory. These categories are not mutually exclusive. Nonetheless, each one assists in understanding the complex process in African-American veterans' postwar fight for manhood. They achieved more success preserving their manly status in some areas than in others, and their relative success often varied as they advanced or lost ground over time.

Politics was one area in which the fortunes of African-American veterans changed as the years passed. It also was inevitable that politics became a key arena of their struggle. In the nineteenth-century United States, political rights, especially suffrage, became a badge of manhood. State legislatures in the early part of the century removed property requirements for voting, leading to universal white male suffrage in all but three states by 1828.[15] Black soldiers, not surprisingly, strongly desired the franchise as a validation of their manhood, as a sign that they were just as good as white men, and as a reward for manly service in the war. African-American troops and recently returned veterans would play an integral role in the advent of African-American suffrage, both as activists for the cause and in providing ideological and emotional justifications to white Northerners for giving black men the vote.

After this initial impressive success, however, their significance as a political force would diminish considerably, though never disappear completely, partly as a response, ironically, to the demands of manhood in the competitive political climate of the postwar South. As veterans fought with black nonveterans and with one another for manly dominance in electoral politics and community leadership, collectively they helped to undermine the position of African Americans in Reconstruction. In any case, it is doubtful how effective black veterans could have been as a political force, given the rise of legal disfranchisement in the late nineteenth century. As the memory of black service in the war quickly faded, so did a sense of gratitude and obligation on the part of federal authorities and the Northern public. On a number of occasions, former African-American soldiers demanded federal intervention to preserve their civil rights and those of other people of their race, but those demands would fall largely on deaf ears.

They would enjoy much more success claiming financial assistance from the federal government on the basis of their Civil War service. The U.S. Congress made black ex-soldiers and their survivors equally eligible under the law as whites for social welfare benefits. By far, the biggest part of this generosity was Civil War military pensions. Though in practice they did not receive a fair share of the program's proceeds, black veterans and their survivors over time collected an enormous amount of money, in addition to significant sums in the form of bounties and back pay due from military service. Government money helped black veterans satisfy societal expectations for economic manhood. Federal pensions and other forms of social welfare directed at former soldiers improved their financial position and made it easier for them to accumulate productive forms of wealth. Access to government assistance ensured that, in general, Civil War veterans were more prosperous than other African Americans and better able to fulfill their responsibilities as providers to their families.

Indeed, family and marriage constituted a notable area of success in black ex-soldiers' quest for manhood. Previous scholarship has demonstrated that black soldiers and other men of their race were able to wrest their families away from the control of slaveholders during the Civil War and to resist white interference with their families early in Reconstruction.[16] *After the Glory* moves beyond this story to a significant but heretofore little appreciated battle among African Americans in the decades following freedom (documented in veterans' sources) to define the meaning of marriage in the black community. The survival of informal marriage, despite the efforts of those who wanted to stamp it out in favor of formal marriage, provides evidence of the limits of male power in the postwar black family. Informal marriage practices, with their roots in slavery, evidently resulted in more egalitarian partnerships for African-American couples and made it easier for black women to leave undesirable unions.

Yet the manhood of African-American veterans cannot be reckoned entirely in terms of their authority within the family, access to economic resources, political influence, or relationship with the federal government. Indeed, to the extent that evidence explicitly suggests how black ex-soldiers judged their progress as men, it was in large part dependent on their relationship with white Union veterans and the degree to which American society as a whole remembered and acknowledged their role in the Civil War.

Black veterans achieved notable success in gaining acceptance into the principal Union veterans' organization, the Grand Army of the Republic (GAR). The GAR officially followed a color-blind membership policy; consequently, many African-American veterans were able to join this fraternal organization. Just as black soldiers had wanted to be part of the Union army during the Civil War, they valued inclusion in the GAR as an important measure of white Union veterans' respect for their manhood. And they did receive genuine respect from former white soldiers in this group. Indeed, the GAR was a notable exception to the usual practice of U.S. fraternal organizations in the nineteenth century, which was to exclude African Americans from white-organized groups.

Yet even with their acceptance into the GAR, African Americans still faced discrimination within the organization. The Grand Army's interracial ideal ignored the reality that most black veterans, Northern and Southern, attended segregated posts (the organization's local-level structure). Hence, because most GAR activity took place locally, the racial separation of American society during the late nineteenth and early twentieth centuries tended to prevail. Likewise, despite the genuine respect that most white Union veterans had for their black counterparts, many harbored racist feelings as well. These sentiments would increasingly push white Union veterans away from African Americans and toward reconciliation with ex-Confederates. Consequently, in terms of interracial veteran relations, black ex-soldiers found their manhood both reinforced and undermined.

Like interracial veteran relations, historical memory proved both conducive and problematic to the manhood of African-American veterans. It certainly allowed them to articulate their vision of the Civil War and what they believed they had achieved in it as men. Black ex-soldiers portrayed themselves in manly terms, as heroes fighting to free their people from bondage and rescue an undeserving nation from dissolution. Their vision of the war, in which emancipation was central, put them at odds not only with Confederate veterans but also with former Union soldiers, especially as these two groups increasingly reconciled with each other beginning in the last years of the nineteenth century. One cost of that rapprochement was that black veterans found themselves and their interpretation of the Civil War increasingly degraded or forgotten in American society, and their sense of manly self-worth was injured as a result. Only in recent decades, in large part a legacy of the civil rights revolution of the mid–twentieth century, has the memory of black Civil War soldiers been revived and these men honored.

*After the Glory* explores all these topics in relation to African-American veterans' quest for manhood. By necessity, it examines their struggle from a national perspective, instead of through the geographically concentrated focus of a state or local study. The broader approach is particularly appropriate given the lack of previous work on this topic. Likewise, since African Americans (unlike white veterans) never formed a permanent organization that helped define their identity and relationship to postwar American society, the book approaches their experience through collective biography. This study is based largely on information gathered about two study groups: a random sample of just over 1,000 ordinary black soldiers, and a second group of about 200 African-American veterans who engaged in notable activities in the postwar period. The aim of examining these two groups is to understand the lives of both ordinary and extraordinary veterans. Studying ordinary veterans uncovers the overall patterns in their postwar lives and how they compared with other African Americans and with white veterans of the Civil War, both Union and Confederate. Exploring the careers of notable black veterans is also important, not only because of their role in postwar politics and as community leaders but also because they most fully articulated the meaning of the Civil War for African-American veterans.

Hence, this book is a social history of the postwar lives of the black men who donned the Union blue during the Civil War. As is often the case with social history, it relies in part on fragmentary sources that illuminate the lives of the mostly obscure men studied: a few black veterans' autobiographies; a small number of surviving books, articles, and letters they wrote; newspapers to which they subscribed; and, for the handful of men who survived until the mid to late 1930s, the Works Progress Administration (WPA) Slave Narratives compiled by the Federal Writers' Project. However, the most noteworthy source for *After the Glory* was Civil War pension files at the National Archives in Washington, D.C. The documents in these files provide a wide variety of biographical information about individual veterans before, during, and after the Civil War, as well as the survivors of deceased soldiers and veterans. Pension files are especially valuable, in that they help preserve the words of ordinary veterans, their survivors, and other members of the black community during the late nineteenth and early twentieth centuries, giving normally voiceless African Americans of the Civil War generation a way to express their ideas and values decades before the more famous WPA interviews.

The information generated from the aforementioned sources is quantitative and anecdotal. Both types are used in the body of this book, but a detailed description of sources and an explanation of the book's methodology have been left to an appendix. This strategy is intended to make *After the Glory* more accessible to casual readers while still allowing interested persons to analyze more fully the basis for its conclusions.

What follows in the prologue is a brief recapitulation of black soldiers' wartime experiences. Although their story has been told many times by now, it is necessary to describe it once again for the benefit of readers who may not be familiar with one of the most fascinating tales of the Civil War. It is retold, though, with an emphasis on the soldiers' quest for manhood. The first chapter also provides necessary background, examining the postwar transition of black soldiers from the Union army. The subsequent six chapters explore different themes related to the struggle of African-American veterans for manhood: veterans' life patterns (with an emphasis on their economic position and social reputation in the black community), political involvement and community leadership, family and marital lives, experience with social welfare (especially federal pensions), postwar comradeship among African Americans and with white veterans, and Civil War memory. Their story is not merely another tale of race in America; it is also a story of gender and how these categories of analysis intersected in the lives of a group of men as they sought to judge their progress against their white counterparts in American society. In the words of James Monroe Trotter, black Civil War veterans wanted both "Manhood & Equality." Although they might characterize manhood differently, depending on the context, it was important to them that their manly prerogatives be comparable to those of white men. It was this sense of parity that was essentially the aim of their quest for manhood. This study explores their progress toward that goal.

# Prologue

THE QUEST OF BLACK VETERANS for equal manhood began during the Civil War. That it began there should not be surprising. The Civil War was a seminal event in the history of black people in the United States. The North found that it could not win the war without destroying slavery and liberating the vast majority of African Americans who were still enmeshed in bondage in the Southern states at the beginning of the conflict. Not surprisingly, emancipation brought fundamental changes to the lives of former slaves as they hastened to take advantage of the new opportunities made possible by freedom. Yet for no group of African Americans was the transformation quite so dramatic as for black soldiers. In a brief period, many of these men went from powerless chattel to armed warriors in what was effectively an army of liberation. Military service exposed them to the possibilities of freedom sooner and more intensely than other people of their race. Despite its costs, especially the risk of injury, illness, or death, overall, black soldiers from both slave and free backgrounds found themselves empowered by their time in the Union army during the Civil War—empowered in ways that bolstered their manhood.

Yet such empowerment would have appeared highly unlikely at the beginning of the war. Black men who attempted to join the Union army in 1861 and the first half of 1862 were turned away. The North, as well as the South, denied that slavery was an issue in the war early on, and both sides openly proclaimed that the fight would be only between white men. Hence, black men were explicitly denied the right to fight because most white Americans refused to recognize them as men. Yet by 1862, with horrendous casualties and battlefield setbacks discouraging whites from joining up, Abraham Lincoln was forced to begin accepting black men into the Union army. Large-scale recruitment of African Americans commenced the following year and continued for the rest of the war. By its end, just over 178,000 black men had joined the Union army (and approximately 10,000 to 18,000 more served in the Union navy).[1]

Whereas black recruitment was largely a matter of military necessity from the perspective of the Lincoln administration, African Americans had their own reasons for wanting to fight for the Union. Many black men, free men of color as well as slaves, were eager to strike a blow against slavery. Indeed, freedom was the foremost motivation behind their enlistment. White Northerners battled to save the Union, and white Southerners fought for Southern independence, but African-American troops joined up not just to gain freedom for themselves but also to release their people from bondage. Thomas J. Morgan, a white Union officer questioning black recruits in Tennessee, discovered this fact for himself. When one man told Morgan that his motive for joining the army was to "fight for freedom," the officer reminded him that as a soldier he might be killed. The recruit replied simply, "But my people will be free."[2]

Significantly, black men also felt that military service would prove them to be the equals of whites as both soldiers and men and would discredit notions of racial inferiority. Many white commentators had mocked the worth of African Americans as potential soldiers early in the war, claiming that black men did not possess the intelligence, courage, or discipline necessary to make good soldiers. In other words, they did not possess the requisite manly qualities. Therefore, black men—slave and free—entered the Union army to prove that they could perform as well as or even better than white troops. They enlisted to prove their equality as men. As Robert A. Pinn, a black veteran from Ohio, later put it, "I was eager to become a soldier, in order to prove by feeble efforts the black mans rights to untrammeled manhood."[3]

Proving their manhood was a motive of no small significance to African Americans who enlisted in the Union army. In an age that increasingly associated masculinity with ambition, aggressiveness, and the exercise of power, black men were often denied opportunities to assert these qualities. On the plantation, slaveholders had usurped to varying degrees the masculine role of male slaves as fathers, brothers, and husbands, depending on their willingness to delegate authority. Poverty and discrimination also interfered with the ability of free men of color to affirm their manhood because they were denied the means to support their families properly.[4] Hence, many black men eagerly accepted the chance to serve as Union soldiers because it allowed them to adopt the ultimate manly role—warrior.

Military service, then, seemingly offered African Americans the chance to be men in the fullest sense of the word, and many of them readily grasped the apparent opportunity. Yet being real men necessitated equality off the battlefield as well as on. Many African Americans joined the Union army not only for the prospect of freedom but also because of the explicit promises of recruiters that they would be treated the same as white soldiers. While white officers of black troops, especially the most sympathetic, may have opted for what Reid Mitchell has called the "familial model of race relations," seeing African-American soldiers in essence as grown-up children in need of paternal care, the soldiers wanted the respect due adult men.[5] They certainly understood and accepted the power differential between themselves and their officers, but they did not want a paternal relationship to characterize it. Black soldiers wanted the same basic dignity that white soldiers could expect from their officers—above all, they desired equal treatment with their enlisted white counterparts as their manly due.

It is the way that black soldiers tied their conception of manhood to equality that explains their passionate reaction to discrimination in the Union army. Perhaps the most galling example of unequal treatment was the issue of pay. White privates received $13 per month plus a $3 clothing allowance; soldiers with higher ranks received more pay. Black soldiers, regardless of rank, received $10 per month with $3 deducted for clothing. The difference angered many African-American troops from both free and slave backgrounds, not only because they had been promised the same wages as white troops when they enlisted but also because the reduced pay made it harder for them to support their families and suggested that they were not worth as much in the eyes of the federal government—issues at the core of their sense of masculine self-identity. Not being able to sustain their families or not being treated as the equals of white soldiers was not to be real men.[6]

Yet the reaction of black soldiers to this affront to their manly dignity was not consistent. In some regiments, most notably the 54th and 55th Massachusetts Infantry, soldiers responded in a restrained manner. They refused to accept any money until the federal government agreed to pay all black soldiers in the Union army the same amount they paid white soldiers. The Massachusetts troops even refused a well-intentioned offer from the state's governor, John A. Andrew, to equalize their pay out of state funds. Andrew's plan, they believed, would force them to betray black Union soldiers from non-Massachusetts regiments whose pay would not be equalized. These men would accept equal pay only from the federal government as a test, as Edward W. Kinsley explained it to Andrew, of whether "a colored man shall be acknowledged a man by even the U.S. Govt."[7] Yet for other black soldiers, the affront to their manhood demanded more drastic action. Some black soldiers from South Carolina, when confronted with unequal pay, refused to continue serving, committing mutiny under military law. The leader of the group, Sgt. William Walker, was executed for this crime in February 1864. Apparently, these South Carolina soldiers, bereft of the support of white officers enjoyed in the Massachusetts regiments, felt that only confrontation could bring them redress for their grievances as men.[8]

Hence, although black soldiers were united in their opposition to unequal pay as an offense against their manhood, the nature of their reaction seems to have been shaped by whether they received support for their resistance from their white officers. That support was essential because the refusal to accept pay, as well as the refusal to continue service, technically constituted mutiny. The more moderate response was possible only when officers declined to prosecute soldiers who refused to accept their pay. For instance, when white officers of the 14th Rhode Island Artillery, a black unit, pursued courts-martial against members of a company that refused to accept unequal pay, they sparked a violent confrontation between the unit's officers and men in which an African-American soldier was killed.[9]

It also was an insult to the manhood of more ambitious black Civil War soldiers that very few African Americans received commissions as officers. Union commanders proved resistant to commissioning African Americans because of the prospect of white soldiers coming under the command of black officers, something many whites—even those sympathetic to black people— found utterly objectionable. A handful of black men received line commissions shortly before being mustered out, and a somewhat greater number received staff commissions as chaplains or in other positions outside of the chain of command, but even in these positions black men were rare.[10]

The most vociferous reaction to the exclusion of black men from officers' commissions seems to have come from free men of color. Many free men of color, especially those from elite backgrounds, saw themselves as logical candidates for commissions. After all, in white volunteer regiments, Northern and Southern, officers were usually chosen from among local dignitaries. When these black soldiers were denied what they saw as natural positions of leadership among their own people, the perceived insult to their manhood could prompt an impassioned response. Such sensitivity was most notable in Louisiana's Native Guard regiments hastily organized by Benjamin Butler

in 1862. These units, the greatest exception to the general practice of not commissioning African Americans, were composed initially of black officers at
the company level. These captains and lieutenants came mostly from the freeborn, mulatto elite of New Orleans. They believed that they deserved their
positions not only by virtue of their background but also because they had
distinguished themselves as leaders in battle at Port Hudson and Milliken's
Bend in the spring of 1863, the first major engagements in which black troops
participated. Yet their reward for manly leadership in combat was that Butler's
successor, Nathaniel P. Banks, continued to force them from their commands
(as he had before these battles) and replace them with white officers, fearing
their effect on the morale of white troops. Their letters of resignation resound
with the rhetoric of wounded manhood. "We did most certainly expect the
Priviledges, and respect due to a soldier who had offered his services and his
life to his government," wrote one group of black officers. "This we have not
received, on the contrary, we have met with scorn and contempt."[11]

The prejudice against black soldiers in the Union army also ensured that
they saw less combat than white soldiers. (In other words, they had less chance
to prove manly courage under fire.) Indeed, some Union authorities felt that
African-American troops were suitable only for fatigue duty, involving hard
and unrelenting physical labor. Black soldiers built fortifications, dug
trenches, and served as stevedores loading and unloading military supplies.
African-American troops chafed against such treatment as an insult to their
manhood. As one black soldier complained to the secretary of war about the
treatment he was receiving in the Union army, "we Expected to be Treeated
as men but we have been Treeated more Like Dogs."[12]

Despite the attempts of some military authorities to limit their use to labor
or garrison duty, many African-American troops eventually came under fire.
Black soldiers' use in combat, like their acceptance in the army, became a
military necessity. By the last years of the war, with casualties mounting and
the enlistments of many white Union soldiers expiring, they could no longer
be spared from the battlefield. Hence, Gen. Ulysses S. Grant extensively utilized black troops in his 1864 and 1865 campaigns in the East. African Americans in the elite regiments of Massachusetts also participated in significant
engagements because Governor Andrew maneuvered to place the state's black
soldiers under the command of generals who would use them in battle.
African-American troops stationed on the Atlantic coast and west of the Ap-
palachians saw less combat and more labor and garrison duty. Nonetheless,

black soldiers played a significant part in the battles of Franklin and Nashville, the most important battles in the West late in the war.[13]

Despite the fact that black soldiers generally saw less combat than their white counterparts, the cost in black soldiers' lives during the Civil War was considerable. More than 36,000 African-American troops died in the Union army, about one-fifth of the men who served. Disease was the major killer of black soldiers. Although the majority of Civil War soldiers (in an era when germ theory was still unknown) died of pneumonia, typhoid fever, smallpox, and other ailments rather than from battle wounds, the percentage of African Americans who perished from disease was higher than that of their white counterparts in the Union army. About 80 percent of black soldiers who died in the Civil War died of disease, compared with only about 60 percent of white Union soldiers.[14] The higher death rate should not be surprising, considering the poorer conditions prevalent in the camps of black soldiers, as well as the fact that African Americans (especially former slaves) generally entered Union service in worse health than did white recruits.[15]

Despite the indignities they faced, African-American soldiers remained committed to the Union cause. They deserted less often than their white comrades did. More than 14 percent of Northern white soldiers deserted during the war, compared with less than 5 percent of black soldiers.[16] Desertion was certainly less appealing for black troops; many African-American soldiers had escaped from slavery to join the army, and returning home would result in re-enslavement and possibly retribution from their owners for having run away in the first place. Yet destroying slavery and proving their manhood also gave black soldiers a stronger motive for staying in the army than white troops had. Ordinary black soldiers realized the momentous stakes for themselves and their people in the war. Freedom and their vindication as men were specific and substantial goals that portended a positive and revolutionary change in their daily lives, well worth fighting and dying for.

Black troops also deserted less frequently because military service offered them the opportunity to enhance their manhood by bettering themselves individually. Certainly the most notable way that this improvement occurred was through education. African-American soldiers realized that book learning—reading, writing, and arithmetic—could improve their lives after the war and help them assert themselves as men. Consequently, different groups of black soldiers appealed to Union authorities to establish schools in the army. "I have the honor to call your attention To the necessity of having a school for The benefit of our regement," wrote John Sweeny, a black soldier from Kentucky in a typical petition. "We have never Had an institutiong of that sort and Stand deeply inneed of instruction the majority of us having been slaves. We wish to have some benefit of education To make ourselves capable of buisness In the future. . . . We wish to become a People capable of self support as we are Capable of being soldiers."[17] In other words, Sweeny and other black soldiers believed that in order to operate autonomously as men in the postwar period, they needed to learn how to read and write so that they could compete against white men, most of whom already enjoyed the benefits of learning. In their opinion, not to be educated was to be lesser men, dependent on others.

For its part, the leadership of the Union army embraced education, like the blacks' role in combat, as a military necessity. Only a small percentage of black recruits from slave backgrounds could read and write, and their illiteracy increased the burden on officers by forcing them to do many errands or clerical tasks that enlisted men ordinarily would have completed in white units. Officers with abolitionist leanings also encouraged the education of black soldiers because they believed that learning would help elevate African Americans. Unfortunately, the Union army formulated no general policy to make educational opportunities available to all black soldiers who desired them. Still, a number of schools for African-American troops were established through the efforts of sympathetic white officers and Northern missionaries. Most of these efforts were aimed at recently liberated slaves, but schools also appeared in regiments composed of free men of color, such as the 55th Massachusetts Infantry and the 5th Massachusetts Heavy Artillery.[18]

When it occurred, the effect of education could be powerful. George R. Sherman, a white officer in the 7th U.S. Colored Infantry (USCI), recruited in Maryland, later wrote about this phenomenon. The 7th established classes for the corporals and sergeants in the regiment, who in turn taught what they learned to the privates. Instruction in reading, writing, and arithmetic continued for three years, right up to the unit's disbandment. Sherman claimed that by the time the men of the 7th USCI left the army, "nearly all of them could read, a large percentage could write fairly well, and many had acquired considerable knowledge of the elementary branches." What impressed Sherman even more was the impact of education on the character and behavior of black soldiers. His troops went home, he wrote, "with views enlarged, ambition aroused, and their interest in the outside world thoroughly awakened."[19] In short, education roused in his men a sense of manly interest in the world. It made them more capable of exercising their manhood and functioning in a competitive world of men.

The Union army also gave many black soldiers the chance to gain leadership skills through service as noncommissioned officers. About 16 percent of black soldiers achieved noncommissioned rank in the Union army.[20] Army life provided those promoted to leadership positions the opportunity, as Joseph Glatthaar put it, "to supervise men in crises and formulate sensible decisions with lives hanging in the balance, which fostered a keen sense of responsibility and instilled confidence in themselves and their decision-making ability." In other words, the army often allowed African Americans with leadership potential to develop it.[21]

Civil War service also provided African-American soldiers with political training. They acquired political skills fighting the discriminatory policies of the Union army, particularly its attempts to pay them less than white soldiers. Fighting for equal pay energized and united black soldiers from different backgrounds in a common struggle. They gained valuable experience writing petitions, practicing passive and active forms of resistance, and cultivating sympathetic politicians and other leading men whose influence might persuade the federal government to change its discriminatory policies. Although political and leadership skills were not absolutely essential to the manhood of black veterans individually, they would prove invaluable collectively as African Americans sought to assert themselves as a group after the war.

Finally, armed service proved psychologically beneficial to black soldiers, especially former slaves. Military service helped erase instincts of subservience built up over decades in bondage and increased the confidence of black soldiers. It allowed heretofore powerless men to awaken their manhood by exerting power over their former oppressors. During the war, black soldiers fought Confederate troops and confiscated supplies from white Southerners. After the war, they served as military police in Southern cities and liquidated surviving pockets of slavery in the countryside.

Although having authority over white Southerners was therapeutic, for most soldiers, just being a soldier was enough to have a profound psychological effect. For the first time in many of these men's lives, they were not treated as property, constantly associated with a white owner and without their own identity. As soldiers, they could finally be real people, real men. Noah Rodgers, a Mississippi veteran, expressed this reality to an interviewer from the Federal Writers' Project late in his life. "He says that he thought he was a soldier in the Southern army, since he had to go everywhere with his young master," wrote a WPA interviewer of Rodgers's time as a servant in the Confederate army. "But after he was captured [and joined the Union army] he knew that he was a real soldier as so minny times he had to go [it] alone."[22] Indeed, despite the indignities black soldiers faced within the Union army, it was often the first time in their lives that at least some white persons treated them in a relatively just and equal manner. They were under the same regulations governing white soldiers, and if black soldiers transgressed these rules, they could expect due process rights instead of the arbitrary judgments of slaveholders. "They accepted punishments without complaint or signs of dissatisfaction," stated a white officer of black troops after the war. "The fairness of such treatment was once commented on by my top sergeant as a contrast to that accorded them as slaves."[23]

Indeed, the morale of African-American soldiers rose and fell in direct proportion to their perception of whether they were being treated equally with their white counterparts, with the requisite manly respect. When they were relegated to fatigue duty, the mood of black soldiers declined. Such work details reminded them all too much of slavery and dashed their hopes of being treated as men worthy of doing a soldier's real duty. When released from work details, their spirits rose. James Peet, chaplain of the 50th USCI, observed as much. "Since being relieved from heavy fatigue work heretofore required," he reported to Adj. Gen. Lorenzo Thomas in 1864, "there is a manifest improvement in the appearance and cheerfulness of the men."[24]

On those occasions when African-American troops acted in combat roles, there was also an improvement in their morale. Another perceptive army chaplain, C. W. Buckley of the 47th USCI, also noticed this fact after the men of his regiment returned from an expedition into Confederate-controlled territory. "The march has promoted a *martial spirit* among the troops," Buckley wrote. "They returned to camp, in spite of their hardship, with a greater fondness for the *profession of arms* and with an increased satisfaction with their present situation as soldiers of the Republic."[25]

Most beneficial to the psyche of black soldiers was the knowledge that they were part of a larger, noble cause. Chaplain Buckley perceived as much in his report on his unit's expedition. "The bringing together of the whole division of colored troops and taking them into the field," he observed, "caused the men to feel that they are engaged in no unimportant service. The sight itself of so many of their own race in one body devoted to one cause, is not without good results; it tends to promote contentment and ardor akin to enthusiasm."[26] Hence, it was beneficial to black soldiers not only to be treated as men personally but also to see other African Americans being treated as men in pursuit of liberating their race from bondage.

Although Buckley was speaking strictly in terms of military morale, his comments have larger implications. It benefited black soldiers psychologically to realize that, after being powerless for so long, they could work together to destroy slavery. The ability to take collective action increased their pride and self-confidence. Still, their simple recognition as soldiers could have the same effect. Performing noncombat duties that black troops regarded as worthy of manly reverence was enough to raise their spirits. Chaplain Peet observed that even the sorrowful task of burying their dead comrades increased the morale of African-American troops if accompanied by the proper military pomp. Peet wrote, "Military escorts have this month accompanied the remains of the deceased to the grave, for the first time I believe, since the regiment was organized. The effect, apparently, is most excellent, causing the men to feel they are regard[ed] *as soldiers.*"[27]

Families and the black community as a whole encouraged African-American troops in their manly role as soldiers. Through the suffering and hardships they encountered, black men generally knew that they had the support of the people that counted most, and they could take comfort and encouragement from that fact. Elmo Steele, a black Mississippi veteran who survived into the 1930s, reported as much to the Federal Writers' Project. During his interview with the WPA interviewer, he recalled his father's reaction to his plans to join the Union army. "I will never fergit how he looked at me an' put his hand on my head an' say, 'My son yo' will make a good soldier.'" Steele continued: "Dem words made me feel good an' helped me over many a rough places in the turrible times dat followed. Deir would times when I'd be cole, tired an' nearly dead, times in de middle ob a battle when my comrades wuz dying at my feet an' me having to step on 'em an' fight right on. I would almost fail when dem word would cheer me on 'My boy will make a good soldier.'"[28]

Black soldiers also performed their manly duty as warriors because they knew the black community was counting on them and, if they faltered, might

call them to account for that failure. For instance, late in his life Henry Butler recalled an incident that had occurred in November 1864 during the battle
of Pine Bluff in Arkansas. After a day of fighting with the Confederates, sometimes in hand-to-hand combat, both sides retreated in exhaustion. Soon
thereafter, a group of black women appeared on the battlefield with refresh-
ments for their men. Yet along with the "eatables," according to the veteran,
came the admonition, "Stand up to them, men. Be real men. Be whole men."[29]
In other words, these women were quite willing to support the soldiers, but
they expected them to fight and not falter—to show the fortitude of real men.

Encouraged by their community to be "real men," African-American soldiers
obtained a variety of benefits from their military service during the Civil War.
It helped many acquire schooling, self-confidence, leadership skills, and other
experiences that eroded ignorance and encouraged interest in public matters.
Certainly former slaves tended to profit more from their time in the service
because, being of the lowliest status before the war, they had the most to gain.
The Union army accelerated the passage of such black men from slavery to
freedom by allowing them to assume manly roles usually denied them before the war. Still, African-American soldiers paid a high price for the quick
progress in achieving recognition as men, potentially having to kill and be
killed to prove their manhood. "How extraordinary, and what a tribute to
ignorance and religious hypocrisy," W. E. B. Du Bois stated poignantly in 1935,
"is the fact that in the minds of most people, even those of liberals, only
murder makes men. The slave pleaded; he was humble; he protected the
women of the South, and the world ignored him. The slave killed white men;
and behold, he was a man."[30] While verging on hyperbole, Du Bois's statement captured the truth that only the crisis of the Civil War had made possible the tremendous progress of black soldiers in achieving manhood. What
his words did not convey was the fact that their battle for recognition as men
had not ended. Indeed, it was just the beginning of a struggle that would
continue for the rest of their lives.

# The Postwar Transition

**W**ITH THE CONCLUSION of the Civil War, African-American soldiers' fight for "Manhood & Equality" entered a new phase as they worked to solidify and extend the gains made during the war. The endeavor took place both inside and outside of military service, for though most black troops were eager to return to civilian life, many were retained for months or even years after Appomattox. Their slow transition out of the Union army brought African Americans both opportunity and danger. As soldiers in the army of occupation, they were in a good position to provide manly leadership to newly freed people in the postwar South, but this role also made them prominent targets for angry white Southerners. Still, despite the special hazards they encountered and the problems common to men returning from war since time immemorial, they did not forgo the chance to assert their manhood in the transitional period after the Civil War. The ways in which these men did so were sometimes quite aggressive, further raising the ire of white Southerners. The war had utterly transformed the American landscape, and in those early, heady days, anything seemed possible. Black soldiers and then black veterans hastened to take advantage of the opportunities that seemingly presented themselves.

At the end of the war, the Union army did not demobilize black soldiers as quickly as white soldiers. Most African Americans had joined the army in 1863 or 1864, so their three-year terms of enlistment had not expired when the war ended in 1865. Given that few black soldiers were near their discharge dates, they proved ideal for occupation duty in the defeated South. Their participation as occupiers varied from region to region. Union authorities utilized them mostly in areas of the South where African-American recruitment had been heavy, such as in the Mississippi Valley, and in border states such as Tennessee. Parts of the South that had seen little black recruitment generally encountered few African-American occupation troops (with the exception of Texas).[1]

The experience of African-American troops in garrisoning the South proved mixed. Former slaves in particular enjoyed the role reversal afforded by their duties related to keeping order. In the army of occupation, they could finally deal with white people as real men, something many white Southerners found intolerable. That is, black soldiers had authority over their former oppressors, which proved an exhilarating experience, but white Southerners refused to accept them in their military role and wrote many letters complaining to Union authorities. They accused the African-American troops of offenses both real and imagined. Objections received from North Carolina, similar to letters from elsewhere, claimed that black soldiers were "leaving their posts and roaming through the country, visiting the houses of citizens, demanding meat, vegetables, and other articles of food and committing depredations upon their Gardens and Fields."[2] In effect, white Southerners argued to Union authorities that the power wielded by African-American troops should be taken away because they could not exercise it with restraint like real men—white men.

However, the charge that black soldiers in the army of occupation were abusing their power was incidental to what was really bothering white Southerners. The actual problem was that black soldiers were asserting themselves as men. By acting in such a fashion, by seizing control of economic resources, black soldiers showed their ability to upset the traditional economic and social order of the South. Whites also realized that black soldiers were capable of asserting leadership, a key requisite of manly power. "The Negro Soldiery here are constantly telling our Negroes, that for the next year, the Government will give them lands, provisions, Stock & all things necessary to carry on business for themselves," E. G. Baker, a Mississippi planter, complained.[3] White Southerners also worried that black soldiers would incite freed people to take vengeance against their former owners and provide them with weapons. The presence of armed African Americans, even as soldiers under white officers, raised the same specter that slave insurrection had generated before the Civil War. "The whole south is resting on a volcano," wrote Baker, reflecting the viewpoint of many white Southerners. "If the Negro troops are not removed from our mids pretty Soon . . . trouble of the direst kind will befall us—They will stimulate the negroes to insurrection & will then lend them a helping hand."[4] In other words, the display of manly power by black soldiers awakened white Southerners' worst fears.

Consequently, it is not surprising that black soldiers found not only words used against them in the postwar South but also brutal violence. For many white Southerners, the substantive exercise of manhood by any black man automatically merited the most forceful response. A typical attack against African-American troops occurred in February 1866 in Columbus, Georgia. The town had been under occupation since August 1865 by white troops of the 151st Illinois Infantry, but black Union soldiers replaced them in mid-January 1866. The change greatly angered the white residents of Columbus. Few African Americans had been recruited in the easternmost part of the state, and many inland counties (with the exception of those in the path of Sherman's army in 1864) did not see Union soldiers until the war's end or afterward. The arrival of the African-American troops proved a shock to the white residents of the town, who had had little chance to adjust to the idea of emancipation, let alone armed black men in federal uniform. Local whites initially tried to rid themselves of the perceived menace by complaining to Union authorities that the black soldiers were disorderly and insolent. Aggravating their anger was the way African-American troops foiled their efforts to intimidate the local black population and reestablish the prewar racial power structure. "When colored Soldiers are about," a black minister from Columbus proudly wrote, "they [white people] are afraid to kick colored women, and abuse colored people on the Streets, as they usually do."[5]

The turnabout in the normal state of race relations, coupled with the presence of African-American soldiers in the army of occupation, proved intolerable to the white citizens of the town, and within a month of the black troops' arrival, their frustration boiled over. On February 12, 1866, a drunken ruffian shot a member of the 103d USCI in an unprovoked attack as the soldier was walking down the street. The black soldier survived, but the shooting triggered a riot. Sparked by the example of the assailant, hundreds of white residents of Columbus poured into the streets, many of them armed and, in the words of one Union officer, "cursing and swearing to attack the troops and drive every 'Yankee' out of town."[6] The first shooting incident was followed by two more attacks by white residents on African-American soldiers, and the only way that Union authorities could end the violence was to remove the black troops and bring white Union soldiers back.

The irony of the situation in Columbus, Georgia, of course, was that in ejecting the African-American troops from their midst, the white men of the town displayed the same unmanly lack of restraint of which they accused the black soldiers. Fearing unreasoned violence at the hands of armed black men, they preempted it with unreasoned violence of their own. The self-control of the black men in this difficult situation was manlier than the lack of restraint on the part of the mob.[7] Indeed, African-American soldiers usually did not retaliate in the face of the verbal and physical onslaught they received at the hands of white Southerners. Instead, they generally allowed Union authorities, ineffective as their efforts were, to deal with the assaults against them. (For instance, Union authorities in Columbus tried to apprehend the assailants who had shot the black soldiers, but those efforts ultimately proved unsuccessful.)

Of course, white Southerners did not see their violence against African-American troops as unmanly. According to Bertram Wyatt-Brown, "Black advances in any aspect of life meant departure from accustomed servitude, endangering the white man's honor."[8] Affronts to the honor of white men, such as the presence of the 103d USCI, justified and even demanded a violent response. Hence, the Columbus riot and other instances of violence directed at black soldiers and veterans in the immediate postwar South were merely early examples of white-on-black violence that would last from Reconstruction to well into the twentieth century. For many decades following the Civil War, white honor in the South simply could not tolerate overly conspicuous examples of black manhood, such as the activities of African-American soldiers in the Union army of occupation.

Faced with an avalanche of complaints and violent incidents, Union authorities sometimes forsook African-American troops, evidently fearing the unrest that black manhood unleashed in the postwar South. Such a fate befell the all-black 25th Army Corps in Virginia. The objections of white Virginians to the soldiers of the 25th Corps found a sympathetic ear with Gen. Henry W. Halleck, who commanded the Union occupation forces in Richmond. Halleck believed the African-American troops to be ill disciplined and feared their potential to disrupt the delicate state of race relations in postwar Virginia. Despite a vigorous defense by the corps' officers, Halleck put forward, and his superiors approved, a proposal to send the entire 25th—approximately 10,000 men—to Texas, where the U.S. government sought to forestall Confederates from establishing a redoubt in that state and to pressure France to withdraw its forces from Mexico.[9]

Garrison duty in Texas was unpopular with black soldiers because it was far from their homes and evoked a fear of the unknown. In such a time of uncertainty, it seemed that anything could happen—bad as well as good. Such was the experience of Alexander Newton, who had joined the all-black 29th Connecticut Infantry in December 1863 and was sent to Texas with his regiment in the spring of 1865. The men of the 29th Connecticut were deeply divided about being sent there, with some soldiers actually menacing those who acquiesced to their reposting. During their sea journey, rumors passed through the ranks that they were headed not for Texas but for Cuba, where slavery had not yet ended and where the officers of the regiment planned to sell them. The rumors proved unfounded, however, and the 29th Connecticut traveled uneventfully, passing through Norfolk, Mobile, and New Orleans. They arrived on the Texas coast at Brazos de Santiago, ten miles north of the Mexican border. There was not enough fresh water for the troops, as the army could condense from the sea only half the regiment's needs. Newton and his comrades were forced to buy water from peddlers at exorbitant prices to quench their thirst. The soldiers marched south to the border and then up the Rio Grande to the town of Brownsville, where they camped. Conditions in Brownsville proved as difficult as at Brazos de Santiago. The men had to contend with the heat, insects, reptiles, and a lack of firewood. Newton described the service of his regiment in Texas as "a time of sore trials." Under the harsh conditions, many men fell ill and died at an alarming rate in the army hospital, where callous stewards neglected the sick and looted from the dead. The more fortunate, according to Newton, spent their time sweating, cursing, scratching at insect bites, and praying for relief. For the men of the 29th Connecticut, these prayers were quickly answered. After a summer under the hot Texas sun, the army mustered them out in October 1865. However, other black Civil War regiments remained posted in Texas much longer.[10]

Whether they were sent to Texas or served closer to home, black soldiers resented being kept in the army. With the Civil War finished, many of them saw little reason to remain in service. "Garrison duty becomes a bore," complained a black corporal from Rhode Island to a federal bureaucrat whom he hoped might help secure him an early discharge. "My mission has so far been to my entire satisfaction and more has been done in such a short space of time, than I could have expected, and I now feel that all that I can do has been done."[11] In other words, with the Confederacy defeated and slavery ended, and having proved to themselves their manly worth as soldiers, most black troops wished to return to civilian life. They no doubt also noticed the rapid departure of white troops from the Union army and wondered why they were being kept in service longer. Such puzzlement must have fed a renewed sense of worry that they were yet again being treated unfairly and not being respected as men.

Indeed, when black soldiers—both former slaves and free men of color—wrote seeking to obtain an early discharge, they often couched their requests in terms of masculine responsibilities. In particular, these men complained that while still in the army they were unable to support their families properly. Having served and fought in a manly fashion, they now wished to care for their wives, children, and other family members like men. "The pecuniary circumstances of an aged grand mother and several orphaned sisters whose sole dependence is on my earnings, prompts me to solicit, with your influence, my honorable discharge," wrote a Northern black soldier in an especially articulate letter requesting assistance in obtaining an early release.[12] Less eloquent soldiers made similar appeals. An unnamed black soldier from South Carolina complained in January 1866 to Gen. Daniel E. Sickles that their sudden enlistment had forced the men of his regiment to leave their families without making adequate provisions for them, and they had since learned that their loved ones were "Perishing for something to Eate."[13]

Men who had left their families in slavery were especially anxious to protect them from the caprices of ex-slaveholders. This was especially true of soldiers from Kentucky, where slavery survived the end of the war for some months until the Thirteenth Amendment to the U.S. Constitution finally went into effect at the end of 1865. One group of men from that state serving in the 116th USCI wrote a desperate letter to President Andrew Johnson and Secretary of War Edwin M. Stanton in May 1866 seeking discharges. They needed to go home to protect their families from their former owners and ensure that their army pay reached them. They informed Johnson and Stanton that "thire is a Numbers of our famuleys has ben turned out of Doors, and they has no place lay thire heads and we has no way to healp them."[14]

Military discipline also increasingly irritated black soldiers after the war ended. Having proved their manhood in combat, African-American troops became more sensitive to treatment that emphasized the unequal relationship between officers and enlisted men. Some white officers continued to treat them with little respect, despite the manly fortitude they had shown during the war, inflicting painful and humiliating punishments for trivial as well as serious offenses. Though such discipline had been more tolerable during the crisis atmosphere of war, when many black soldiers were still unsure of their military roles (slaves in particular), after the war, it led to unrest and even mutinies in several black regiments.

Perhaps the most notorious postwar mutiny involving black troops occurred in Jacksonville, Florida, in late October 1865. Troops of the 3d USCI, a Northern regiment recruited in Pennsylvania, rioted after seeing a comrade tied up by his thumbs as punishment for an offense that the court-martial records never clearly specified but was probably insubordination.[15] White officers quickly suppressed the mutiny, and several of the ringleaders were executed after being convicted in swift courts-martial. Yet Jacksonville was merely an extreme example of the fact that, with the war over, black soldiers were less tolerant of punishments that offended their manhood. Although most black soldiers acted with more restraint than the troops of the 3d USCI to instances of harsh discipline, there can be little doubt that African-American troops became increasingly restive after the war, and the potential for unruly behavior increased.[16]

Not surprisingly, growing discipline problems helped speed the black troops' departure from the army. Indeed, the surviving soldiers of the 3d USCI were discharged several days after the Jacksonville mutiny. Putting an end to the stream of letters from African-American soldiers asking for early release and to the complaints of white Southerners about black occupation troops also made black troops' departure from military life more attractive to Union authorities, especially after the collapse of the French threat in Mexico and the growing confidence that the white South had ended formal military resistance to the reassertion of federal authority. By the fall of 1866, there were only 13,000 African Americans left in federal uniform, down from 83,000 a year earlier. The black military experience in the Union army came to a definitive close with disbandment of the 117th USCI, the last active black regiment, in August 1867.[17]

The mustering out or dissolution of a black Civil War regiment was an occasion of great significance for black soldiers, especially for units composed of former slaves (see fig. 1). It signified to them not only a transition from military to civilian life but also, for many, the first real taste of freedom. For men who had been in bondage prior to enlistment, it was the first moment they could fully enjoy their freedom. As slaves, their owners had had authority over them. As soldiers, they had been subject to the orders of their officers. As veterans, they finally gained control of their lives. Discharge from military service, then, presented black soldiers with the prospect of finally being free men, fully able to exercise independent manhood without slaveholders or military authorities telling them what to do.

Some white commanders of black regiments appreciated the special significance attached to the mustering out of their troops. As they assembled the men one last time to address them just before discharge, such officers sought to provide black soldiers with a fitting valedictory. Common themes ran through such orations. Commanders almost invariably praised their black soldiers for proving their manhood during the war. For instance, Col. T. H. Barrett, commander of the 62d USCI, a unit recruited in Missouri, unreservedly lauded the conduct of his regiment. "Always and everywhere," he said, "upon the march, in the camp, in the trenches, on the picket line, and on the field of action it has done its duty." He extolled the low arrest and desertion rate of the regiment and the large number of men who had learned to read and write or had saved sizable sums from their army pay. Acknowledging the efforts of his soldiers in adopting manly traits, he asserted, "It is you yourselves, that have made yourselves men."[18] Mustering-out speeches also referred to the prejudice and hostility faced by black troops and commended the soldiers for the calm, manly restraint they had shown.

Finally, officers counseled former slaves how to live as free men, advice that they believed would allow their soldiers to solidify the freedom and manhood they had won during the Civil War. A considerable portion of mustering-out speeches was often devoted to advice for the future. Many white officers of African-American regiments saw themselves as teachers to their troops and used the mustering-out speech as an opportunity for one last lecture on how to behave as free men. They advised black soldiers to put slavery behind them and reconcile with their former owners and other white Southerners. T. W. Trowbridge, commanding officer of the 33d USCI, a South Carolina regiment, was particularly adamant on this point, italicizing this part of the printed version of his final message to the regiment. He stated, *"I adjure you, by the associations and histories of the past, & the love you bear for your liberties, to harbor no feelings of hatred toward your former masters."* Commanding officers advised their men that instead of seeking vengeance for past transgressions they should look to the future, provide for their families, and seek economic advancement like true men. "Be civil, polite, industrious, frugal, just and religious, and you will prosper," promised Col. James S. Brisbin, commander of the 6th U.S. Colored Cavalry (USCC), recruited in Kentucky.[19] In short, these regimental commanders told their troops that they could be proud of their Civil War service, having helped free their people from bondage and proved their manhood, and if the men behaved properly after they left the army, good fortune would follow.

Unfortunately, these white Northerners underestimated the tremendous hostility from white Southerners that African-American veterans would face when they returned home, especially from former members of the Confederate army. Confederate veterans, having seen the blood of their comrades shed by black soldiers on the battlefield, particularly abhorred African-American veterans. More than any other group of white Southerners, ex-Confederates felt that black soldiers had insulted their honor, and they used their hatred as a convenient outlet to exorcise their frustration at losing the war. Hence, the violence that black soldiers faced in the army of occupation continued to plague them as they returned to civilian life. Federal authorities received news of outrages committed against black ex-soldiers throughout the South, even in the border states that had stayed loyal to the Union. The complaint of Charles A. Watkins, an African-American veteran living on Maryland's Eastern Shore, was typical. He wrote to Gen. Oliver O. Howard, commissioner of the Freedmen's Bureau, in March 1866, stating that "the colard Solgers . . . darcent walk out of an evening if we do, and we are Met by Some of these roudies that were in the rebbel army they beat us badly and Sumtime Shoot us."[20] Besides avenging injured honor, the object of such attacks was sometimes to disarm black veterans. African-American soldiers could purchase their army weapons when they mustered out, but upon returning home, they discovered that local whites feared armed black men even if they were not wearing a blue uniform and attempted to disarm them by any means necessary, including violence.[21]

Black veterans' demeanor increased the hostility of white Southerners. At least a few former soldiers, evidently quite proud of their Union service, were not shy about telling people at home about it, including local whites. And some of those whites took considerable offense at such boasting African Americans. "We will not allow niggers to come among us and brag about having been in the yankee army," stated a white doctor in Virginia. "It is as much as we can do to tolerate in white men."[22] Yet it was not just boasting that bothered white Southerners. In a real sense, military service had made black veterans men, because it made them unwilling to act subserviently anymore. "No negro who has ever been a soldier, can be again imposed upon; they have learnt what it is to be free and they will infuse their feelings into others," wrote a Freedmen's Bureau official in Mississippi soon after the war.[23] Evidence from throughout the South confirmed his opinion. In Florida, ex-soldiers proved more willing than other African Americans to break labor contracts when they had disputes with their employers, and they were least likely to seek the aid of the Freedmen's Bureau in settling such conflicts.[24] Black veterans in De Valls Bluff, Arkansas, demanded higher wages for their labor than did nonveterans.[25] In Shelbyville, Kentucky, veterans played a central role in protests against the exclusion of African Americans from the town's public facilities and the relegation of black people to menial employment.[26] And in Caddo Parish, Louisiana, as Nell Irvin Painter uncovered, "former soldiers rode across the countryside, reading contracts and bills for illiterates, explaining their legal rights to them, and backing up their demands for fairness from planters."[27]

Veterans' assertiveness manifested their leading role in the postwar black community, begun even before they left the army. In the wake of emancipation, African-American troops often became the leaders of former slaves. Freed people turned to the soldiers because these armed black men symbolized the overturning of slavery and could assist them with their problems. African-American soldiers, experienced in the military command structure, articulated the problems freed people faced and directed them to persons who could help. Such was the case of a black sergeant from Michigan, E. S. Robinson, serving in South Carolina. Robinson complained to the commander of the Department of South Carolina, Q. A. Gilmore, that black people in the state capital of Columbia were being badly abused by white Southerners and that the highest Union authority in the city, General Horton, refused to take any action to stop it. Robinson's letter prompted Gilmore to investigate the allegations. Such letters came not only from free men of color from the North but also from their Southern comrades fresh out of bondage. Indeed, wherever freed slaves had problems and black troops could help them, letters from African-American soldiers streamed in to Union authorities.[28]

To help solidify the independence of former slaves, black soldiers also participated in the building of churches, schools, orphanages, and other institutions to serve the African-American community. Their contributions to institution building were both modest and substantial. In Nottoway, Virginia, soldiers let local African Americans use their barracks as a school and for church services. Troops of the 56th USCI raised money for the construction of an orphanage in Phillips County, Arkansas.[29] Soldiers of the 62d and 65th USCI donated nearly $6,400 of their army pay in June 1866 to help found Lincoln Institute (later Lincoln University) in Jefferson County, Missouri.[30]

As the leadership role of soldiers and returning veterans increased in the black community during the immediate postwar years, so did the scope and intensity of white Southerners' violence against them. As soldiers and veterans emerged as visible leaders, they became the targets of organized mob violence instead of mere harassment and impromptu attacks. The coordinated assaults implicitly recognized the importance of black troops to newly emancipated African Americans. These men became a serious threat to white supremacy in the South. They attempted to assert manly leadership over the postwar black community, and white Southerners feared the subversive potential of this leadership. Through violence, they sought to put black soldiers and veterans back in their traditional place in the Southern social order—as subordinates and certainly not real men. The blacks' occasional aggressiveness also greatly offended white men's sense of honor, making the day of reckoning, when it came, all the more awful.

The Memphis riot of May 1866 illustrates in great detail how black soldiers assumed leadership responsibilities in the African-American community and how white hatred for black soldiers and the role and demeanor they adopted culminated in one of the worst instances of large-scale unrest in the early Reconstruction period. Memphis had become a magnet for freed slaves from the surrounding countryside after its occupation by Union troops in 1863. The African-American population of the city mushroomed from 3,000 in 1860 to around 20,000 at the war's end.[31] Many migrants were the family members of black soldiers, as Memphis had become a major recruitment and training center for African Americans in the Union army. Migrants came to Memphis not only to be close to family members in the army but also to escape the plantations where they had been enslaved before the arrival of Northern troops. The families of black soldiers and other migrants gathered in the southern part of the city near Fort Pickering, where the troops were garrisoned.

The arrival of large numbers of African Americans alarmed the white population of Memphis, particularly the ethnically diverse, upwardly mobile inhabitants of the city's southern section, where many of the refugees settled.

Their resentment was due to not only racism but also the collapse of
Memphis's cotton-dependent economy early in the Civil War, which left the
white inhabitants of south Memphis fearful the black migrants would become
a public burden and a social menace.[32]

The white inhabitants of Memphis came to harbor a special hatred for
the black troops stationed in the city. These African Americans, empowered
by their status as federal soldiers, uniformed and armed, rejected the subservience expected of them by prewar Southern racial etiquette. Black soldiers
refused to make way for white persons on public sidewalks or to treat them
with the deference to which the white citizens were accustomed. In one particularly trenchant encounter, a white female Tennessean was accosted by
black soldiers, who told her, "We's all ekal now. Git out o' our way, white
woman."[33] The incident demonstrates that besides refusing to kowtow to
white people, the black soldiers saw equality in sexual terms. To be equal with
white men in the eyes of these soldiers meant exercising masculine authority
over all women, not just women of their own race. Whereas in the old system race had trumped sex in defining power in relationships, these black
soldiers now believed that sex trumped race.

They were encouraged in this belief because the African Americans of
Memphis came to depend on African-American troops in the army of occupation as masculine protectors. With slavery gone, the black community in
the city was eager to throw off prewar racial subordination. Black soldiers
proved a natural source of leadership to Memphis's burgeoning African-
American population. Armed black men in uniform were a stunning sight
to these black Tennesseans, most of whom had been slaves until recently. They
could see black noncommissioned officers exercising authority over other
African-American troops and over white civilians as well. Hence, it was natural for them to turn to these black soldiers for guidance and to defend them
against white Southerners' attempts to reassert their prewar supremacy. Black
Union troops, as no group in their memory, embodied the manhood denied
African Americans before the war. These black males were recognized by at
least some whites—their officers—as men. As it was expressed at a mass
meeting celebrating the anniversary of the Emancipation Proclamation, "we
are highly gratified by the appellation by which the colored soldiers are addressed by their officers, viz: men."[34]

As manly protectors, black soldiers in Memphis resisted attempts by white
Southerners and Union authorities to force the recent black migrants back

into the countryside. Black migrants initially were encouraged to leave voluntarily, but there were few takers. In October 1865, Gen. Nathan A. M. Dudley, the Freedmen's Bureau superintendent in Memphis, ordered that black persons without visible means of support be arrested and compelled to accept work contracts as plantation laborers in rural areas. But Dudley's attempt to drive the African-American migrants out of the city was disrupted by the black troops there. When bureau personnel went through the black section of south Memphis informing residents that only those with adequate means of support would be allowed to remain, black troops followed after them asserting that the Freedmen's Bureau had no authority to implement the policy.

To the soldiers, the bureau's action was too close to a reimposition of slavery. Voluntary movement was important to their conception of freedom. Forced removal reminded them of the tight control kept over slaves' movements. African Americans had also come to Memphis to escape the harsh conditions in rural areas, especially the abuse and exploitation of white planters. Some black soldiers, wanting to assert their role as manly providers and protectors, also wished to remove their wives, children, and parents from field labor and relocate them in the refuge of the domestic sphere. Migrating to Memphis seemed to promise the best chance of achieving this masculine goal, along with reuniting families separated by slavery and military service, even if black families had a harder time supporting themselves in the city than in the countryside.

Yet the resistance to forced removal stemmed not only from their belief in equality—including equality in the freedom of movement—and the presence of their families in the city but also from the close ties they developed in the Memphis black community in churches, schools, taverns, and private homes and even on the streets. The soldiers became leaders, protectors, friends, and, with their army pay and access to military supplies, an economic resource to the black people of Memphis. In the process, the dividing line between the two groups blurred. Military rations and clothing found their way into the African-American community, which, according to one scholar, "made it more difficult for the casual observer to distinguish between soldiers and black civilians."[35] This phenomenon would have dire consequences during the coming riot.

Relations between black soldiers and the white inhabitants of Memphis, which were never good, deteriorated further from the fall of 1865 into the spring of 1866. As white Southerners shook off the melancholy of their defeat in the war, they became increasingly determined to rid the city of its black occupiers. Such feelings were especially strong among the Memphis police force. Serious confrontations between the police and African-American troops had already occurred when the police tried to enforce an order restricting the operation of dance houses patronized by soldiers and other freed people. Joint jurisdiction over soldiers' activities outside of Fort Pickering also led to tension between the Memphis police and black military police. The aggressive manner in which the city police treated disorderly conduct by African-American troops, along with their attempts to enforce prewar social customs, worsened the situation.[36]

The mounting tension exploded in the spring of 1866. On April 30, the remaining black soldiers stationed at Fort Pickering were mustered out of the Union army. Although most of the new veterans quickly left for their homes in the countryside, about 150 men remained in the vicinity of the fort waiting for their discharge pay. On the afternoon of May 1, Memphis police attempted to take into custody two black veterans for disorderly conduct. A group of former soldiers had evidently been drinking to pass the time and, with their inhibitions lowered, began taunting the police by cheering for Abe Lincoln. What should have been a routine arrest turned violent because of an incident that had occurred the week before. The police had taken a black soldier into custody without cause and beaten him badly. The soldier's comrades had let the police know that if anything like that ever happened again, there would be trouble—and trouble indeed occurred. The man who had been beaten witnessed the arrests that day, and when he saw his principal assailant from the previous week among the police, he became visibly excited, causing considerable agitation among the other ex-soldiers. Some of the veterans started shouting "Club them" and "Shoot them." When the police began to lead away the arrested men, some ex-soldiers shot their revolvers in the air, causing the police to conclude that they were being fired upon, and they started shooting at the veterans. The two sides exchanged gunfire, and the ex-soldiers killed a policeman. The police retreated with the dead officer to obtain reinforcements. However, when they returned, they discovered that the number of veterans had grown. After another exchange of gunfire, the police were still unable to gain control of the situation and retreated again. They then raised a white citizens' posse consisting of themselves, firemen, laborers, and small businessmen. After the end of the second clash, the veterans returned to the safety of Fort Pickering, where Union authorities disarmed them.[37]

With the veterans unable to mount further resistance, the posse turned into a mob and took out its rage on the African-American community of south Memphis. It systematically sacked and pillaged the black neighborhood over a two-day period while white Union authorities stood by and did nothing. By the time Union authorities belatedly declared martial law in Memphis on May 4, forty-six African Americans were dead, seventy to eighty were injured, five women had been raped, more than a hundred people had been robbed, and many churches, schools, and houses had been burned.[38]

African-American veterans were a prime target for the mob. Although most were safely inside Fort Pickering, fourteen of the forty-six black persons killed in the riot were veterans. Witnesses remembered the mob directing its venom at black ex-soldiers. The posse looked for black men still in uniform and specifically sought out the homes of veterans and their families. The mob also attacked civilians wearing pieces of Union uniforms, and all but one woman raped during the riot had a connection to the Union army. The targeting of black veterans was unquestionably linked to their status as leaders of the African Americans in Memphis and the assertive way they defended the community's interests. Now that they were no longer in the army, and with the Union occupation authorities turning a blind eye, white citizens of Memphis took out their vengeance on the unlucky ex-soldiers who had not found sanctuary in the fort, and they also took the opportunity to destroy other bedrocks of the black community, such as churches and schools.[39]

The members of the mob were not merely seeking to punish black veterans for attempting to overturn the racial order of Memphis. The majority of the identified members of the mob were Confederate veterans.[40] In seeking out black veterans during the riot, they sought to punish the former slaves who had offended their sense of honor by taking up arms for the hated Yankees. Yet the irony was that they succeeded in terrorizing the black community of south Memphis because Union army officers disarmed the African-American veterans, refused to confiscate the weapons of the city police, and offered no protection to black residents for two crucial days. This lack of action portended the eventual abandonment of black veterans by their white comrades in the years after Reconstruction. At that moment, though, the Memphis riot was more indicative of the zealous response of white Southerners to the leadership role that African-American soldiers and veterans took in many parts of the region during the postwar transitional period.

The hostile treatment that African-American veterans faced from white Southerners was but one of their problems after the war. Indeed, many of these men faced a more universal dilemma encountered by returning soldiers before and since—finding the means to survive after they left military service. However discriminatory pay had been in the Union army, it had provided them with at least some means to support their families and fulfill the manly role of provider. With no GI Bill after the Civil War, black veterans found themselves in a difficult situation, because the transition to peacetime almost inevitably meant that for a time there would be fewer jobs than men seeking them. Even worse, evidence suggests that the problem of postwar unemployment was more acute for African Americans than for whites. Larry Logue, in a study of Civil War veterans in Rhode Island (where relevant data were available), found that black veterans "were four times as likely to be unemployed as were white *veterans,* and five times as likely to be jobless as black *civilians.*"[41] Evidence from the border region and farther south suggests that black veterans there also experienced postwar readjustment problems. In the District of Columbia, for instance, during the spring and fall of 1866, a stream of unemployed black veterans waiting to collect bounty payments was forced to beg the Freedmen's Bureau for help. Many of these men were ragged and vermin infested, and the bureau had to find fresh clothing and feed them.[42] Even when jobs were available, it proved difficult to reintegrate returning soldiers into the local economy, particularly when they all came home at once, as was often the case for black units recruited in the same locality. The discharge of the 33d USCI, for example, led to an increase in unemployment around Port Royal, South Carolina, because the local agricultural economy was unable to absorb the sudden influx of returning soldiers.[43]

Economic uncertainty and the hostility and violence faced by black Civil War veterans help explain the impulse of some ex-soldiers to reenlist in the postwar army's infantry and cavalry regiments serving in the West. No doubt, some men had grown to like military life during their Civil War service and found the prospect of continued soldiering more appealing than the uncertainties they faced if they returned home. Whatever their reasons for staying in the army, these veterans facilitated the formation of new black regiments in the regular army, providing a cadre of experienced soldiers who could teach raw recruits the ways of military life. Called "buffalo soldiers" by Native Americans, because the black troops' hair reminded them of the buffalo's curly coat, African-American cavalry and infantry units played an important role in the Indian wars that lasted from the end of the Civil War into the late 1880s. They protected settlers, garrisoned frontier forts, and helped wrest control of the West from Native American societies.[44]

There was no single path into the postwar army. Some black soldiers joining the regular army simply transferred from their Civil War regiments shortly before their muster out.[45] Other men went home for a visit and then reenlisted.[46] Still others lived as civilians for several months or even several years before deciding to join up.[47] Although a few black Civil War veterans made their careers as buffalo soldiers, most of them returned to civilian life for good after a few years in the regular army.[48]

Whatever the circumstances of their reenlistment and service, the presence of black soldiers in the postwar U.S. Army represented a significant achievement for the African-American troops that had fought in the Civil War. The formation of black infantry and cavalry regiments in the postwar army was a tangible signal of the shift in attitude of the Northern public about African Americans and military service. Although the Civil War had by no means eliminated prejudice on the part of white Northerners (after all, the buffalo soldiers served in segregated units), the enlistment of black men was at least a partial recognition of their manhood. In the eyes of the federal government, they were now men enough to fight Native Americans on the frontier, men enough to be given a permanent place in the military structure of the United States.

Still, only a small number of black Civil War veterans joined the regular army after the war. To the extent that Civil War pension applicants reflect all black veterans, probably no more than 1 to 2 percent (approximately 2,000 to 3,000 men) ever served in the postwar regular army.[49] In short, the vast majority of black soldiers did not cling to military life. They had helped liberate their people and proved their manhood through military service. Whether free or slave, most of these men were eager to leave the army as soon as possible to explore and take advantage of the new possibilities engendered by the war.[50] (In fact, it would have been hard for large numbers of veterans to stay in the army after the war, because the post–Civil War army was considerably smaller than the Union army at the peak of the conflict. Only four permanent black regiments existed in the regular army by the early 1870s, two infantry and two cavalry.)

More common than postwar military service among black Civil War veterans were attempts to acquire the means to achieve a manly economic independence, especially among former slaves. For the African-American veterans—men overwhelmingly from rural origins—achieving such independence meant acquiring land. Hence, it should not be a surprise that former soldiers displayed a strong propensity to seek landownership after the war. African-American soldiers had been encouraged to pursue this course during the war by some of their white officers. For instance, Col. T. H. Barrett, commander of the 62d USCI, gave his men such advice in January 1866 at the regiment's disbandment. (Because its effective strength had fallen sufficiently, the army had decided to consolidate it into a separate battalion with four companies.) "When discharged I advise every one to get for himself a piece of land, for a home." With the men having a year left in their enlistments, Barrett believed that it was possible for them to save enough from their army pay in that time to purchase small pieces of land after discharge. He told his soldiers, "It is a great deal better for you to live upon your own land, than to hire land from another, or to work for another."[51]

Although the efforts of officers such as Barrett played an important role in encouraging their men to seek landownership, the truth was that such efforts merely reinforced a dream that many black soldiers already shared. Most African-American troops already recognized the connection between landownership and independent manhood. They realized that without their own land, they would still be dependent on their former owners or other white planters for their livelihood, with the requisite loss of self-sufficient manhood. Landowners could dictate the circumstances of their work and interfere in their domestic authority by deciding who in the family would work, frustrating the efforts of these men to remove their wives and children from field labor and assert their patriarchal authority within the family.

Like other African Americans, Civil War veterans were disappointed by the federal government's failure to reward their race for its wartime loyalty and service by giving them land that had been confiscated from disloyal Southern planters.[52] Still, former soldiers enjoyed a better chance of purchasing land after the war than did other former slaves. Fed, clothed, and housed by the army, thrifty soldiers could accumulate significant savings. The army inadvertently encouraged accumulation by paying troops infrequently, creating what amounted to an involuntary savings plan. The refusal of many black regiments to accept lower pay than white soldiers also meant that the army owed them sizable sums when the government finally equalized pay scales late in the war. In addition, the government paid bounties or lump-sum rewards to some black soldiers for joining the army (see chapter 5). In short, what little capital existed in the African-American community after the war often belonged to veterans. Perhaps more than any other group of African-American men, they had the economic resources to undergird their manhood. For example, soldiers accounted for $3,000 of the initial $5,000 deposited in the Freedmen's Savings Bank branch in Baltimore, Maryland.[53] In fact, one white officer later claimed that, collectively, the men in his Maryland regiment had saved $90,000 by the time they left the army, an enormous sum at the time.[54] Former soldiers invested their army pay and military bounties not only in land but also in business ventures. A Freedmen's Bureau agent reporting from De Valls Bluff, Arkansas, in April 1866 indicated that although many black veterans worked on local plantations, others had purchased town lots, and a group of fifteen ex-soldiers had formed a mercantile partnership.[55]

Many black soldiers used their army pay, as well as any bounty money they received for their enlistment, to try to purchase land. But despite the relatively superior resources they commanded, black veterans often found the road to landownership difficult. In many cases, individuals still did not have enough money to purchase land alone. Not surprisingly, some African-American soldiers had explored the possibility, before leaving service, of establishing veterans' colonies. By living together and pooling their money, these soldiers hoped that they could more easily acquire land, while at the same time providing mutual protection against the depredations of white Southerners. For instance, S. H. Smothers, a Northern black soldier, proposed founding a black veterans' colony in the lower part of the Rio Grande Valley in Texas, where cheap government land was available and the African-American settlers could live in relative isolation. Settlement would occur under the auspices of the First United States Colored Pioneer Association. The association would locate the exact site for the colony and help the settlers purchase land, and the men of the association would organize a militia for self-defense purposes. Smothers's plans, however, never came to fruition.[56]

Other veterans' colonies got further than the planning stages, but numerous obstacles prevented them from ultimately succeeding. First, it was often difficult if not impossible to convince white Southerners to sell their land to African Americans. Second, when black veterans could find willing sellers, financing the purchase often proved difficult, even for soldiers working together. Even though many men had saved their army pay to buy land, over the course of a typical enlistment, the sum amounted to several hundred dollars at most, leaving soldiers' groups with insufficient resources to buy enough land to support a veterans' colony adequately. This left many men with their enlistment bounties as the margin between becoming landowners and remaining landless. According to Claude Oubre, the Freedmen's Bureau "received numerous requests from groups of black soldiers proposing to use their bounty claims to purchase entire plantations which they wanted to divide among themselves."[57] The problem then became collecting bounties in a timely way that would enable groups of soldiers to have the money on hand when the seller demanded payment. Because many black soldiers had not become eligible for a federal enlistment bounty until after they enlisted, they had to go through a protracted and expensive claims process to actually get the money from the government. Such bureaucratic red tape frustrated attempts to organize black veterans' colonies because it tied up their bounty money when they needed it most.

Lack of access to bounty money could frustrate veterans' colonies even before they got off the ground. Such was the experience of a group of former soldiers that had served in the 58th USCI, a regiment recruited in southern Mississippi's black belt. They attempted to purchase a tract of 10,690 acres from a planter in Adams County, A. K. Farrar. The soldiers requested the help of the Freedmen's Bureau in getting Congress to assign their bounties to Farrar so that he would let them occupy the land. The deal fell apart because the bureau received reports that the man pushing the scheme, George Hitchen, was unreliable, and the bounties due the veterans were insufficient to both purchase the land and farming supplies and feed the former soldiers and their families until they harvested their first crop. The bureau blocked the transaction and instead proposed that the veterans purchase land with their bounties individually—effectively scuttling the plan.[58] As individuals, most veterans were even less able to afford to buy land. That had been the point of banding together in the first place. Some veterans would eventually become landowners, but for the most part, they would achieve that status gradually in the years and decades after the war.

As the experience in Memphis and countless other incidents illustrate, black Civil War veterans found ways to demonstrate their manhood both before and after they left the army. White Southerners' violence against them is the surest evidence of that. At first, the violence was scattered and unorganized, but as black troops' and returned veterans' importance as leaders of the freed slaves became apparent, and as their assertive behavior and determination not to submit to prewar norms of racial behavior increasingly grated, the ferocity of dishonored white Southerners grew more intense and systematic. Certainly, most black veterans returned home peacefully, despite the widespread violence, adjusting as best they could to civilian life in an era before there was a social safety net to cushion the transition from military service. A small number of men lingered in the postwar army as buffalo soldiers, but most black veterans returned home as quickly as possible to assume manly responsibilities in a world that had changed beyond recognition, especially in the former slave states. Although they soon blended into the civilian population, as a group, their lives would in many ways be different from those of the rest of the African-American community in the postwar period.

# Life Patterns

**A**FTER THE TUMULTUOUS YEARS of the Civil War and the transitional period that followed, life finally settled down for former soldiers. They returned home, established civilian identities, and lived lives that at first glance seem little different from those of other African Americans during the late nineteenth century. Yet as a group, black Civil War veterans exhibited life patterns that set them apart from the rest of the black community in ways both obvious and subtle. These dissimilarities not only were the result of military service but also reflected differences in their prewar backgrounds and postwar experiences. Whatever the source, the distinct circumstances of veterans gave them a greater inclination and ability to achieve the economic attributes of manhood than nonveterans had. Civil War veterans came to constitute an elite group in postwar African-American society, enjoying the respect and even the envy of their peers.

In 1890, the U.S. Census Bureau took a special census of all Civil War veterans as part of the regular decennial enumeration of the U.S. population. Congress ordered the special count to assist former soldiers and sailors in applying for federal disability pensions. Many Union veterans in the 1870s and 1880s had been unsuccessful making belated disability pension claims because they had lost contact with ex-comrades who might be able to provide testimony that their injuries were war related (as the law then required). The end product of the special census was to be a directory of Union veterans in which pension applicants would be able to locate former comrades. Although Congress ultimately did not fund publication of the directory, the Census Bureau compiled the information it gathered from veterans into a revealing statistical portrait of the survivors of Civil War veterans, both Union and Confederate, twenty-five years after the guns had fallen silent.[1]

In the case of black Union veterans, the special census of 1890 notably revealed that an unusually high percentage of these men could be found living in the Northern states (see statistical appendix, table 1). Nearly 27 percent of Civil War veterans resided in the North at a time when only about 7 percent of the general black population in the United States lived there. The upshot of this phenomenon was that former soldiers were overrepresented in the North and underrepresented in the South, especially the Lower South. Just over 60 percent of African Americans still lived in the Lower South in 1890, but only around 35 percent of black veterans. Only in the Upper South and the West was there a rough parity in the proportions of former soldiers and the general black population.[2]

The disproportionate percentage of black veterans living in the North in the late nineteenth century was principally a legacy of Civil War recruitment patterns for African Americans. Black soldiers generally had joined the Union army in the region where they had lived prior to the war, and the special census showed that they usually returned there after leaving service.[3] Hence, many black veterans lived in the North because of the greater success recruiting black soldiers there. African Americans in the Confederacy needed to get to Union-controlled territory to enlist, and even in the loyal border states, slaveholders afraid of losing their labor force resisted black recruitment. None of these impediments existed in the North, and by the time black recruitment began in earnest in 1863, an effective recruitment infrastructure was in place there. Luminaries such as Frederick Douglass, Martin Delany, John Langston, and countless local leaders also served as recruiters or aided the efforts of state and federal authorities in the black community. Hence, despite the fact that only 5 percent of black men of military age (eighteen to forty-five years) lived in the Northern states at the beginning of the war, 16 percent of all black soldiers enlisted from that region. (In fact, about two-thirds of black men in the region capable of serving ended up in the Union army.)

Migration patterns after the war also contributed to the unusually high percentage of black veterans in the North in 1890. Although the information from pension files on geographic movement is incomplete (since federal bureaucrats did not always gather data on this subject), it is reasonably certain that the Northern states were the leading destination for black veterans who migrated during this period.[4] The North was by far the most common destination for black migrants leaving the interior states of the Upper South, and the large concentration of former soldiers in the border states meant that much more of the migration of African-American veterans was directed northward rather than southward to frontier states such as Arkansas, Texas, and Oklahoma, which drew most black migrants from the Lower South, where fewer black veterans lived. These general trends are confirmed by the individual cases of black veterans documented in Civil War pension files. African-American former soldiers living in the interior border states tended to migrate into contiguous Northern states. Kentucky veterans crossed the Ohio River into Illinois, Indiana, and Ohio.[5] Missouri veterans went east into Illinois, west into Kansas, and north into Iowa.[6] Ex-soldiers from Tennessee also migrated to the North, often passing through Kentucky or Missouri on their way.[7] Overall, these migrants increased the concentration of African-American veterans in the North, building on the trend established by Civil War enlistments.

It should be noted, however, that the movement of black ex-soldiers from the Upper South into the North was not a precursor of the tremendous stream of African Americans from the rural South to the urban North that started with World War I, known as the Great Migration. Only a few black veterans, such as George H. Fisher, who settled in Chicago, headed to the big cities of the North.[8] Instead, veterans moving from the Upper South into the North tended to settle in the "butternut" or southern portions of Illinois, Indiana, and Ohio—areas that were in many ways similar to the places they had left behind. Indeed, veterans like Harry Givens had to travel only a short distance to leave the "South" for the "North." Immediately after the war, Givens lived in Paducah, an Ohio River town in western Kentucky. In 1871, he crossed the Ohio to live in Metropolis, Illinois, just downstream from Paducah.[9] There was also a small counterwave of veterans from the North into the Upper South. This counterwave consisted primarily of ex-soldiers returning home to the Upper South after living in southern Illinois, Indiana, or Ohio. For instance, Harry Givens returned to Paducah from Metropolis in the 1880s.[10]

The unusually high percentage of black former soldiers in the North had noteworthy implications for the experiences of these men. It meant that, as a group, veterans were relatively freer than other African Americans from the racial repression and poverty of the postwar South, and hence better able to preserve and bolster their manhood. Certainly the North was no paradise for black Civil War veterans. Scholarship on African Americans in this region after the Civil War has amply documented their marginal position, especially in employment.[11] Expanding Northern industries in the late nineteenth century largely excluded black workers, except as strikebreakers, in favor of European immigrant labor. In Northern cities, with the exception of a small professional and merchant elite, black men and women overwhelmingly worked in lowly service-sector jobs or as unskilled day laborers. The jobs to which African Americans could aspire generally offered low pay, no security, and little prestige or opportunity for advancement. Indeed, a large part of the black workforce in the postwar North—veterans included—remained in small towns and the countryside because of the lack of opportunity in Northern cities. It is also the case that African Americans faced considerable de jure and de facto discrimination in education and public accommodations and through antimiscegenation statutes in the North after the Civil War.

Nonetheless, as bad as the situation was for black veterans in the North, when one takes the entire postwar period into account, they were still better off than their counterparts below the Mason-Dixon line. Northern black veterans escaped the war-ravaged conditions and the violence directed at their Southern comrades returning from Union service. They generally enjoyed a quieter homecoming, usually slipping unobtrusively back into civilian life. In some cases, a warm welcome awaited these men. In fact, several prominent veterans of the 55th Massachusetts Infantry (who were commissioned as officers late in their service), James Monroe Trotter, William H. Dupree, and Charles L. Mitchell, received federal patronage jobs in the Boston post office or U.S. customhouse as a reward for their Civil War service.[12] There was even a victory parade in New York City for black troops returning from the South.[13]

Perhaps the most interesting and successful career of a black veteran in the North was that of Lewis Latimer (see fig. 5). More than any other African American who served the Union, he managed to break through the color line and achieve an extraordinary career for a man of his race at that time. Born to escaped slaves in Boston in 1848, Latimer joined the Union navy as a young teenager during the Civil War, seeing action aboard the USS *Massasoit* on the James River. After the war he returned home, where he found a job as an office boy for a firm of patent attorneys. There he taught himself mechanical drawing and was gradually drawn into the burgeoning field of late-nineteenth-century American invention.

His list of associations reads like a who's who of famous American inventors in the second half of the nineteenth century. Early in his career, he did the drawings that Alexander Graham Bell used to patent the telephone.

He worked in the early 1880s with Hiram S. Maxim, who was experimenting with technology for incandescent electric lighting (and would later invent the machine gun). It was his experience with Maxim that brought him to the attention of Thomas Edison. Latimer joined Edison's staff in 1883, serving in his organization in various capacities for nearly thirty years and becoming one of its foremost experts on electric technology, authoring a treatise in 1890 describing Edison's electric lighting system. He joined Edison's legal department that year and served as an expert witness for much of the remainder of his career, defending the inventor's patents against infringement. A true renaissance man who patented several of his own inventions, he was a musician, artist, and poet in his spare time. Indeed, he was so respected that he was accepted into the Edison Pioneers, a social organization of Edison's early employees, as its only black member.[14]

The career of Lewis Latimer, the victory parade, and the patronage jobs are anecdotal evidence that the prejudice of some white Northerners toward African Americans had softened because of their military contribution to the Union cause. This softening mirrors—although it was certainly never as strong as—the hard feelings among white Southerners caused by black service in the Union army. Nonetheless, the warmer opinion toward black people in the North, especially African Americans returning home from the army, was authentic.[15] Such sentiment would help generate white support for black suffrage after the war (see chapter 3). Although racism remained alive and well in the North, at least some white Northerners reconsidered their views toward African Americans in light of blacks' wartime service. This was especially true of white Union veterans, particularly former officers of black regiments, who had the most direct experience with black soldiers. Consequently, Civil War service would have a tremendous influence on the development of interracial comradeship between white and black Union veterans (see chapter 6).

One consequence of the improved feeling toward black veterans in the North was that they were better able, in the long run, to maintain their political and civil rights than their Southern comrades were. However, former soldiers in the North did not win such rights quite as fast as Southern black veterans in the immediate postwar period. Most Northern legislatures in the late 1860s refused to grant black men voting rights, whereas Reconstruction state governments in the South gave the franchise to black men.[16] It is also true that only a handful of black officeholders served in the North, compared with a sizable number of African Americans who held public office in the South during Reconstruction. Northern blacks finally gained the right to vote with the ratification of the Fifteenth Amendment in 1870. More important, Northern black veterans did not lose their voting rights in the wave of disfranchisement that swept the South in the late nineteenth century. Hence, although black ex-soldiers in the North were slower to make the same political achievements as their Southern comrades and never came close to paralleling the extent of their political officeholding during Reconstruction, the Northerners generally managed to hold on to their manhood and suffrage for the rest of their lives. It is also true that although discrimination, segregation, and disfranchisement made inroads in some places in the late-nineteenth-century North, such practices never became as deep and pervasive as they were in the South.[17]

Just as a disproportionate number of black veterans lived in the North after the Civil War, an unusually high percentage lived in cities. The special census of 1890 indicates that about 23 percent of African-American veterans lived in cities with more than 25,000 people. By contrast, only 11 percent of the overall black population in the United States lived in such cities that year. In short, black veterans were significantly more urbanized than other people of their race, especially in the South.[18] Nearly 25 percent of ex-soldiers in the Upper South lived in cities with more than 25,000 people, compared with only 14 percent of the overall black population in this region; in the Lower South, the urbanization figures were 11 percent for veterans and 5 percent for African Americans overall.[19]

Indeed, the special veterans' census of 1890 probably understates the extent to which black veterans experienced urban life after the war. Essentially a snapshot of one moment in time, it does not capture the dynamic process of migration between the city and the countryside. Evidence from pension files suggests that there was significant movement back and forth between rural and urban areas. Many former soldiers who moved to the city did not stay there permanently. For instance, eighty veterans in the sample group definitely moved from rural to urban areas after the war, but fifty-six of them moved back to the countryside at least once. Some veterans went back and forth several times or even on a regular basis, taking advantage of seasonal job opportunities. Although such frequent movers were in the minority, evidence from pension files suggests that a typical African-American veteran's move to the city from a rural area was not likely to be permanent.

However, the steadily rising percentage of black ex-soldiers who could be found in urban areas as the decades progressed suggests that many veterans—perhaps even the majority—lived in cities at some point during the postwar period. About 10 percent of black soldiers had resided in urban areas before the war.[20] Pension files suggest that by the 1870s, about a quarter of black veterans lived in towns with more than 8,000 people; by the 1890s, the figure was over a third.[21]

It is also worth noting that a greater percentage of black veterans than white veterans lived in urban areas. Nearly 23 percent of black veterans lived in cities with more than 25,000 people, according to the special census of 1890, but only 18 percent of white Union veterans did so. Black veterans' greater presence in the cities is even more pronounced when compared with that of former Confederate soldiers, whose rate of urbanization was quite low, even by the standards of the late nineteenth century—only 5 percent in 1890.[22]

Civil War service was probably largely responsible for the relatively high percentage of black veterans living in cities after the war. The army provided many African-American men with their first significant exposure to urban life. Regiments were often assembled in cities, drawing most of their recruits in from the countryside. As noted earlier, many black soldiers also did garrison duty in Southern cities. In the army, they discovered that cities were vibrant and interesting places, offering entertainment, access to black institutions (churches, schools, and so forth), and a greater range of social contacts than the countryside provided. Even considering the shortage of job opportunities and the unhygienic conditions found in many postwar Southern cities, urban areas were still an attractive alternative to the countryside, where former slaveholders sought to reassert control over their former slaves through black codes, labor contracts, child guardianship laws, and violence. After the war, black veterans' relatively greater familiarity with cities and their advantages compared with other African Americans was no doubt responsible for the higher rate of migration into urban areas by ex-soldiers.

Disparate conditions probably explain why a larger percentage of black veterans could be found in cities compared with their Confederate counterparts. White Southerners had less to gain through urban residence after the Civil War than did African Americans. Or, to put it another way, they had less to lose by staying in the countryside. They had no repression to escape, and a greater percentage could earn a decent living there. Hence, only a very small percentage of Confederate veterans lived in Southern cities by 1890. Black former Union soldiers, however, had more to gain from migrating to the cities, where "freedom was freer."[23] Although urban conditions were far from ideal, white oppression there tended to be milder than in the countryside.

In other words, like the Northern states, cities proved a better place for African-American veterans to sustain their manhood. Although segregation and disfranchisement manifested themselves in Southern cities, as they did throughout the South, conditions were better for black people in cities than in the countryside in terms of racial repression. In cities, former soldiers had a better chance of escaping the problems that beset rural blacks after the war, especially after the end of Reconstruction. In Southern cities, sharecropping, the crop lien, and debt peonage could not erode their dreams of manly independence and self-sufficiency. Although many urban black veterans were as poor as their rural counterparts, greater economic opportunity existed in Southern cities for African Americans than in the post-Reconstruction countryside. As men who were accustomed to taking chances, having risked their lives in the war, and with a greater personal knowledge of what to expect, it should not be surprising that so many black veterans tried urban life after the war.[24]

In short, black Civil War veterans gravitated disproportionately (compared with their nonveteran peers) to the Northern states and Southern cities—places that offered them more freedom and opportunity or, in other words, greater potential to realize their manhood. Their choice produced tangible results. More African-American former soldiers worked at higher-status occupations in 1890 than did their nonveteran counterparts. The special 1890 census reveals that over 13 percent of veterans held such jobs in 1890; in comparison, data from the regular census show that only 7 percent of black men aged forty-five years or older who had not served in the Union army obtained such jobs.[25] Northern and urban residence evidently gave black veterans better access to higher-status occupations compared with nonveteran African Americans, who were more likely to be found in the rural South.

The vast majority of both groups, of course, did not hold high-status jobs. Nonetheless, a close examination of employment patterns of African-American Civil War veterans and their nonveteran contemporaries in the black community (men forty-five years and older in 1890) suggests that the former soldiers did better. A small but discernibly higher percentage of veterans compared with nonveterans was employed as artisans and professionals (see statistical appendix, table 2). About 8 percent of black veterans were artisans in 1890, versus around 6 percent of black men who had not served; about 3 percent of former soldiers were professionals, compared with just over 1 percent of nonveterans. At first glance, however, considerably fewer nonveterans appeared to be engaged in unskilled labor and a higher percentage in business. About 50 percent of African-American veterans in 1890 could be characterized as unskilled, according to the census, and about 34 percent as engaged in business. By contrast, around 40 percent of their nonveteran contemporaries were unskilled workers, and 49 percent were in business. Yet these categories are deceptive. Farmworkers, with the exception of wage-earning "agricultural laborers," were not differentiated in the 1890 census. That is, the U.S. Census Bureau did not distinguish between farmers who owned land and those who rented land or were sharecroppers. The 1890 census lumped together planters, farmers, renters, and sharecroppers as "businessmen." Hence, the greater percentage of nonveterans in the business category must be read as evidence of their relatively inferior position compared with veterans, since most of them were not landowners but poverty-stricken sharecroppers or renters. What employment data exist from the 1890 census, carefully considered, suggest that former soldiers were appreciably better off than their nonveteran contemporaries and more prepared to take care of their families and bolster their status there through relatively greater economic power.

Despite their relative success, of course, the vast majority of black Civil War veterans remained enmeshed in rural poverty. There is also little evidence that the conflict helped black ex-soldiers experience upward occupational mobility. A few lucky men learned new skills while in the service or gained the patronage of influential white men. Tales of veterans rising from slavery or other humble backgrounds to become ministers, lawyers, newspaper editors, politicians, well-off farmers, and entrepreneurs abound in the Whiggish biographical anthologies of the African-American community published in the late nineteenth and early twentieth centuries.[26] Although such stories are inspiring, they were not typical, as evidence from the Civil War pension files and special veterans' census of 1890 suggests.

In fact, the war probably had a more discernible impact in terms of downward mobility for African-American former soldiers. Although fewer black men than white men saw combat in the Union army, a significant number were disabled nonetheless, with a much more immediate and catastrophic impact on their postwar prospects. The case of Alexander Fuller, a black veteran from Ohio, was typical in this respect. He tripped on a fallen tree branch while charging Confederate fortifications at Deep Bottom, Virginia, in 1864.

Other soldiers coming from behind trampled him, and he suffered permanent back damage. "I never did heavy work after the war," complained Fuller. "I did such work as driving, waiting on table[s], and odd chores about the house . . . at times my back would cause me to quit even light work for a day or two."[27] However, his problems were minor compared with those of other soldiers who lost eyes or limbs. The most disabled veterans were incapable of working at all; those ex-soldiers who could still perform minimal tasks wanted to work but had considerable trouble finding employment. They were forced to live on federal military pensions, and some, especially those who had no family to care for them, were obliged to take up residence in government homes for disabled veterans.[28]

No matter how well veterans performed relative to nonveterans in the black community, in no respect did they come close to the level of white veterans—Union or Confederate—in terms of prosperity after the war. That is, although fewer black veterans worked as unskilled laborers compared with nonveterans of the same age group in the African-American community, they did not necessarily enjoy as much prestige in their work as white veterans did. Only around 23 percent of white Union veterans were unskilled laborers in 1890, compared with nearly 50 percent of black veterans. Likewise, about 20 percent of white Union veterans worked in skilled occupations, but less than 9 percent of black veterans did so (see statistical appendix, table 2).[29]

There was little security in the work world in the late nineteenth century, but it was certainly less secure for the mass of black laborers, veterans included. Their economic position was quite tenuous. Jobs were often scarce, and the men could not afford to be particular when choosing employment. Especially for agricultural or day laborers, their working history was invariably a long succession of employers. Some lucky veterans achieved a degree of stability, but James Henry Mabin's comment was no doubt more typical: "I have worked for so many people at odd jobs that I can hardly name them all."[30] As long as they were physically able and work was plentiful, these working-class veterans could expect to scrape by. Howard Mason, a Kentucky veteran, testified in 1895 that he earned from seventy-five cents to one dollar a day in the decades after his discharge from the army. However, after Mason developed rheumatism, he had trouble finding work or getting the wages of a full hand. Disabilities caused by work mishaps, other accidents, illness, and advancing age could easily reduce veterans to a pitiful state. Some ex-soldiers who were no longer able to work, such as James Walton, who lived in Ohio and Michigan after the war, ended up in the poorhouse.[31] Other veterans were reduced to scavenging for bones or rags to sell. John L. Paine, a field investigator for the U.S. Pension Bureau, was so personally troubled by the situation of St. Louis veteran Henry Taylor that he took pains to describe it in a report to his superiors in Washington, D.C. "He has been a familiar figure to me for six months," Paine wrote of the sixty-six-year-old man. "I have seen him time and again hobbling with cane and rag hook, and bag, doing the alleys and gutters for rags. He does not earn two dollars a week."[32]

As the Taylor case shows, the poorer working and living conditions of black veterans took a considerable toll on their health. Hence, it is not surprising that a much smaller percentage of them survived the quarter century following the end of the Civil War compared with white veterans (see statistical appendix, table 3). More than half of the white men who had joined the Union and Confederate armies and navies were still alive in 1890 (about 54 percent of white Union veterans and 57 percent of Confederates), but less than 30 percent of African-American veterans survived. Although the higher survival rate of white Union veterans after the conflict can be partly explained by their lower wartime death rate, this was not so for Confederates, who suffered a higher death rate than both white and black Union soldiers during the Civil War.[33]

Given the general context of African-American life in the late nineteenth century, it is not surprising that a greater percentage of white than black veterans survived until 1890. Black mortality rates were significantly higher during the nineteenth century than they were for white Americans. In 1900, the Census Bureau found that in areas of the United States with death registration, 17 per 1,000 white persons died per year, compared with 30 per 1,000 African Americans.[34] Black men could expect to die as much as a decade earlier, on average, than white men during the late nineteenth century. One demographer found that during the period from 1870 to 1900, white males had a life expectancy of about fifty years, while black male life expectancy was closer to forty years.[35]

Hard physical labor took a toll on the health of black veterans, as did diseases caused by unsanitary living conditions. Black Americans in the late nineteenth century generally lived in unhealthier locations than white people did. Consequently, African Americans proved more vulnerable to outbreaks of smallpox and cholera.[36] Endemic diseases had an even greater effect on black mortality in the long run, particularly tuberculosis and other respiratory ailments. In 1910, tuberculosis was the leading cause of death for both black and white people in the United States, but 182 of every 1,000 African Americans who died that year perished from that disease, compared with only 102 of every 1,000 whites.[37] Indeed, half of black Civil War veterans documented in pension files who died before 1890, with an identified cause of death, died of respiratory diseases such as tuberculosis; the next leading cause of death was infectious disease. Only after 1890, when surviving ex-soldiers had aged sufficiently, did circulatory ailments, such as strokes and heart disease, overtake epidemic and endemic infections as the leading causes of death among African-American former soldiers.[38]

Yet despite the fact that black veterans lived shorter lives and were poorer in general than their white counterparts, as the aforementioned statistical evidence also shows, they tended to be more prosperous than black men who had not served. In addition, anecdotal evidence suggests that veterans may have tried harder to better themselves than did their nonveteran counterparts. Certainly the unusually high percentage of former soldiers who moved to the cities is strong evidence that black veterans as a group worked harder to achieve the means to bolster their manhood. One particular case, Robert Anderson, also suggests a connection between military service and the thirst for economic improvement.

Born and raised a slave in Kentucky, Robert Anderson (see fig. 6) devoted his postwar life, to the virtual exclusion of all other pursuits, to becoming a well-off farmer. In a memoir, *From Slavery to Affluence* (1927), he clearly attributed his quest for prosperity to military service. "The idea of owning my own land and being independent had been given me while I was still in the army," he later commented, "and I had never been able to get rid of it."[39] Hence, in at least one case, and no doubt in others, a black soldier imbibed the free labor ideology preached by some white officers to their African-American troops. Anderson internalized the notion that any man, through hard work, ability, and frugal living, could become a success.[40]

Yet as Anderson's autobiography shows, the road to prosperity could be a particularly difficult one for a black ex-soldier, even with the advantages he and other veterans enjoyed compared with other African Americans. After his discharge from the 125th USCI, Anderson seemingly had the resources to achieve his dream of landownership quickly. A thrifty man, he had saved his army pay and used it to buy acreage in Mills County, Iowa. Being inexperienced, however, he trusted the sales agent and paid for the land without seeing it first. When he finally laid eyes on the property, Anderson realized that the real estate agent had swindled him. He confessed in his autobiography, "It was all rough land that was no good at all for farming." The veteran had no choice but to sell the property at a substantial loss. After that debacle, Anderson worked at a brickyard for three years, saving more money, and in 1870, he went to Butler County, Nebraska, about sixty miles west of Omaha. He initially homesteaded, but finding the land too remote to market his crops, Anderson risked all his capital to buy land closer to the railroad. This time, bad luck rather than inexperience frustrated his dreams. "One year the grasshoppers came and ate everything up," he complained. "Then came four years of drouth [*sic*] when everything burned up." By 1881, Anderson had lost the land to foreclosure and had to hire himself out as a cook for a railroad construction crew in Kansas.[41]

Despite his reverses, Robert Anderson did not abandon his dream of becoming a successful farmer and landowner. His sense of manhood and desire for independence would not allow that possibility. Anderson saved the money he earned feeding railroad workers and, after three years, returned to Nebraska to homestead again. The odds against his success were now greater, because most of the better lands in eastern Nebraska had been taken by this time. He was forced to homestead in Box Butte County, in the more arid western section of the state. Anderson built a sod house to live in, planted trees, and lived off wild rabbits and other prairie game. Finding himself short of money to buy implements, he left his claim to earn more money cooking for the railroad construction crews, but he lost $1,600 by unwisely loaning his accumulated savings to another man, who absconded without repaying the money. Not deterred by yet another major setback, Anderson decided that rather than work as a cook to raise capital, he would risk everything he still had in one last stab at succeeding as a farmer. He mortgaged his land in Box Butte County to finance the purchase of a plow and the oxen to pull it. This time, his gamble worked, and the homestead proved a success. Within ten years, Anderson had paid off the mortgage and had money in the bank. Eventually, he could even afford to leave his land and take long trips across the United States and abroad.[42]

Robert Anderson proudly attributed his ultimate triumph to military service. "It is to that determination, formed when a soldier," the veteran asserted in his autobiography, "that I owe my independence today."[43] Military service had left him with the absolute resolve to demonstrate his manhood by accumulating wealth. In the end, Anderson achieved his dream of manly independence, but at a tremendous personal cost. By living cheaply and working hard, he managed to pull himself out of poverty several times and finally become a prosperous landowner. Yet he was so busy taking advantage of various opportunities that he lived alone all those years, and by the time Anderson achieved his goal, he was an old man. He achieved the masculine self-sufficiency that went with being a landowner but had no wife or children with whom to live out the masculine role of husband and father. Few black Union veterans went to such extremes to achieve independence through land-ownership, but Anderson's case demonstrates just how far some veterans were willing to go to achieve a manly competency.

The lack of a family apparently did not bother Anderson for most of his life, but as he approached his eightieth year, he confessed, "I began to feel lonesome, and wanted a companion, some one to make my hours less long, some one to share my life with me." Just short of his seventy-ninth birthday, he met and courted Daisy Graham, a young Arkansas woman nearly sixty years his junior. Graham, who had grown up in conditions of extreme poverty, accepted the veteran's attentions, and they married. However, the relationship between the couple was more like that between a doting grandfather and devoted granddaughter than a husband and wife. Graham took care of the old man in his declining years, and in return, she shared in his prosperous lifestyle and inherited his property when Anderson died eight years after they wed. Their marriage was a classic example of a union between a Civil War veteran looking for a caretaker in his old age and a poor young woman in search of economic security. Unfortunately, Daisy Graham Anderson lost her husband's property within several years of his death through a combination of mismanagement and extravagant living. By December 1936, according to a local relief official, she was "living in a one-room shack in the country . . . without food, clothing, or bedding."[44]

Although Robert Anderson was exceptional in the extent to which he went to achieve landownership and the means of patriarchy, he was not unusual in his desire to become a landowner. Indeed, ex-soldiers' ability to acquire land impressed Thomas Wentworth Higginson, former commanding officer of the 33d USCI, during a visit to Florida and South Carolina in the late 1870s. "I rarely met an ex-soldier who did not own his house and ground, the inclosures varying from five to two hundred acres," he commented.[45] Although Higginson no doubt overestimated the number of black veterans owning land in the areas he visited, it is significant that enough of them had become property holders to create this misimpression. Civil War pension files provide more realistic information on the extent of property ownership among African-American former soldiers. They suggest that at least one in nine black veterans, or around 11 percent, owned real estate at some point after the war.[46] Because this information tended to be gathered at the end of their lives, and landownership was generally not an issue in federal pension claims (since these benefits were not means-tested), the actual percentage of black veterans who owned land was no doubt higher and probably closer to the black rate of farm ownership, which by the 1880s was around 20 percent of all black farmers.[47] Hence, although military service may have helped inculcate a strong desire to become landowners, it is difficult to say whether veterans were more successful than nonveterans in acquiring real property. Certainly, though, with the bounties they received after the war and their access to Civil War pensions, they had resources for acquiring land that were not available to other African Americans in the late nineteenth century. The important point, however, is that demographic and anecdotal evidence suggests that former soldiers tried harder than other men to bolster their manhood—by moving to cities and trying to acquire land—and that they had some success, although the vast majority of them remained poor. Still, they clearly made a greater effort to obtain the means of manly independence and influence.

What is certain is that Civil War veterans did not have to become property owners to enjoy respect as men. Former soldiers as a group were quite well regarded in the postwar black community, both for their manly valor and for helping to liberate their own people from bondage. That is, the postwar African-American community evinced considerable pride in its Civil War veterans. The prestige they enjoyed is hard to exaggerate. These men had risked their lives to help destroy slavery and had taken on a more visible role in the war's outcome than any other segment of the African-American population. Consequently, it should not be surprising that former soldiers and sailors were often lionized by their people from the earliest days after the war. Besides veterans' receiving heroes' welcomes when they returned to the bosom of the black community, in some places, martial style became the rage. For instance, as Julie Saville documented in South Carolina soon after the war, "ex-slaves living near federal garrisons manned by black soldiers began to dress work

routines and frolics with a military air." Military-type drilling became a rec-
reational activity among the freed people there, not just among men but also
among women and children.[48] Military-style parades and other occasions
dressed up with martial pomp would remain quite popular among African
Americans in many parts of the country for the remainder of the nineteenth
century and well into the twentieth.[49]

The pride of the African-American community in Civil War veterans
continued for many years, explaining their enduring interest in former soldiers. Articles in the black press usually appeared in late May or early June,
relating the Memorial Day activities of the ex-soldiers. They announced ceremonies to be held or described such events after the fact for the benefit of
those who had been unable to attend. A typical article of the latter type appeared in *New York Age* in late May 1891. It reported on the Memorial Day
activities of the all-black Robert A. Bell Post No. 184 of Boston, part of the
Grand Army of the Republic (GAR), the principal Union veterans' organization (see chapter 6). In the morning, the post joined with its female auxil-
iary, Relief Corps No. 67, and an affiliated Sons of Veterans group in a
memorial service for three post members who had died in the previous year.
Following an afternoon repast, the veterans and their families adjourned from
the GAR hall to a local black church to hear sermons written especially for
the occasion, with intriguing titles such as "Time, the Great Problem Solver"
and "Offensive and Defensive Weapons."[50]

Reports on veterans appeared not just on Memorial Day but at other times
as well, chronicling veterans' social and political activities, reporting on black
veterans in government soldiers' homes, complaining about the ill treatment
of veterans and their survivors in bounty and pension applications, decrying
instances of discrimination in the GAR, celebrating when white veterans accorded black veterans manly respect, and airing an argument among black
veterans about which African-American regiment had been the first one organized during the Civil War, as well as other topics.[51] Although the articles varied in length and in the subjects they covered, collectively, they demonstrated
the virtually unanimous positive interest of the black community in its aging
"boys in blue." Hardly a critical word ever appeared in the African-American
newspapers of the late nineteenth and early twentieth centuries concerning
black Civil War veterans. They were simply beyond reproach.

The veterans became even more sacrosanct as their numbers dwindled
to a relative handful in the early years of the twentieth century. Whereas the

earlier articles had gushed in their praise of former soldiers, the tone became even more adulatory as the few surviving veterans reached their golden years. For instance, an article published in Baltimore's *Afro-American Ledger* just after Memorial Day in 1903 celebrated the city's black veterans with flowery but tragic words that captured the emotional impact as the number of surviving Civil War soldiers in the black community grew smaller each year. It lamented, "The grim reaper has entered and cut down one here, one there until He has greatly diminished their number, and those that have escaped His scythe feel the weight of years, their heads have grown white, their steps have become slackened as they request the band, 'boys not too fast for the old men.'" But the article quickly added, "A noble set of men!"—as if these words could provide a counterpoint to the woeful description of Baltimore's black veterans as the twentieth century dawned.[52]

The black press used not only words but also images to celebrate African-American veterans of the Civil War. The *Freeman,* which served the black community of Indianapolis and much of the Midwest, employed the services of a talented editorial cartoonist whose drawings appeared at the top of the front page and provided trenchant commentary on the issues of the day. In a series of three cartoons around Memorial Day in 1906, 1907, and 1908, he celebrated the black veterans in images that mirrored the flattering words reserved for these men in African-American newspapers. His 1906 cartoon, entitled "The Idol of Memorial Day," depicted an aging but still fierce-looking former soldier, his head held high, confident that he had done his manly duty by serving (see fig. 7).[53] The 1907 cartoon, simply titled "Memorial Day," idealized the bonds of veteranhood between white and black former Union soldiers. It depicted a white Union veteran missing a leg shaking hands with a black veteran missing an arm. The cordial expression on both men's faces commemorated the alliance between black and white men in the war, which still found institutional manifestation in the GAR (see fig. 8).[54] Yet it was the 1908 cartoon that captured the same sorrowful but celebratory tone of the aforementioned 1903 article in the *Afro-American Ledger.* The cartoon shows three elderly black veterans slowly marching down the street in what appears to be a Memorial Day parade (see fig. 9). The sorrowful expressions on their faces show that they know their time left on earth is short. To drive the point home, the cartoonist captioned his drawing "Still Marching to the Grave," and the subcaption adds, "Almost to their destination." With an eloquent and touching image, the cartoonist sought to remind the black readership of the

*Freeman* that the Civil War veterans in their midst were scarce and growing scarcer every year, and that as long as they remained, they needed to be cherished and honored.[55]

Like the press, black churches also showed pride in African-American veterans of the Civil War. Given the church's position as the most important institution in postwar black communities, the connection between former soldiers and churches was not surprising. Whereas newspapers served the literate and upwardly mobile segment of the postwar black community, churches reached the black masses. They were not only houses of worship but also places where African Americans could freely articulate their feelings and thoughts and where clergy, through their ministry, helped shape public opinion. Clergymen not only addressed purely religious issues but also reflected on issues of concern to African Americans—past, present, and future. An issue from the immediate past was the Civil War and the service of black soldiers in that conflict. Like the black press, clergymen were unfailing in praising African-American soldiers for their courage and valor and as manly liberators of their race. A Baptist minister in Washington, D.C., was quite typical in his praise when he stated, "The white soldier will be praised for defending his liberty, but the colored soldier will be praised because having no liberty, he purchased it by his own blood."[56]

Black clergymen did more than simply hold up African-American veterans on a pedestal. Evidence from newspapers suggests regular interaction between black churches and veterans' groups, but the most telling source on the close association of black churches and former soldiers comes from the Robert G. Shaw Post No. 206 of the GAR. This black GAR post in Pittsburgh, Pennsylvania, has the only known surviving records of a local African-American chapter of that organization. The minute books, which run from 1881 to 1904, although virtually silent in detailing the ceremonial rituals of Post No. 206 (which, after all, were secret), provide an intimate account of the close and cordial bonds between the black Grand Army men of Pittsburgh and the city's black churches. They reveal that local black ministers issued fairly frequent invitations to black GAR men to attend special services and commemorative events. The minutes for December 13, 1882, for example, recorded "a communication from the Pastor of Allen Chapel to attend a emancipation celebration on Jan 1st 1883."[57] The black churches of Pittsburgh also organized picnics for the veterans and opened their buildings for special events held by the Shaw post. In 1898, for instance, the John Wesley Zion Church in Pitts-

burgh let the veterans use its church building to add solemnity to the instal-
lation of Moore J. Barkes as the post commander.[58] In return, the post honored the black churches of Pittsburgh by often attending special religious
services in their GAR dress uniforms, thereby lending the prestige of their
fraternal order and status as manly heroes to the congregations they graced
with their presence. No doubt the close relationship of Pittsburgh's black
community was replicated in many other places across the United States.

The pride of African Americans in their Civil War veterans was a source
of unease to black men who had not served in the Union army or navy. This
discomfort manifested itself in a tendency to seek excuses for not serving
or to embellish and misrepresent what they had done during the war to
make it seem that they had served as soldiers. William W. Grimes, an African Methodist Episcopal (AME) minister in Massachusetts during the Civil
War, exemplifies the men in the black community who prevaricated in this
fashion. In his autobiography, under the heading "A Soldier of the Rebellion," Grimes indicated that he had not served because of his failure to gain
the chaplaincy of the 54th Massachusetts Infantry. He claimed that he had
been the first man to offer himself to John A. Andrew as a prospective chaplain, but the governor wanted to appoint a Baptist to the post instead.
Prominent federal officeholders interceded on his behalf, citing his successful recruiting activities for the regiment. Grimes claimed that, as a com-
promise, Andrew offered to make him and William Jackson, a Baptist
minister, co-chaplains of the 54th Massachusetts. Grimes wrote that he had
declined the appointment because "he considered himself a man, and did
not believe that it took two colored men to do the duty of one white man."
Grimes explained his refusal to serve on the principled grounds that made
sense to nineteenth-century Americans. These grounds also demonstrate
the importance of masculinity in the nineteenth-century African-American
community and the unwillingness of a proud black man to tolerate affronts
to his dignity. For Grimes to serve with Jackson would have been to admit
in his reckoning that blacks were lesser men than whites (although he also
confessed that he and Jackson did not get along).[59]

Unlike Grimes, some black men had served in the Union army and navy,
but not as soldiers or sailors. They had been cooks, servants, laborers, or teamsters or had supported military operations in other menial capacities, but
sometimes at considerable personal risk in combat zones. After the war, these
men saw the glory showered on those who had borne the rifles, while their

important services were trivialized or ignored. In response, they adroitly exaggerated their descriptions of the war to imbue their wartime activities with manly bravery. A classic example was a black man living in Albany, New York, William Henry Johnson. Johnson wrote in his autobiography (speaking of himself in the third person) that, "not allowed to enlist as a soldier because of his color, he joined a Connecticut regiment as an independent man and participated in the battles of Bull Run, Roanoke, and Newbern."[60] If the reader was confused by what he meant by an "independent man," a subsequent passage strongly intimated that it was more than simply a body servant. "When the regiment returned home," he indicated, "Mr. Johnson went to the front with the Eighth Connecticut [a white infantry unit] . . . and was commended for his bravery by every officer in the command."[61] Johnson's account could easily leave the reader with the impression that he had been a soldier in the war and had seen action. In a sense, he probably had participated in combat. Black civilians working for both Union and Confederate forces near or at the front found themselves exposed to many dangers encountered by soldiers, especially artillery. However, it was awkward to try to explain this reality to civilians who had never experienced the war firsthand and saved their adulation for the men who had formally served under arms in the army or navy. To get the credit for the manly bravery they felt they deserved, men such as Johnson evidently found it necessary to parse their activities in the war and hope that the public drew the proper conclusions.[62]

Yet the true significance of the autobiography of William Henry Johnson was that he and other authors like him demonstrated the prestige accorded Civil War service in the black community in the years following the conflict. Some men wanted to be counted among the former soldiers and rhetorically placed themselves in the illustrious ranks of war veterans, even if, strictly speaking, they did not belong there because they had not borne arms. The service of black men in the Civil War was a well-known fact in their community, and veterans were idolized as liberators of their race. Who could blame men who had been servants, teamsters, or military laborers for wanting to share in the manly honor of the soldiers?

It must also be admitted that authentic black soldiers in the war were not above misrepresenting their Civil War records. A classic example in this regard is Caesar C. Antoine, who served as lieutenant governor of Louisiana during Reconstruction and was later a high-ranking GAR officer in the Department of Louisiana and Mississippi. During the war, Antoine served as a captain in a sixty-day regiment, the 7th Louisiana Infantry, hastily raised to stem a Confederate offensive in that state in the fall of 1863 and disbanded after its term of service expired. Antoine made no further attempt to join the army after leaving the 7th Louisiana, but in late April 1865, he found himself drafted into the 10th U.S. Colored Heavy Artillery (USCHA) as a common soldier. He spent three months in the unit before finally finagling a medical discharge. This was hardly a military career that a man seeking political advancement or a prominent place in the GAR could brag about. Hence, Antoine's profile in *Men of Mark,* the most famous and widely distributed biographical dictionary of prominent black Americans in the late nineteenth century, simply mentions his captaincy in the 7th Louisiana and indicates, "he served at Breashear, now Morgan City, and other places in the department with credit to himself to the close of the war."[63]

Despite the prevarications of Caesar C. Antoine, the prestige that black Civil War veterans enjoyed in the postwar African-American community is undeniable. They were praised in black newspapers and from the pulpits of African-American churches, and their position was unassailable among their own people. It is little wonder, then, that their presence proved uncomfortable to their contemporaries who had not served as soldiers or had not served with distinction. The idolization they received each Memorial Day and at many other times must have been a balm for the poverty many still faced and for the fact that their numbers diminished more quickly than those of their white Union and Confederate counterparts—something that must have been apparent to discerning black veterans. Yet, as a group, they were better off economically than their nonveteran contemporaries and worked harder to achieve success. Happenstance placed a high percentage of black veterans in the North, but more moved there in the years after the war; their disproportionate presence in postwar cities compared with other African Americans and the anecdotal evidence suggest that they strived harder for economic manhood, which alone makes their postwar experience distinctive. Their prestige and relative success made them a special group among postwar African Americans. Yet success in achieving manly attributes and respect in their community was not enough for many of these men—to be a real man meant achieving and preserving political rights as well.

# Politics

IN THEIR PURSUIT of manhood, it was inevitable that black Civil War veterans became involved in politics. Politics was the forum through which these men could achieve what they saw as their just reward for military service: suffrage and full citizenship. They began agitating for these rights even before leaving the army. This quest, however, was merely the beginning of a lifelong involvement in politics and community leadership. Unfortunately, black veterans would reach the peak of their effectiveness as a group in the immediate aftermath of the war. Their influence quickly faded, and it is notable that military service had only a modest impact at best on their political behavior after the late 1860s. Bonds created in past struggles for freedom and voting rights quickly unraveled as veterans vied with former comrades (and other ambitious black men) for government offices during Reconstruction. Ex-soldiers also exhibited deep disagreement about how best to respond to the deteriorating status of African Americans in the late nineteenth century. Yet even as political office was increasingly closed off to black men, veterans in community leadership positions continued to work for their people's welfare both to do good and to assert their manhood.

Some black soldiers emerged from the Civil War with the feeling of a battle half won. Although they had helped to destroy slavery and proved their manhood, they had not won suffrage and full citizenship rights or opened avenues for the economic and social advancement of their race. In fact, the exact status of African Americans in the wake of the war was uncertain. This state of affairs proved intolerable to the black men who had worn the Union blue. Politicized by their military service and desirous of equality, black soldiers and veterans did not hesitate to demand what they saw as their manly due. Thus, they ended up playing an integral role in the campaign for African-American suffrage.

The campaign for voting rights touched black troops and veterans in both the North and the South. On at least one occasion, black soldiers organized their own political convention to press for suffrage rights. This meeting was held by 700 troops of Iowa's 60th USCI on October 31, 1865, at Camp McClellan in Davenport.[1] Rather than organizing their own meetings, it was more common for soldiers to attend the postwar political conventions put on by black civilian leaders after the war. African Americans used these forums not only to agitate for full citizenship rights—especially suffrage—but also to discuss solutions to their economic, educational, and other concerns. Convention delegates often drew up resolutions later presented to government authorities. Although a few conventions drew black delegates from across the United States, more often they were local or state affairs.[2]

Soldiers and veterans participated in postwar black political conventions across the country. At least ten former black officers of Louisiana's Native Guard regiments took part in the New Orleans convention in January 1865. In fact, James Ingraham, a black officer in the 1st Louisiana Native Guards, served as its president.[3] Several black veterans also figured prominently at the North Carolina convention that occurred in September 1865. George W. Price Jr., for instance, a former sailor in the Union navy, helped organize the meeting.[4]

More important, black Civil War soldiers and veterans not only participated in the suffrage conventions but also helped articulate and justify African-American claims for voting rights after the war. Perhaps the most eloquent example in this regard comes from Tennessee. In October 1865, African Americans from across the state assembled for the State Colored Men's Convention at Nashville's St. John AME Church. Black Union soldiers on leave from their regiments in Tennessee were among the delegates who attended. A number of these men spoke at the meeting, but one in particular, Henry Maxwell, a sergeant in the 3d USCI, made an especially meaningful contribution. "We want two more boxes besides the cartridge box—the ballot and the jury box," stated Maxwell.[5] With one sentence, this soldier simply but eloquently made the connection between military service in the Civil War and African Americans' postwar desire for voting and other citizenship rights.

Indeed, there were few things more important to many black veterans in the conflict's aftermath than gaining suffrage. It was a linchpin of achieving political equality with white men in terms of manhood. They had fought as men, and now they wanted what they saw as a man's most important political right. The significance of suffrage had been made plain to them early in the war. Opponents of black enlistment argued, among other things, that African Americans could not render military service because, as the *Dred Scott* decision had declared, they were not citizens. They based their position on the dual nature of citizenship. To nineteenth-century Americans, citizenship meant not only the enjoyment of rights but also the assumption of responsibilities. Citizens voted and exercised other rights, but in return, the government expected them to fulfill certain duties, including answering the call to bear arms at the appropriate time. Hence, the military service of African-American soldiers in the Civil War was a powerful argument for black suffrage in the nineteenth century. The belief that African Americans were not citizens had been an important justification for denying black men entrance into the army at the beginning of the war; reversing that logic provided compelling grounds to grant black men suffrage once they had served in the army.

Other black soldiers besides Henry Maxwell powerfully expressed this argument connecting military service with citizenship rights. As Iowa's black soldiers put the case in their convention's resolutions: "He who is worthy to be trusted with the musket can and ought to be trusted with the ballot."[6] Having performed a man's most onerous duty as a citizen, they felt that they clearly deserved a man's citizenship rights. Yet suffrage remained paramount as the key to all rights, without which the others were essentially meaningless. Bereft of voting rights, contended Iowa's black soldiers, "we have no power to defend ourselves from unjust legislation, and no voice in the Government we have endeavored to defend."[7]

Given the keen interest in suffrage among African-American veterans and their importance in articulating arguments in favor of black citizenship rights, it was logical that these men organized nationally among themselves to achieve that goal. African-American veterans in the North joined with their Southern comrades in 1866 to form the Colored Soldiers and Sailors' League. The purpose of the league was to focus the efforts of black former soldiers and sailors in favor of African-American suffrage rights. The formation of this organization also reflected the fact that African-American veterans were beginning to develop the idea that they were special advocates for the black community as a whole on the issue of suffrage. Veterans were not alone in this opinion. The *Christian Recorder,* mouthpiece of the African Methodist Episcopal Church, expressed a similar sentiment while promoting the league's national convention held in Philadelphia in January 1867. "The men, who in open field could bear their bosoms in heroic charge upon the enemy's cannon," the *Recorder* opined, "have certainly the force of character, and will know better than any body else can tell them, to charge upon and overthrow the citadel of American prejudice."[8] In short, the Colored Soldiers and Sailors' League was meant to give organizational force to the moral authority of black veterans in favor of voting rights.

In particular, black veterans believed that their moral authority would be difficult for white Northerners to ignore. They were certainly not mistaken in this notion. The military service argument helped change the opinion of many white Northerners on the issue of black voting rights. Suffrage for black men in the antebellum period had been dismissed out of hand in most Northern states, but with the valiant service of African Americans in defense of the Union, a groundswell of support for the idea developed in the North. In a short period of time, the notion of black men voting went from being outlandish to being quite conceivable, largely because of the contributions of African-American soldiers and the connection between military service and citizenship made by nineteenth-century Americans.

A trenchant example of this pro-suffrage sentiment among white Northerners is visible in the work of the most famous political cartoonist of the period, Thomas Nast. In 1865, Nast used the image of a tattered, disabled black veteran in a cartoon advocating black suffrage (see fig. 4). Nast carefully crafted his image. The black soldier exudes noble suffering. His face shows the pain of both a lost limb and justice denied. Columbia, a popular personification of the United States during the nineteenth century, presents the soldier not beseechingly but matter-of-factly. She does not have to beg for this disabled man; the rights he has earned should be evident to all. With a powerful image, Nast reminded the nation of the connection between military service and citizenship rights. His picture argued in images more powerful than any words that black soldiers had suffered like white soldiers during the war and consequently deserved the same rights, particularly the vote.

However, despite Nast's powerful image, suffrage did not come quickly for black veterans in the North. Black soldiers and veterans there initially were hopeful that state legislatures would bestow voting rights on African Americans as a reward for their wartime service. But although there was growing support for the idea, racial prejudice still trumped gratitude throughout the North in the immediate aftermath of the war, as state after state rejected attempts to extend suffrage rights to black men.[9] Ohio presents a good example of this phenomenon. The state managed to recruit its own black regiment during the war, the 5th USCI. Regardless of this unit's faithful service, however, the state proved quite ambivalent about extending citizenship rights to African Americans. The Ohio legislature ratified the Fourteenth Amendment in 1867, granting black Americans citizenship, but rescinded the ratification a year later. Likewise, white voters in the state rejected by 50,000 votes a referendum on an amendment to the state constitution that would have granted suffrage to black men. Later, the state legislature approved by one vote the Fifteenth Amendment, granting black men voting rights nationwide, but only when it became clear that the amendment would gain approval in enough states to become part of the U.S. Constitution without Ohio's support.[10]

Southern black veterans did not fare much better than their Northern counterparts, at least initially. Reconstruction policy during most of 1865 and 1866 was in the hands of Abraham Lincoln's successor, Andrew Johnson. Johnson, a Tennessee Unionist and ex-slaveholder, believed that African Americans were unqualified for citizenship and suffrage regardless of whether they had served in the army. Furthermore, he leniently restored the citizenship rights of Southern white men, except for a few of the highest former Confederate officials. His policies quickly reestablished state governments in the South dominated by white Southerners. These governments vehemently opposed African-American suffrage and, through highly restrictive laws—the so-called black codes—sought to control the mobility and labor of former slaves, as the prewar regimes had restricted the lives of free persons of color in the South.

Yet suffrage did eventually come to black men—in the South by 1867 and nationwide by 1870. Civil War veterans played a significant part in the final achievement of suffrage for African-American men as victims in the New Orleans riot of July 1866. The riot stemmed from the reconvening that month of the 1864 state constitutional convention, which had as an important aim the enfranchisement of black men. The convention represented a threat to the state's traditional Democratic party elite, which had recouped much of its prewar power under President Johnson's lenient policies.[11] On July 30, twenty-five delegates of the 1864 convention assembled at the Mechanics Institute in New Orleans. A group of about 300 African Americans, led by flag bearer A. L. Thibaut, a former officer in the 1st Louisiana Native Guards, escorted them to the hall. Almost half the crowd accompanying the delegates was composed of African-American veterans.[12] The former soldiers flocked to defend the meeting against threats of disruption. Lacking the means to acquire a more lethal arsenal, they and other supporters of the delegates at the Mechanics Institute were armed only with clubs, canes, sticks, and a few pistols.[13]

Intense fighting broke out on the first afternoon of the convention between its black supporters and a white crowd. As in the earlier Memphis riot, the black defenders initially gained the upper hand, fiercely resisting the mob's onslaught and pushing it back. However, the New Orleans police did not take a neutral stance and fired on the African-American veterans and other convention supporters. Overpowered, most of the black crowd prudently fled the scene, but some supporters sought shelter in the convention building. The white mob quickly besieged the individuals remaining inside the Mechanics Institute. The delegates and other defenders managed to beat back the initial attempts to storm the building, but the mob eventually overwhelmed them. Once inside, the mob turned the full force of its rage on the poorly armed delegates and their supporters. A few persons managed to escape in the initial confusion, but the mob and the police killed or badly beat those who could not get away. When federal troops finally arrived late in the afternoon to restore order, 38 people were dead and 146 were wounded—many of them black Civil War veterans.[14]

Black ex-soldiers suffered greatly during the New Orleans riot, but their sacrifice furthered the campaign for suffrage and equal rights for African Americans in the U.S. South. The New Orleans riot, as well as the violence in Memphis earlier that year (see chapter 2) and other signs of Southern whites' continued intransigence, combined with Johnson's veto of the extension of the Freedmen's Bureau and the 1866 civil rights bill, swung Northern public opinion against Johnson's lenient approach to reintegrating the South into national life. The 1866 elections brought Reconstruction under the control of the Radical Republicans in Congress. With Radicals in power, the Fifteenth Amendment passed Congress and was submitted to the states for ratification. It finally became part of the U.S. Constitution in 1870. Black men in the South gained the vote even earlier. Congress made provisions for African Americans to vote for delegates to the 1867 state constitutional conventions in the South, with the aim of establishing biracial government in that region. These new state constitutions in the Southern states opened not only suffrage but also political office to black men.

Hence, black veterans, despite the continued intransigence and violence of white Southerners, played a pivotal part in the battle for suffrage during Reconstruction. Although the African-American veterans paid a bloody toll, white Northerners' gratitude for their wartime sacrifice and sympathy for their postwar suffering at the hands of white Southern mobs played an important role in swinging enough support for black voting rights. Certainly theirs was not the only contribution to the advent of black suffrage and political officeholding. Yet it is fair to say that without black service in the Civil War or these men's agitation for suffrage afterward, the Fifteenth Amendment might never have been ratified. Their argument for suffrage and the suffering they endured went a long way toward creating the political climate in the North that made equal rights—including voting rights—possible for African Americans.

Although black veterans proved influential in the campaign for suffrage and equality, they were a much weaker political force as Reconstruction officeholders. To understand this change, it is important to know some salient facts. What first stands out about the African-American veterans who went into postwar politics is that they were underrepresented among the 1,465 documented black officeholders who served between 1867 and 1877. Of the aforementioned total, only 144 claimed Civil War service.[15] Hence, veterans made up only around 10 percent of the black men holding public office during Reconstruction, while they constituted about 16 percent of the adult-male black population in the United States immediately after the war.[16]

The underrepresentation of veterans among African-American lawmakers during Reconstruction did not represent a lack of commitment on their part to the problems and needs of their race but was instead a product of the geography of wartime recruitment and differing opportunities for black officeholding in particular states after the Civil War. With the exception of black carpetbaggers who came down from the North, African-American officeholders, Civil War veterans included, tended to serve in their home states. In Florida, Georgia, Virginia, and Alabama, where the Union army had recruited only small numbers of black soldiers, fewer veterans existed to serve in public office. Likewise, in states with high levels of recruitment but little or no opportunity for African Americans to serve as lawmakers, few veterans held office. Such was the case in the North and the loyal border states, where a high percentage of black men served in the Union army but African Americans were mostly shut out of office during the Reconstruction years.[17]

The vast majority of black veterans in public office during Reconstruction served in Louisiana, Mississippi, and North and South Carolina (see statistical appendix, table 4). Together, these four states accounted for nearly 80 percent of black veteran lawmakers. More former soldiers held office there than in other ex-Confederate states partly because of the greater opportunities for black officeholding that existed there. (In fact, over 60 percent of all African Americans in political office during Reconstruction served in the four aforementioned states.) Further contributing to the large number of veteran officeholders in Louisiana and Mississippi was the higher percentage of veterans in the black populations of those two states than elsewhere in the Lower South—a legacy of the heavy recruitment of black soldiers in the Mississippi Valley during the war. In the Carolinas, however, Union recruiters operated in coastal enclaves under Northern occupation, isolated from inland areas of North and South Carolina under Confederate control. Yet after the war, a surprisingly high percentage of veterans held office in the Carolinas because both states became a popular destination for politically ambitious black ex-soldiers from the North. In South Carolina, for instance, more than a third of the black veteran officeholders in the state had lived in the Northern states before the war.[18]

The underrepresentation of veterans among postwar black lawmakers in the South somewhat belies their overall importance. Many of the most important black officeholders during Reconstruction were Civil War veterans. Former soldiers were particularly prominent at the federal level. Six of the sixteen black members of the U.S. House of Representatives in the Reconstruction years claimed military experience during the Civil War.[19] Thirty-seven veterans also held federal patronage posts during Reconstruction, filling a disproportionately large 28 percent of the federal positions awarded to black men. These offices ranged from the U.S. ambassadorship to Liberia, held by James Milton Turner during much of the 1870s, to the position of postmaster in local communities.[20]

Still, despite their notable presence in high office, military service had little apparent influence on veterans as Reconstruction officeholders. Indeed, the tragedy of the political involvement of these men was that with their victory in the battle for suffrage, black Civil War veterans reached the peak of their influence as a political force. Not the least reason was that, once they gained citizenship and voting rights under the Constitution, they largely dropped their political identity as veterans. For instance, the Colored Soldiers and Sailors' League disappears from the historical record in the early 1870s, apparently a victim of its own success. Although black veterans would organize again in the mid-1880s, this decentralized "reunion" movement would be less overtly political and much less effective than the league had been more than a decade earlier (see chapter 6).

During Reconstruction, influences other than their military experience were more important in shaping the behavior of black veteran officeholders. Indeed, socioeconomic status stands out as the most apparent determinant of the political behavior of these men between 1867 and 1877.

More so than other black political leaders of that era, veterans were drawn from the elite of their race. African-American politicians during Reconstruction tended to be disproportionately literate and from freeborn, mixed-race backgrounds, and these characteristics were even truer of politicians who had served in the Civil War. Around 68 percent of black veteran officeholders were born free or gained their freedom before the Civil War. By contrast, less than half of nonveteran officeholders had enjoyed freedom before the war (see statistical appendix, table 5). Nearly two-thirds of black veterans in Reconstruction politics had mixed racial ancestry, compared with around half of nonveterans (see statistical appendix, table 6). Almost 97 percent of veteran officeholders were literate, but only about 81 percent of nonveteran officeholders (see statistical appendix, table 7). Veterans also enjoyed higher overall occupational success in the Reconstruction years. Virtual parity existed in the percentage of veteran and nonveteran officeholders who were artisans and service workers (see statistical appendix, table 8). However, a greater percentage of former soldiers worked in the professions (46 versus 33 percent) and a lesser percentage in unskilled jobs (13 versus 26 percent).

Many black veterans in Reconstruction politics also had acquired significant property by 1870, although few were enormously wealthy. Just over four out of five veterans in politics identified in the 1870 census owned property, with about 36 percent owning property valued at $1,000 or more (see statistical appendix, table 9). On the whole, the census also showed them to be somewhat wealthier than their nonveteran contemporaries in politics. Certainly fewer former soldiers did not own property (18 versus 26 percent).[21]

The actions of these black veterans as Reconstruction officeholders are consistent with their relatively exalted status. Given that an unusually high percentage of them were property owners, or persons who soon hoped to own property, it was not in their interest to back land confiscation, a position supported by many freed slaves who believed that the real property of former slaveholders should be taken away and redistributed to them as just compensation for their years in bondage and as a reward for their loyalty to the Union during the war.[22] With only rare exceptions, such as Joseph T. Wilson, a black Virginia veteran (and later the author of *The Black Phalanx*, a history of black soldiers in the Civil War), veteran lawmakers did not advocate land confiscation.[23] Instead, they sought to shore up the rights of African Americans within the existing political system. Most of them concentrated on passing laws guaranteeing African Americans suffrage and citizen rights at the state level and promoting education and economic development. Almost uniformly, they believed that hard work and thriftiness was the best path to prosperity for themselves and the entire African-American community.[24] In other words, black veteran officeholders embraced the Horatio Alger myth of the Republican party, which held that any man, through sufficient frugality and resourcefulness, could rise in society. As Eric Foner put it, they, like their nonveteran counterparts, "fully embraced the prevailing free labor ethos, which saw individual initiative in the 'race of life,' not public assistance, as the route to upward mobility."[25] They felt that the best route to manhood for black men lay not in the confiscation of the means of production but in the guarantee that African Americans would be able to fight for advancement playing under the same rules as everyone else.

Hence, positions taken by black veterans as Reconstruction officeholders are unremarkable, and their political behavior showed little discernible difference from that of nonveterans. Even in the state where the concentration of veteran officeholders was greatest, Louisiana, this situation was true. Historians have long recognized the significance of former soldiers in that state's postwar politics, especially among the mulatto elite of New Orleans, which had initially supplied the company officers for the Louisiana Native Guard regiments (see the prologue).[26] Over 30 percent of African Americans in public office in Louisiana during Reconstruction were Civil War veterans, including the highest-ranking black politicians in the state. The only African-American governor during this period, P. B. S. Pinchback of Louisiana (see fig. 13), was a veteran. Likewise, three of Louisiana's Reconstruction lieutenant governors, Pinchback, Caesar C. Antoine, and Oscar J. Dunn, claimed military service during the war.[27] Yet their experience as officers in the Native Guard regiments had little discernible effect on their actions as politicians. Instead, the quest for dominance within the state's Republican party seemed to be the overriding imperative behind their actions.

Although top black officeholders in Louisiana had fought together during the war to end slavery and cooperated afterward in the battle for suffrage, once those aims were achieved, their attention shifted toward satisfying personal ambitions. Having seemingly gained a permanent voice in the political process, they vied with one another to have the most powerful voice among their people. Oscar J. Dunn headed the group allied with white Republicans based in the New Orleans customhouse, until his sudden death in 1871.[28] White Republicans in the state were split between the supporters of Reconstruction governor Henry C. Warmoth and his pro-Grant opponents based in the customhouse. Dunn, elected lieutenant governor in 1868, had turned against Warmoth because the governor's support for black civil rights was too lukewarm. Warmoth refused to support, neglected on his desk, and finally vetoed legislation to enforce racial equality provisions in the Louisiana state constitution. P. B. S. Pinchback led a rival black faction that continued to support Governor Warmoth. Like Dunn, Pinchback was bothered by Warmoth's veto of the civil rights bill. However, he and Dunn were rivals dating back to 1867, when they had both sought to represent New Orleans' fourth ward at the state's constitutional convention. Warmoth had supported Pinchback in that contest, and they became political allies. Rather than oppose Warmoth on the civil rights bill, Pinchback and his followers turned their attention to the business of enriching themselves in public office.[29] The governor rewarded Pinchback's loyalty by supporting his candidacy for lieutenant governor after Dunn suddenly died. Dunn's replacement as head of the black anti-Warmoth faction was Caesar C. Antoine. Unlike Dunn, Antoine and Pinchback were former friends and allies. They had operated a cotton factorage together in the late 1860s and cofounded the *New Orleans Louisianan,* a political weekly. Eventually, however, the business and professional relationship of the two men soured after Antoine sided with Dunn when the latter repudiated Warmoth. Antoine was supposedly also mad at Pinchback for allegedly cheating him out of $40,000 promised as part of a property deal in which Pinchback had made $200,000 buying land earmarked for a public park and reselling it to the city of New Orleans at a higher price.[30]

Certainly the Louisiana experience does not suggest that Civil War service had no influence at all on the conduct of black veterans as Reconstruction officeholders. Without doubt, the Civil War helped prepare black soldiers for political office. Over 90 percent of veteran lawmakers during Reconstruction had served at least as noncommissioned officers in the Union army. Within the military command structure, they developed their abilities to lead men, and they gained political skills during the campaign for equal pay with white soldiers and while protecting the interests of freed slaves and the black community more generally. Military service also allowed some future officeholders to improve themselves in other ways. For instance, at least five of these men learned to read in the army.[31] The indignities they often suffered in the army also strengthened their commitment to equal rights and universal male suffrage. In addition, some black veterans developed their political constituencies while in military service. This was most noticeable among black carpetbaggers. At least half of these men sought office in states where they had served in the army. Their exposure to the problems of the people there probably encouraged them to return after the war to deal with them. Veterans were much more likely to become carpetbaggers than were nonveterans. About 23 percent of the veteran lawmakers (33 of 144) had lived outside the South, compared with only 8 percent (104 of 1,321) of nonveteran officeholders.[32]

Veterans also built postwar political careers based on their wartime exploits. Perhaps the best example of this phenomenon was Robert Smalls of South Carolina (see fig. 12). A slave in Charleston before the war, Smalls made his reputation through an act of considerable courage and daring. In May 1862, he stole a cotton steamer, the *Planter;* bluffed his way past Confederate fortifications guarding Charleston harbor; and delivered the ship to the Union blockade flotilla outside the port. Smalls's act made him an overnight hero in the North. Congress passed legislation awarding prize money to Smalls for delivering the *Planter* into Union hands. Smalls was appointed pilot and later captain of the *Planter* and subsequently saw action supporting Union military operations along the coast of South Carolina. His heroism at Charleston and later wartime activities established Smalls as an important public figure in the Sea Islands region of South Carolina, where he had been born and spent his early years. Smalls built on his initial popularity there through numerous speaking engagements, where he regaled audiences with the account of his escape in the *Planter* and subsequent feats. Smalls also made trips to the North to raise money for the benefit of the freed people in his home region.

After the war, he settled in the town of Beaufort in the Sea Islands, actually buying the home where he had been enslaved as a small boy. Smalls sunk his prize money into the local economy. In 1866, he entered a cooperative venture with a black Union army veteran, Tom Long, to purchase and operate a coastal steamer and bought local real estate. He also supported philanthropic projects that directly benefited the community. For instance, Smalls purchased a two-story building for use as a school and raised money in the North to fund its operation. Smalls solidly established himself as a prominent member of the Sea Islands postwar black elite.[33]

By carefully building on his wartime exploits, Robert Smalls established the most durable career of any black politician in the postwar period. He was elected to South Carolina's 1868 constitutional convention and then served two years in the lower house and four years in the upper house of the South Carolina legislature. In 1874, Smalls won election to the U.S. Congress and served there on and off for the next twelve years, until internal dissension in the local Republican party allowed the Democrats to overcome his congressional district's overwhelming black majority. As the most powerful local Republican leader in South Carolina, however, subsequent Republican presidents recognized his continued power and party loyalty by appointing Smalls collector of customs in Beaufort. Except for the second Cleveland administration in the 1890s (which appointed a Democrat to the post), Smalls held the post of collector of customs in Beaufort until his death in 1913.[34]

Yet in the rough-and-tumble world of politics in the Reconstruction-era South, although the war influenced the public service of black veterans, socioeconomic status and political realities of intraparty competition played a much greater role in shaping the conduct of the former soldiers who chose to pursue political office in the years following the war. On the one hand, this was a positive development. It was a sign that black veterans had advanced beyond the quest for the rights of manhood to the exercise of them. Like white men, they could play the masculine power game within the political system, rather than fighting to be included in that system. On the other hand, they lost the moral authority that their identity as Civil War veterans had given them in the early years after the war. Although they still might be able to use the leadership skills honed in the army and benefit politically from the prestige of military service, as the decades passed, they became increasingly indistinguishable from African-American leaders who had not rendered military service.

**After the Glory**

The stances taken by African-American veterans in the years following Reconstruction demonstrate this reality. Their positions were little different from those of nonveteran leaders in the black community. Like their counterparts who had not served, Civil War veterans were not of one mind on how to challenge the rise of disfranchisement, Jim Crow laws, and lynching in the South in the wake of Reconstruction. Certainly their wartime sacrifices made them especially reluctant to accept inferior treatment and had trained them in the skills of resistance, but they developed different responses to the challenges confronting African Americans in the last decades of the nineteenth century. Black veterans, it seems, drew a variety of lessons from the failure of Reconstruction. Nearly all of them had opted for moderation as lawmakers after the Civil War, but that course had not produced results, and the collapse of Reconstruction caused them to diverge on three different paths. Yet black veterans remained united by the goal of defending the gains they had made during the Civil War and defending their manhood, even if they could not agree on the best strategy to accomplish this task. In short, they disagreed on the means, not on the final goal.

One group of former soldiers opted to stand their ground and fight discrimination wherever it appeared, participating in the post-Reconstruction civil rights struggle. Some of these veterans challenged discriminatory laws in state legislatures; a few even experienced success in this endeavor. James Harvey Anderson, a minister of the AME Zion Church and a veteran of the 39th USCI, successfully lobbied the Rhode Island legislature to lift the state's ban on interracial marriage in 1881.[35] Most other former soldiers, however, were less successful. As a member of the Ohio legislature in the 1880s, for instance, George W. Williams failed dismally in his effort to gain the repeal of Ohio's ban on interracial marriage.[36] James Townshend, a veteran and AME minister who served in the Ohio legislature, was equally unsuccessful in gaining repeal of the state's "black laws."[37]

With legislative approaches often unfruitful and African Americans increasingly unable to gain election to such bodies, ex-soldiers shifted the focus of their attacks on discriminatory laws to the courts. The most significant court challenge in which Civil War veterans were involved was the infamous case of *Plessy v. Ferguson* (1896). Caesar C. Antoine and P. B. S. Pinchback (who had apparently settled their differences), as well as James Lewis, participated in the citizens' committee in New Orleans that sponsored Homer C. Plessy's challenge of a Louisiana segregation law in the 1890s. The statute prohibited black people, except for white children's nurses, from sitting in first-class railroad cars, even if they had purchased first-class tickets. This law especially troubled Louisiana's black elite, many of whom were freeborn, light skinned, and relatively well-off. The law essentially reduced their status to that of poorer, darker-skinned persons of African descent, ignoring their education, wealth, and social refinement. The citizens' group arranged for Plessy, a light-skinned African American (his ancestry was only one-eighth black), to break the law and then challenged his prosecution in the courts. The case moved through the appellate process to the U.S. Supreme Court, where it became the basis for the "separate but equal" doctrine that legally legitimized racial segregation until the 1950s.[38]

Although the efforts of the Louisiana veterans backfired, at least one former soldier proved successful in challenging discrimination in the courts. Two decades after the *Plessy* decision, John B. Anderson won his suit seeking to invalidate a 1908 Maryland law enacting a grandfather clause in municipal elections in the state capital of Annapolis (where Anderson resided). Under the law, the city of Annapolis refused to register black men to vote in municipal elections unless they owned property with an assessed value of $500 or more—an amount few African Americans in the city possessed. The statute also exempted from the property requirement men qualified to vote before 1868 or their descendants. As a loyal border state not subject to the Reconstruction Act of 1867, African Americans in Maryland had been unable to vote in the state before the ratification of the Fifteenth Amendment in 1870. In short, the 1908 law allowed white men in Annapolis to vote in municipal elections regardless of their property holdings, while disfranchising all but the wealthiest black voters. Anderson's initial suit in federal circuit court in 1909 was successful in overturning the Annapolis grandfather clause, but Maryland authorities appealed, and the case eventually ended up in the U.S. Supreme Court, where oral arguments were heard during the October 1913 term.[39]

It is highly significant that at each judicial level, Anderson's lawyers saw fit to mention his Civil War military service in their court briefs. Anderson's service, in both the Union army and navy, was not strictly germane to his legal challenge. The basis for the lawsuit was that the Maryland law governing Annapolis elections violated Anderson's and other black men's Fifteenth Amendment rights. Though his lawyers certainly pressed this key point, they always inserted one or more references to their client's military service. For instance, the initial brief to the federal circuit court in 1909 stated, "The plaintiff [i.e., Anderson] further says that prior to the said first day of January in the year one thousand eight hundred and sixty eight, he had served creditably in and been honorably discharged from both the military and naval service of the United States." In his court testimony, his attorneys also elicited the fact that Anderson was drawing a federal pension on the basis of his Civil War service. Likewise, his lawyers' brief to the U.S. Supreme Court mentioned his military service not once but twice. Though not exactly relevant in a legal sense, mentioning Anderson's military service was far from gratuitous. It gave Anderson's case moral weight. As men raised and socialized in the nineteenth century, the federal judges from the circuit level up to the Supreme Court would have been aware of, and likely believers in, the connection between military service and manhood rights. Knowing that the plaintiff was a veteran and had faithfully discharged the most onerous burden of citizenship would make it harder for them to rule against him—and so it proved. When the U.S. Supreme Court unanimously ruled against a similar Oklahoma law in June 1915 in *U.S. v. Guinn*, it also invalidated the 1908 Maryland law, and John B. Anderson regained the legal right to vote in Annapolis municipal elections.[40]

Yet moral arguments on the basis of military service did not always prevail. Such was the case during South Carolina's constitutional convention of 1895. The convention was essentially called for the purpose of disfranchising the state's African-American voters. The six black delegates to the convention were given a chance to speak and bravely argued their case, despite the fact that the outcome of the meeting was more or less a foregone conclusion. It is significant that both black delegates who spoke, Thomas Miller and James Wigg, used military service as an important argument for retaining African-American suffrage in the state. They wisely downplayed black service in the Civil War, instead emphasizing the military contribution of African Americans in the American Revolution and the War of 1812. Wigg made the case most succinctly, stating that black men had served the cause of American liberty "upon an hundred battlefields, from the first skirmish on Boston commons when Crispus Attucks fell, to the battle of New Orleans, when the flower of the English army faded away before the leaden storms from the black battalions of General Jackson." Although Miller and Wigg's eloquent argument failed, and virtually all of South Carolina's black men had lost the right to vote by the end of the 1895 constitutional convention, it is significant that their argument did have an impact. At least one white delegate proposed exempting black Civil War veterans from the poll tax and literacy test, arguing that African-American ex-soldiers were generally more intelligent than other men of their race.[41]

The obvious failure of most political and legal challenges to discrimination, and the increasing number of lynchings and other violence directed against African Americans, led a second group of former soldiers to conclude that if black men could not vote with a ballot, they could at least vote with their feet. That is, black Civil War veterans participated prominently in the black emigration movements of the late nineteenth century that sought physical escape from disfranchisement, segregation, and violence.

Black Civil War veterans, particularly former soldiers from Louisiana, played a significant leadership role in the Kansas exodus movement of 1879. In the aftermath of the final collapse of Reconstruction, some African Americans looked at Kansas as a place of hope, free from the repression increasingly found in the "redeemed" South. Alfred Fairfax, for example, a black veteran from Louisiana and a Republican party activist and officeholder in Tensas Parish, had been forced to flee that locality in 1878 when armed white bands had restored Democratic party rule by force, killing about seventy-five African Americans and forcing many others to leave. Fairfax bravely returned to the parish in 1879 to help organize emigrants before leaving permanently for Kansas the following year. He later became the first black member of the Kansas legislature. Other black veterans who did not move to Kansas lent their support to those who did. James Milton Turner, living in St. Louis, assisted black emigrants passing through on their way to Kansas. O. S. B. Wall, a black officer during the Civil War, was president of the Emigrant Aid Society in Washington, D.C., which helped black persons who wanted to move to Kansas.[42]

The veterans who left for Kansas were clearly motivated by the prospect of losing the manhood they had gained in the Civil War. One such veteran was John Solomon Lewis, yet another Louisiana veteran. He had grown tired of the system of debt peonage that had arisen in his state. "I was in debt," Lewis later related, "and the man I rented land from said every year I must rent again to pay the other year, and so I rents and rents and each year I gets deeper and deeper in debt." Frustrated, Lewis eventually confronted his landlord and told him that he would no longer work for him and was determined to "go somewhere else and try to make headway like white workingmen." When a riverboat captain tried to prevent the departure of the veteran and his family, Lewis faced the man down. "I am a man who was a United States soldier, and I know my rights, and if I and my family gets put off, I will go in the United States Court and sue for damages." The ploy worked—Lewis and his family were allowed on the boat, and made it to their promised land.[43]

For other veterans, Kansas was not far enough away. These men doubted that African Americans would gain equal treatment or economic advancement anywhere in the United States. They looked for places on foreign soil where they could control their destiny. The most popular place proposed was Africa. Returning to the ancestral homeland of their people stirred the emotions and imaginations of some former soldiers, as it did for other African Americans in the late nineteenth century, as racial repression in the South grew in intensity.

Perhaps the most prominent advocate of African emigration in the late nineteenth century was Henry McNeal Turner, a black veteran of the Union army. During the war, he had served as chaplain of the 1st USCI, organized in and around Washington, D.C., where Turner had been a rising young minister just before the war. After leaving the army, Turner went to Georgia as a missionary for the AME Church, seeking to build up congregations where only a short time ago that denomination had been banned. He proved enormously successful at the task, converting thousands and organizing the African Methodists in that state. Turner parlayed his religious following into a seat in the Georgia constitutional convention and later in the state legislature, where he served until that body expelled him and the other black members in 1870, despite the conciliatory stance he had taken toward white Southerners. This experience and the stinging rejection he received from local whites while serving as postmaster of Macon, Georgia, proved seminal in transforming Turner—heretofore quite typical of other black veterans in his moderate positions as a Reconstruction officeholder—into the premier African emigration advocate of his time in the black community.

Turner became convinced that only by leaving the United States could African Americans hope to escape violence, discrimination, and the equally destructive assault on their identity. From the 1870s until his death in 1915, Turner promoted the emigration of a "significant minority" of the black population in the United States to Africa. He believed that God had allowed the enslavement of black people in America so that they might be brought quickly to Christianity. White owners' mistreatment of their slaves had gone against the divine will, however, and the Civil War served as God's retribution. Turner held that continued association with white society would only retard the development of the black race. White terms of reference, he believed, damaged the self-esteem of African Americans. In the United States, white was the color of God, and black was the color of the devil. Turner feared that the association of evil with their skin color would have a destructive influence on black America's sense of self-worth. Yet simply symbolizing God as a black man was not enough to correct this problem. A return of a significant portion of the African-American population to Africa was necessary, to remove them from the denigration of white society, both physical and psychological, and to allow them to spread the positive benefits of Christian civilization to black Africans.

Turner's elevation to the office of bishop in the AME Church in 1880 demonstrated the power of his following within the organization and the appeal of his message to the oppressed and poverty-stricken black masses. However, Turner never realized his hope for a large-scale migration of African Americans. The black community lacked the resources to finance the project, and it was hindered by reports of disease and death sent back by the few emigrants who made it to Africa.[44]

Other Civil War veterans also worked for African emigration. After being used and discarded by Southern Democrats in South Carolina in the wake of Reconstruction, Martin Delany, the most prominent pre–Civil War advocate of emigration to Africa, returned to promoting that idea. His African emigration project proved a financial failure, however, and the aging Delany had no choice but to abandon the field to younger leaders such as Turner.[45] One of those younger leaders with an interest in Africa and Civil War military experience was George W. Williams, who also gained prominence as a pioneering historian of the black experience in the United States (see chapter 7). In the mid-1880s, he formulated a plan to aid the development of the Belgian Congo by recruiting black American settlers to go there. His early death prevented him from bringing those plans to fruition.[46]

A third group of veterans opted for neither civil rights agitation nor a departure to Kansas, Africa, or some other location. Instead, they sought to adjust as best they could to growing discrimination in the South by disavowing equal citizenship rights with white people for the time being and concentrating on economic advancement and moral uplift for black people. This philosophy, most associated with the public stance of Booker T. Washington, encouraged African Americans to turn inward and isolate themselves from white people. The ultimate manifestation of this self-segregation was the all-black town. These communities appeared throughout the United States in the late nineteenth century. Residents of these towns saw them as refuges, where African Americans could pursue self-improvement with minimal white interference.

The most notable all-black community founded by a Civil War veteran was also one of the most famous: Mound Bayou, Mississippi. Formed in the late 1880s on land owned by the Louisville, New Orleans, and Texas Railroad Company, Mound Bayou was a quintessential African-American town of that era. Mound Bayou's organizer was Isaiah T. Montgomery, a veteran of the Union navy. Although born and raised in slavery, he had enjoyed special privileges unknown to most persons in bondage. Montgomery and his family had been the property of Joseph Davis, the older brother of Confederate president Jefferson Davis. Isaiah Montgomery's father, Benjamin, was literate and served as Davis's business manager. Isaiah, who had also learned to read and write, became Davis's personal secretary and office attendant. During the Civil War, he served as the cabin boy of Union admiral David Porter.[47] Shielded from the harshest aspects of slavery and enjoying the patronage of prominent white men, Montgomery was predisposed to seek accommodation with white Southerners.

Isaiah Montgomery served his apprenticeship in community building under his father after the war. In 1866, Benjamin Montgomery purchased the properties of Joseph Davis, establishing Davis Bend, Mississippi. Davis Bend functioned more as a plantation enterprise rather than a true town. The Montgomery family managed the operations, with former Davis slaves and other freed people working the land. The community survived until 1881, when a combination of crop failures, mismanagement, and the loss of workers to the Kansas exodus finally put the enterprise into foreclosure. By the mid-1880s, Isaiah Montgomery was living in Vicksburg, running a small mercantile establishment.

It was while he was living in Vicksburg that the Louisville, New Orleans, and Texas Railroad approached him to sell railroad lands to black farmers. Montgomery expanded the railroad's modest proposal into an ambitious plan for an all-black community in the northern Mississippi delta region. He initially promoted the idea to relatives and former Davis Bend residents. Later, Montgomery recruited settlers more widely, not only in Mississippi but also throughout the Lower South. He laced his appeals with themes of racial self-help and advancement through economic progress. Despite Montgomery's continued financial problems and the primitive conditions in the early years, the community grew and prospered.

The survival of Mound Bayou, however, depended on Montgomery carefully maintaining the goodwill of white Mississippians. The power imbalance between the races was so great by the late nineteenth century that white Mississippians could have wiped out Mound Bayou quickly had they so desired. Indeed, white racial conservatives found the idea, let alone the actual existence, of an independent black town objectionable. In their opinion, African Americans needed to be tightly controlled because, otherwise, they would fall into barbarity.[48] Consequently, Mound Bayou relied on Montgomery's ability to win the goodwill and support of more moderate whites willing to tolerate the town. Although Montgomery was a mediocre businessman, he proved adept at ingratiating himself with prominent white men, drawing on his training with Joseph Davis and David Porter. Internally, Mound Bayou operated with complete independence, and the town was formally incorporated in February 1898, with Montgomery as mayor.

Yet the price of Mound Bayou's independence was high. As the only black representative to Mississippi's 1890 constitutional convention, Montgomery was forced to endorse the disfranchisement of black men throughout the state. To gain internal autonomy within Mound Bayou, he had to support the end of political rights for African Americans elsewhere in Mississippi. He rationalized his decision with the notion that the political power of African Americans in the state was already at an end. It seemed better to Montgomery to surrender what formal voice African Americans had in the political process gracefully and win the goodwill of white Mississippians in the process rather than aggravate them by resistance and risk jeopardizing his fledgling community (which was then only three years old). His acquiescence to the disfranchisement of black Mississippians led Montgomery to be widely reviled in the African-American press nationally, and in later years, Montgomery himself privately acknowledged that his support of the 1890 convention had been a mistake. He admitted that he had sacrificed too much, selling out his race to protect the community he loved.[49]

Although Isaiah Montgomery can be viewed as a black quisling, it is equally arguable that his intentions were good. He was trying to safeguard his community during a difficult time. In that respect, he was typical of other black veterans in leadership positions after the Civil War. Certainly their actions can be criticized. Certainly they did not always have the best interests of their people at heart and sometimes acted in selfish and foolish ways. However, on the whole, the statement of one black veteran politician, Richard Griggs of Mississippi, captures the ideal that generally guided them. In an 1872 pamphlet promoting his candidacy for Mississippi commissioner of immigration and agriculture (a race he would win), he stated, "While in the Legislature I have endeavored to ameliorate the condition of my oppressed race in every way in my power, and I have the proud consolation of knowing that I have done something towards elevating them to a higher standard in life."[50] Although it is possible to dismiss Griggs's words as mere campaign rhetoric, they authentically capture an important impetus of the African-American veterans who became leaders in the post–Civil War black community. Whatever other motives they had for going into politics and for seeking leadership roles in the black community, nearly all these men—like Griggs—genuinely sought the advancement of their people. Having risked their lives in a manly fashion on the battlefield to win the freedom of their race, they guided former slaves through the awkward early months of freedom. Black veterans served as officeholders during Reconstruction to the extent that they were able to take advantage of such opportunities. Likewise, they served as leaders within the black community throughout the entire postwar period, into the early decades of the twentieth century.

Such leadership roles also allowed them to exercise and reinforce their manhood, permitting them to do good for their people while rising in economic and social status. Hence, it is no accident that, in terms of their leadership roles in the black community, African-American veterans flocked to the ministry. In the postwar black community, churches were the most important institution. Here African Americans enjoyed autonomy and the greatest potential for independent collective action. This promise remained even in the face of disfranchisement and Jim Crow laws. Hence, black veterans were attracted to the ministry not only out of genuine religious conviction but also because, as clergymen, they could make the most difference in their community. Leading black churches offered them the greatest potential for manly action, especially after the collapse of Reconstruction began to severely limit access to political office by African Americans. Clergymen wielded tremendous influence throughout the postwar period as leaders in the black community and intermediaries between it and the larger world. This gave them potent political power.[51] "It may appear singular that so many colored preachers are in politics," wrote William J. Simmons in 1887. "But our people being an ignorant people very largely, cannot read the newspapers and know the positions of parties, and consequently they are dependent upon the preachers." Simmons (see fig. 14), a veteran of the 41st USCI and a prominent black clergymen in Kentucky, added, "Their power over the people is almost unlimited, and for this reason the good man can do much good, and the bad man can do much evil."[52] This last statement was an implicit acknowledgment by Simmons that, as the principal source of power in the postwar African-American community, the ministry attracted men with less than the best motives.

Still, the ministry brought pitfalls as well as power to former soldiers. Although black ministers helped shape public opinion in the black community, their influence was not unlimited. Black churches rebelled against veterans in the ministry who supported unpopular causes or allied themselves with perceived enemies. Elijah Marrs, a Baptist minister in Kentucky after the war, was criticized by his predominantly Republican congregation when he supported a temperance ordinance sponsored by local Democrats.[53] While Marrs managed to hang on to his post, William B. Derrick, an AME clergyman and veteran of the Union navy, had to seek reassignment from his Virginia congregation after he opposed the Readjuster movement during the 1880s and that movement (which gained considerable support among black Virginians) swept to power.[54]

The life of veterans in the clergy, as for other black ministers, was difficult because it often involved frequent relocation. Typical of this pattern was Alexander Newton, who, after his discharge from the 29th Connecticut Infantry, became a minister for the AME Church. Newton went south in the 1870s and served successively in Tennessee, Arkansas, Louisiana, and North Carolina before returning to the North, where church authorities continued to reassign him every few years.[55] Black Baptist ministers did not have to endure frequent long-distance moves because their churches, unlike those of African Methodists, usually were organized at the state level. Still, decentralization did not prevent routine reassignments within state boundaries. Thomas Wilbourn, a Texas veteran, told a pension investigator in 1909 that he had "been in all parts of the state" during his thirty-year career as a Baptist clergyman. "I have . . . lived in Galveston 2 or 3 years, Waxahachie 7 yrs,

Corsicana about 2 yrs, Celeburne [*sic*] 1 year, Ft. Worth about 15 years, Marshall about 1 year, here [Wharton] since 1896." Even after permanently settling in Wharton, Wilbourn's position as a missionary for the Twentieth-Century Baptist Association of Texas and his membership on the state board of the Colored Baptist Church still entailed considerable travel. When asked by a federal pension investigator how much he had been home in the past four years, Wilbourn replied candidly, "I hardly know. Sometimes I am at home 3 or 4 days a week then I go away Friday or Saturday and come back Monday or Tuesday. Then again I am away longer than that. Sometimes [I am] away two weeks at a time. I am in and out."[56]

In addition, veterans discovered that the power they wielded as clergymen could be personally dangerous. It attracted the attention of white Southerners interested in keeping the black community in subordination. For instance, Alexander Newton learned upon his arrival in Tennessee that "the Klu Klux Klan [*sic*] was especially after the preachers to force them to use their influence to make the Negroes vote the Democratic ticket in elections."[57] Newton, like other African-American clergymen, also had to minister to the victims of white Southerners' violence. This proved a difficult task, as he could offer little comfort to survivors, knowing that in all likelihood the perpetrators would never be brought to justice.[58]

Despite its dangers, traps, and burdens, ambitious black Civil War veterans found that the ministry was their best avenue for advancement. The 1890 special census identified 844 black Civil War veterans as "clergymen." This was by far the occupation with the highest number of African-American ex-soldiers within the census category of "professional service." The second largest occupation for black veterans was teacher, which employed only ninety-three former soldiers that year.[59] The material rewards of the ministry also served as an inducement. Many black ministers enjoyed a comfortable middle-class lifestyle compared with the widespread poverty in the postwar African-American community. Some black congregations paid their ministers particularly well. Alexander Newton marveled in his autobiography at the $1,000 annual salary he received during his tenure in Raleigh, North Carolina—a tremendous sum for that time and place.[60] That amount was about four times the income of the average African-American household in the late nineteenth century.[61]

The church not only provided veterans with their source of influence in the postwar black community; it also gave former soldiers a platform to develop further avenues of leadership. William Simmons rose to prominence during the 1880s by assuming such nonministerial roles. In 1879, Simmons moved to Lexington, Kentucky, becoming pastor of the First Baptist Church. The following year, he accepted the presidency of a failing black Baptist college, the Normal and Theological Institution in Louisville. Under Simmons's leadership, the institution revived, eventually becoming the State University of Kentucky at Louisville. Starting in 1883, Simmons also edited the *American Baptist*. His position as a college president and editor gave him twin platforms from which to promote his views and himself within Kentucky and nationally. He quickly rose to chair of the executive committee of the State Convention of Colored Men of Kentucky, an organization that fought for the interests of African Americans. He used the *American Baptist* to organize the American National Baptist Convention in 1886 and became the organization's first president. (The American National Baptist Convention was an important forerunner of the National Baptist Convention, U.S.A., and the first major umbrella organization for black Baptists in the United States.) Simmons might have achieved further prominence but for his sudden death in 1890 of a heart attack at the age of forty-one.[62]

Despite the importance of the clergy in the postwar black community, other veterans developed prominence and power completely outside of the ministry. The black press provided one such outlet. For instance, John H. Murphy, a Maryland veteran, founded the *Baltimore Afro-American*. At the time of his death in 1922, the paper had a circulation of 14,000—the largest circulating black newspaper on the East Coast. His sizable readership gave Murphy a powerful editorial voice, which he used to support the programs of Booker T. Washington.[63] Alexander Augusta and Charles B. Purvis, who both lived in Washington, D.C., provided significant leadership in the fields of medicine and education. As early members of the Howard University medical faculty, they trained many of the black doctors in the United States after the Civil War. Denied entry into the American Medical Association, Augusta and Purvis helped form the National Medical Society of the District of Columbia, a black medical organization.[64]

Veterans in business also exerted influence in the black community by generating wealth, employment, and economic opportunity. Former soldiers engaged in a variety of entrepreneurial activities. Some veterans operated such traditional Southern enterprises as plantations; other veterans were merchants. Wiley Jones was a prominent black businessman in Pine Bluff,

Arkansas, in the late 1880s, operating a general store and the town's street-cars.[65] Many prominent veterans invested in real estate. Indeed, the Mound Bayou community, besides serving as a social experiment and refuge for African Americans, was also a real estate venture. Isaiah Montgomery did well for himself, at the same time he benefited his people, by profiting from the sale of land to new residents.

Although most former soldiers involved themselves in the civilian institutions of the black community, a few veterans, perhaps nostalgic for the Civil War, sought military leadership posts. The postwar U.S. Army provided the most prized opportunities in this regard. The federal government maintained four African-American regiments in the regular army after the war—two infantry and two cavalry (see chapter 1). As was the case during the Civil War, the officers of these regiments were almost invariably white men, but in some cases the government commissioned black chaplains. Two black veterans of the Civil War, Allen Allensworth and Henry V. Plummer, served as chaplains of black army units—Allensworth in the 24th U.S. Infantry and Plummer in the 10th U.S. Cavalry. Striking parallels existed in the two men's backgrounds. Both had been slaves before the war (Allensworth in Kentucky and Plummer in Maryland), both had served in the Union navy, both became Baptist ministers after the war, and both joined the postwar army as chaplains in the mid-1880s.

The duties of chaplain involved Allensworth and Plummer in much more than simply tending to the spiritual needs of the soldiers in their regiments. Chaplains also oversaw education, an activity that was even more important among black than white soldiers because of their relatively lower levels of literacy. Allensworth took his responsibilities as an educator particularly seriously. He initially brought in volunteer teachers to instruct soldiers during Sunday school classes and later trained enlisted men to teach their fellow soldiers. Allensworth eventually created a full curriculum to guide the education of soldiers at Fort Bayard, New Mexico, where he was stationed. His plan was used at other army posts, and one of Allensworth's superiors even recommended its general adoption by the U.S. Army. In addition to their religious and educational duties, commanding officers often expected chaplains to manage the post library, garden, commissary, bakery, and treasury and to defend soldiers brought before military courts.[66]

Although being chaplains placed Allensworth and Plummer outside the chain of command, they were not immune from the race issue. Indeed, Henry

Plummer's advocacy of African emigration led to his downfall. He had already antagonized his commanding officer with a temperance campaign. In 1894, he applied for a leave of absence from his army post to lead a group of black soldiers to Africa and spread Christianity among the native population. Plummer believed that this activity would help improve race relations in America and give the United States a toehold in African commerce. Although his plans met with the approval of emigration advocates such as Henry McNeal Turner, they troubled his superiors in the U.S. Army and prompted his trumped-up court-martial for drunkenness and his dishonorable dismissal from the army. "Plummer's aggressive and energetic behavior," as a scholar of the postwar army put it, "challenged the leadership structure in which blacks were clearly relegated to a secondary position."[67]

Rather than antagonize his superiors, as Plummer did, Allensworth was exceedingly careful in his conduct as chaplain of the 24th U.S. Infantry. He worked principally at educating black soldiers and sought to cultivate the friendship of prominent white citizens wherever the army stationed his regiment. He also attempted to maintain cordial relations with the white officers of the 24th Infantry and did not complain about being excluded from their social activities. Although his acceptance of racial restrictions helped Allensworth's work, he and his family suffered considerable isolation. They could not fraternize with black enlisted men, and on frontier posts, there were often few if any African Americans with whom they could form friendships. Even when the army posted Allensworth near major cities, his dual status as a black man and an army officer led to awkward situations. In several cases when he attended official functions with prominent white people, Allensworth was unable to acknowledge their black servants—people he knew socially and who were prominent members of the local African-American community.[68] Still, because he was careful to maintain excellent relations with his white superiors, Allensworth retired honorably from the army in 1906 as a lieutenant colonel, while Plummer fruitlessly challenged his dismissal until his death in 1905.

Even after retiring from the army, Allensworth continued to offer leadership to soldiers. After moving to California, Allensworth, a supporter of Booker T. Washington, became involved in the creation of an all-black town in the state's vast Central Valley. Allensworth hoped that the town, which was eventually named in his honor, would become a model black community in the West. In this sense, the town of Allensworth was not very different from

Isaiah Montgomery's Mound Bayou. However, the former chaplain also envisioned Allensworth as a home for black veterans of the regular army—a place where they could sink roots after so many years of moving from one military post to the next. Indeed, a promotional newspaper for Allensworth, the *Sentiment Maker,* deliberately aimed itself at army veterans. It promised that the community would be a place where veterans could retire while enjoying the comradeship and protection of other former soldiers. "You will not be living among strangers," the *Sentiment Maker* promised, "but in the midst of fellow comrades with whom you have soldiered in the past, or if not, whose names and deeds are familiar."[69] The paper promised the establishment of a group home for dead soldiers' families, paid for by the developer, if enough army veterans bought lots in the town. It also announced that the Pacific Farming Company, the Allensworth developer, would give a soldier's family the deed to his property when he died, provided he was at least half paid up on his mortgage. Some black veterans of the regular army moved to the town, but Allensworth's sudden death in a 1914 traffic accident, difficulty getting water for the arid settlement, and other problems kept the community from ever becoming the refuge for former soldiers that Allensworth hoped it would be.

The Civil War also influenced the leadership activities of veterans in less dramatic ways. For instance, Christian A. Fleetwood participated in military and paramilitary groups in the nation's capital after the war (see fig. 15). Freeborn in Baltimore, Maryland, in 1840, Fleetwood rose to the rank of sergeant major in the 4th USCI and won the Medal of Honor for his bravery during the battle of Chaffin's Farm, Virginia, in September 1864. After the war, he was a leading figure in the Colored Soldiers and Sailors' League. Fleetwood also served in the District of Columbia National Guard during the late nineteenth century. He became the commanding officer of the D.C. National Guard's Sixth Battalion in 1887, with the rank of major. In 1891, the D.C. National Guard consolidated its black units into the First Separate Battalion. Passed over as head of the new organization, Fleetwood resigned from the D.C. National Guard the following year. He vainly attempted to gain a colonel's commission in a black volunteer regiment during the Spanish-American War, but the army offered him only the rank of lieutenant, which Fleetwood contemptuously rejected. His explanation for turning down the lieutenancy was the epitome of insulted manhood. "Being an applicant for the highest position in a regiment, and accepting the lowest," he wrote to a friend in June 1898, "is very much like the case of the man who applied for appointment as a foreign Minister and compromised on a pair of cast off trousers."[70] Though frustrated in his quest for personal advancement through postwar military service, Fleetwood still managed to derive considerable satisfaction by passing on the martial tradition to a new generation of African Americans. He and Charles B. Fisher, a black veteran of the Union navy, organized a Colored High School Cadet Corps for Washington, and Fleetwood worked with the group for many years.

In short, politics and community leadership positions provided an avenue for black Civil War veterans to help their people while helping themselves— a way to exercise their manhood. A few of these men, like Allen Allensworth in particular, managed to find a way to fill this manly role in a martial setting that hearkened back to their wartime military service. Yet it was much more common for former soldiers to seek influence in civilian life, initially in Reconstruction politics and increasingly within African-American society itself as the decades wore on. It was in the civilian realm, especially in the churches, where the power lay in the postwar black community. It was there that veterans could exercise the most influence as men. Yet they exerted this power as individuals, not as a group; collective political action by black veterans had ceased by the early 1870s. Although they continued to draw on the leadership experience they had gained in the army and on the prestige that military service brought them as leaders, by the end of Reconstruction, and certainly by the late nineteenth century, their identity as leaders and politicians was practically indistinguishable from that of nonveterans. Within African-American society, then, although they were greatly admired, former soldiers as a group never became a potent political force like their white counterparts—Union and Confederate—did. Yet there was another place where, even in this time of discrimination and repression, these men could endeavor to be a force— within their families.

Fig. 1. Black soldiers celebrating their discharge from the Union army. For many ex-slaves, this moment was their first true taste of freedom.
 *(Library of Congress)*

Fig. 2.
A Northern white artist celebrates the sacrifices of black Civil War soldiers—an example of how black military service softened the racism of some white Northerners. Thomas Waterman Wood, "A Bit of War History: The Veteran," 1866.
 *(Metropolitan Museum of Art, New York)*

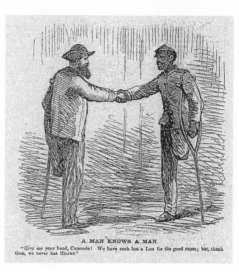

A MAN KNOWS A MAN.

"Give me your hand, Comrade! We have each lost a Leg for the good cause; but, thank God, we never lost Heart."

Fig. 3.
An unknown artist celebrates the wartime alliance of white and black Union soldiers in what was then the nation's best-circulating periodical. "A Man Knows a Man," *Harper's Weekly*, 22 April 1865. *(Library of Congress)*

Fig. 4.
The most famous American editorial cartoonist of the nineteenth century demonstrates the connection between wartime military service and black suffrage demands. His cartoons would not always be so kind to black people. Thomas Nast, "And Not This Man?" *Harper's Weekly*, 5 August 1865.
*(Library of Congress)*

Fig. 5. Lewis Latimer, a black Union navy veteran, with other "Edison Pioneers," c. 1920s. Latimer is standing on the ground, second from the left. Thomas Edison is standing on the lowest platform, eighth from the left. Latimer's presence in a white social group was unusual in the early twentieth century and is evidence of his value as a technical expert to the Edison organization. Inset: Lewis Latimer, draftsman, electrical expert, inventor, and associate of Alexander Graham Bell, Hiram S. Maxim, and Thomas Edison.

*(Photographs and Prints Division, Schomburg Center for Research in Black Culture, New York Public Library)*

Fig. 6. Robert Anderson (far left) stands with a group of his white comrades at the GAR post in Hemingford, Nebraska.

*(Robert Anderson, From Slavery to Affluence, c. 1927)*

Fig. 7. Editorial cartoon in a black newspaper demonstrates the honored status of Civil War veterans in the black community during the early twentieth century. G. Haywood, "The Idol of Memorial Day," *Freeman* (Indianapolis, Ind.), 26 May 1906. *(Library of Congress)*

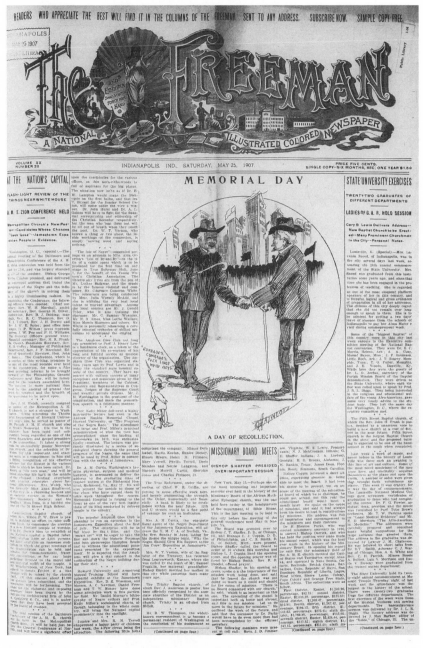

Fig. 8. Editorial cartoon in a black newspaper celebrates the wartime alliance of black and white Union troops—a relationship that by the early twentieth century was undermined by the growing rapprochement of white Union and Confederate veterans. G. Haywood, "Memorial Day," *Freeman* (Indianapolis, Ind.), 25 May 1907. *(Library of Congress)*

Fig. 9. Editorial cartoon in a black newspaper notes the rapidly declining numbers of Civil War veterans in the black community in the early twentieth century.
G. Haywood, "Still Marching to the Grave: Almost to their destination," *Freeman* (Indianapolis, Ind.), 30 May 1908.

(*Library of Congress*)

Fig. 10. Black veterans march at the dedication of the monument to Robert Gould Shaw and the 54th Massachusetts Infantry on the Boston Commons, 31 May 1897.

(*Massachusetts Historical Society, Boston*)

Fig. 11. James Monroe Trotter, prominent veteran of the 55th Massachusetts, businessman, musician, and federal officeholder in Massachusetts.
(*William J. Simmons,* Men of Mark, *c. 1887*)

Fig. 12. Robert Smalls, pilot and captain of the *Planter,* state legislator, U.S. congressman, and federal officeholder in South Carolina.
(*William J. Simmons,* Men of Mark, *c. 1887*)

Fig. 13. Pinckney Benton Stewart Pinchback, officer in the Louisiana Native Guards, state legislator, lieutenant governor, acting governor of Louisiana.
(*William J. Simmons,* Men of Mark, *c. 1887*)

Fig. 14. William J. Simmons, 41st USCI. Simmons was an author, educator, and prominent Baptist clergyman in postwar Kentucky.
(*William J. Simmons,* Men of Mark, *c. 1887*)

Fig. 15. Christian Fleetwood, sergeant major in the 4th USCI and Medal of Honor winner, in military dress uniform. After the war, he was a prominent member of Washington, D.C.'s black elite.

*(Library of Congress)*

Fig. 16. Allen Walker (alias King), 122d USCI. A Kentucky-born slave, he lived in Indiana and Ohio after the Civil War.
*(National Archives)*

Fig. 17. John Taylor (alias Grant), 135th USCI. He lived in Savannah, Georgia, after the war.
*(National Archives)*

Fig. 18. Adam Cole, 137th USCI. This Georgia veteran was in his fifties when this portrait was taken in 1902.
*(National Archives)*

Fig. 19. Charles Wilson (alias Blackson), 34th USCI. This photograph was taken in 1897 while the veteran was an inmate in the Government Hospital for the Insane in Washington, D.C. He died there the same year.

*(National Archives)*

Fig. 20. Jacob Overall (alias Hutchinson, alias Abraham I. J. Wright), 4th USCHA. This veteran changed his name again after the war and fled from Kentucky to Indiana to escape prosecution for the murder of a white man. The photograph was taken in April 1899.

*(National Archives)*

Fig. 21. Hiram Kirkland (alias Kirkham), 101st and 110th USCI. This veteran was born in Tennessee and lived there after the war.

*(National Archives)*

Fig. 22. Samuel Patterson, 32d USCI. Patterson was a resident of the Central Branch of the National Home for Disabled Volunteer Soldiers in Dayton, Ohio, when this photograph was taken.

*(National Archives)*

Fig. 23. Frank Nunn (alias Nearn, alias
Charles Franklin Crosby), 86th USCI.
This ex-slave lived in Texas and Mexico
after the war and had a Mexican wife.
*(National Archives)*

Fig. 24. Lewis Smith (alias Dick Lewis Barnett), 77th USCI. This veteran took the
last name of his white father after the war. He is pictured here with his wife, Eliza.
*(National Archives)*

# Family and Marriage

N O LESS THAN POLITICS, family and marriage became an integral way for black veterans to assert their manhood after the Civil War. By helping to destroy slavery, these men opened up new possibilities for themselves and other black men to assert their authority within their families. They brought loved ones under their masculine protection, created important symbolic links to their male forebears, and legalized slave marriages—all actions that increased their standing and power. Although former soldiers were not the only African Americans taking such steps, historical evidence shows that they were at the heart and sometimes on the cutting edge of change for black families during and after the war, and for black men within those families. Moreover, while veterans fought a losing battle to retain their political rights in the wake of Reconstruction, the gains they and other African Americans in the South made in terms of marriage and family law remained largely intact despite the rise of Jim Crow. Yet the realities of African-American life in the late nineteenth century placed limits on the power of black veterans within their families. Despite the decisions of many former slaves to legalize their marriages, the survival of informal marriage customs from the prewar period gave black women opportunities to evade male power, undercutting the manhood of veterans and other African-American men.

Black Union soldiers began the process of asserting their manhood in family life during the Civil War. Naturally, the priority of many of these men was to free loved ones from the control of slaveholders. Having joined the army in part to prove their manhood, they now wished to be true men to their families as well by liberating their wives and children from their owners. Many soldiers, some barely literate, sent letters to army officers and Freedmen's Bureau representatives beseeching their assistance in this effort. For instance, Joseph J. Harris, a black soldier from Louisiana, wrote to Gen. Daniel Ullman, commander of the Louisiana Black Brigade, twice from Florida in late 1864, asking that Ullman send forces to free his family from their owner.[1] For many men like Harris, the need to reclaim their families was all the more urgent because slaveholders had evicted them from their plantations or ill-treated them in retaliation for the soldier's enlistment. The latter fate befell Frances Johnson, the wife of Nathan Johnson, a Kentucky soldier in the 116th USCI. In an 1865 affidavit, Frances claimed their owner's son had badly beaten her after Nathan's enlistment, and to avoid further abuse she had fled to the Union army encampment at Camp Nelson, Kentucky.[2]

With their families suffering, African-American troops must have felt the frustration of belittled manhood, since they could often do no more than beg government officials from afar to aid and protect their loved ones. A few men such as Spotswood Rice, a Missouri soldier stationed at Benton Barracks in St. Louis, were able to take a more assertive course. He did not appeal to federal authorities but instead boldly sought to gain custody of his wife and children by his own efforts. In Rice's case, his maturity (he was thirty-nine years old when he joined the Union army in February 1864), his literacy (unusual for a slave), and assertive personality (he became an AME minister after the war) no doubt encouraged him to take this daring course.[3] Yet liberating his family still proved to be a difficult task. Rice's family was scattered among different owners. He managed to reclaim his wife and ten of his children, but two daughters remained in the hands of F. W. Diggs and his unmarried sister, Kitty. Although offended by Rice's boldness, F. W. Diggs did not seem averse to surrendering the daughter under his control, claiming that he was merely waiting until Rice's wife could support the child. Kitty Diggs proved more resistant, however, refusing Rice's offer of $40 for Mary, the daughter she owned. His patience exhausted, Rice wrote to Kitty Diggs in September 1864, demanding that she give him Mary and threatening that if she did not, black soldiers would liberate Mary by force. He jotted passionately, "The longor you keep my Child from me the longor you will have to burn in hell and the qwicer youll get their."[4]

Spotswood Rice demonstrated that he wished to bring his daughters who were still enslaved into his custody, where he could care for them like a real man. He clearly associated his manhood with taking parental control of his daughters. Writing from St. Louis to Kitty Diggs, he demanded that she return his daughter because "she is a God given rite of my own."[5] At the same time, he wrote a letter to his daughters infused with fatherly authority and concern. Rice promised Mary and her sister that he would free them from Diggs and reunite them with the rest of their family. "Your Miss Kaitty said that I tried to steal you," he wrote to them. "But I let her know that god never intended for man to steal his own flesh and blood."[6]

Although Spotswood Rice demonstrated extraordinary courage in confronting his daughter's owner in such forceful terms, as a group, black soldiers who tried to reclaim their wives, children, and aged parents showed not only a strong commitment to family but also a determination to assert their authority as head of the family unit—an authority that had long been usurped by slaveholders. In other words, claiming responsibility for their kin was as essential to asserting their manhood as taking up arms in the Civil War or claiming suffrage rights afterward. To be a true man was to take charge of your family.

Not surprisingly, black soldiers discovered that some slaveholders were quite resistant to their efforts to reclaim their families. One particularly poignant example was Thomas McDougal, a sergeant in the 107th USCI, who found himself jailed in Larue County, Kentucky, in the fall of 1865. McDougal had gone, under the authority of the Freedmen's Bureau, to collect his wife and children from their owner, Hillary Johnson. With the Thirteenth Amendment not yet ratified, the soldier was acting under congressional legislation that had freed the families of black soldiers even in loyal border states like Kentucky. From McDougal's perspective, he was liberating his family and assuring them the masculine protection that was his duty as a husband and father. Johnson, a local judge, saw the matter quite differently. The judge hastened to use the authority of his position to get revenge. Soon after the McDougal family's departure from his home, Johnson swore out an arrest warrant for Thomas McDougal on a charge of theft. The "stolen" items were 75 cents worth of clothing on the backs of the soldier's family. "The Judge it is reported," wrote a local Freedmen's Bureau official, "takes the astute distinction that though the act of Congress may free wives and children of soldiers 'it does not divest the owner of the title to the clothes they wear.'"[7] McDougal sat in jail for weeks, as bureau officials and the army were apparently unable to arrange his release. He was finally freed after a grand jury in Larue County failed to indict him.

The resistance of white Southerners like Judge Johnson to black soldiers' efforts to claim their families is further evidence of the significance of this act in terms of manhood. No doubt the slaveholders wished to retain the labor of the soldiers' family members, but by attempting to reclaim their relations, the soldiers also directly confronted the patriarchal authority at the heart of antebellum slavery in the South. By taking control of their families, black soldiers threatened the traditional power structure in which male slaveholders were the patriarchs of both white and black people on their property. As black Union soldiers demanded that slaveholders surrender their families, they also effectively challenged white supremacy. To gain control over their kin so as to assert their manhood, they found it necessary to wrest it from the hands of slaveholders, for whom such control had been a fundamental source of their prewar dominance.[8]

Many black soldiers and veterans found that there was a far easier and safer way to assert their manhood than the often difficult business of confronting slaveholders over their families. They could simply adopt new last names that reflected male-line family connections. Civil War pension files show that it was common for black men who had been slaves to discard their owners' surnames and adopt their fathers' last names, either during the war or sometime afterward.[9] Before the war, a slave, if referred to by last name at all, was generally known by his owner's surname, at least to white people.[10] African-American soldiers who had been slaves usually entered the Union army under those names. The lack of their own last names had signified that, in a society in which family identity was passed on through the male line, slave families had no official standing, nor did male slaves have any rights that white men need respect. Hence, it should not be surprising that during their service or soon afterward, many former slaves changed their surnames in a quest for a noteworthy bit of manly dignity.

The experience of black Civil War veterans shows that many men did not assume these new names casually, but instead took names that reflected family connections through the male line. "My father's name was Gilbert Jackson, and after I was set free I took the name of my father," explained Smith Jackson, an Alabama veteran, in his application for a Civil War pension. "I preferred to go by my father's name, rather than the last name of my owner."[11] Before his service, he had been known as Smith Buchanan, the surname of his last owner. Former slaves adopted their fathers' last names even if they had never known their fathers, and even if they were white. "I was using the name of Lewis Smith," Dick Lewis Barnett told a federal pension investigator in 1911 (see fig. 24). "But I found that the Negroes after freedom were taking the names of their father like the white folks. So I asked my mother and she told me my father was John Barnett, a white man and I took up the name of Barnett."[12] As Barnett's case demonstrates, the symbolism and not the source of the last name was the most important consideration. Black veterans associated a father's last name with the assumption of an identity as a free man, because free men inherited their fathers' last names.

In short, an important way for black men to assert their manhood in the era of emancipation was to adopt the surnames of their fathers. To be equal, to be a man, was to be known by a family name that was passed down from father to son, even if that name was really the surname of the father's last owner or the last name of a white man who had done little more for his son than pass on his genes. Regardless of the actual relationships between the black veterans and their fathers, assuming their surnames was a vital part of becoming real men. Making that symbolic connection was the important thing.

Yet the gains made by black veterans and their families were not merely symbolic. Legal benefits accrued to them and other African Americans as a result of the war. This was particularly true in the case of marriage. Slave marriages, of course, had not been recognized under the law in the antebellum period. Couples could be separated from each other at any time if a slaveholder so desired. Hence, it should come as no surprise that many former slaves legalized their marriages as soon as it became possible.

Black soldiers were at the forefront of marriage legalization in the black community during the Civil War. Although Union chaplains often proved reluctant to perform marriage ceremonies for young men who had met women while in the army, they were quite eager to formalize existing bonds made in slavery. James Peet, chaplain of the 50th USCI, reported as much to Brig. Gen. L. Thomas in September 1864: "I . . . urge marriage upon all those who, already, have families."[13] John Means Thompson, former chaplain of the 15th USCI, echoed Peet's sentiments when he told a Pension Bureau examiner in 1888, "I encouraged all of the colored soldiers to have the ceremony of marriage performed."[14] These chaplains saw it as their duty to regularize marital bonds between slave couples. Although they recognized that many slaves considered their existing bonds to be sacred, the chaplains believed that since these people were now free, it was time for them to enter into a new covenant of marriage—a legal one.

Union authorities believed that by legalizing marriage, both black men and women would be more inclined to adopt the ideals of middle-class

Victorian married life, including marital fidelity and male authority within the family. Some Union officers had been shocked by what they perceived as the loose sexual mores of their troops and women in the black community. "There was practically no sense of chastity," wrote A. W. Greely, a Union officer serving with African-American troops from rural Louisiana. He continued: "Most of the infractions of regulations [by black soldiers] were due to intimacies with the women camp followers, who were without a sense of shame. The men said that their plantation life had been marked by such practices, and why, they asked, should they change, seeing that it had nothing to do with their duties as soldiers."[15]

Hence, officers like Greely believed that marriage was essential to encouraging moral propriety among freed slaves, starting with their own troops. They also hoped that it would encourage their soldiers and other black men to bring the women of their community under greater control, because in their opinion, the freed slave women were entirely too independent. Thus, as Leslie Schwalm noted, another important function of marriage for freed people in the eyes of Union authorities was that it "institutionalized men's privileges and obligations as heads of households, and assured their entitlement to the unpaid labor of women on behalf of the household."[16] In other words, Union authorities believed that legal marriage would make former slave women more chaste and submissive and ensure the supremacy of black men in newly freed families.

For their own reasons, many black soldiers and their wives eagerly took advantage of legal marriage. They wished to bring their marriages under the protection of the law, guarantee the legal sanctity of their unions, and ensure that they were never separated from loved ones again. Consequently, numerous soldiers and their wives consented to marriages performed "under the flag," as these wartime ceremonies by Union chaplains came to be known.[17] The formalization of slave marriages occurred among black soldiers stationed throughout the South. Not only soldiers, but also many other African Americans flocked to army chaplains and ministers registered with the Freedmen's Bureau to give their marriages legal status. For those couples who did not ratify their marriages during the war, in its aftermath, Southern legislatures hurriedly passed laws allowing former slaves to legalize existing marriages through new ceremonies or by registration with local authorities. Hence, there was ample opportunity for former slaves to bring their marriages under the new covenant.

The question remains, however, to what extent African-American couples legalized their marriages in the wake of emancipation. The best existing evidence comes from Herbert Gutman's seminal book *The Black Family in Slavery and Freedom.* Gutman estimated the extent of marriage legalization in Virginia and North Carolina. He compared the number of couples in ex-slave marriage registers in both states against the number of adult slaves in the 1860 census, county by county, to get a rough approximation of the percentage of slave couples that legalized their marriages. By this method, Gutman calculated that about half of slave couples had legalized their marriages in these states by 1866. From these quantitative data and from other anecdotal evidence, Gutman concluded that most former slaves wanted and obtained legal marriages soon after they became available.[18] Yet Gutman overlooked another inference that could be drawn from his sources. Although the marriage registers and census data revealed that at least half of adult freed people in Virginia and North Carolina had legalized their slave marriages immediately after the Civil War, they also suggested that as many as half had not.

The inference that many African Americans did not rush to legalize their marriages is supported by an examination of the marital histories of black veterans in Civil War pension files. They show that although freedom gave all African-American couples access to the privileges and protections of legal marriage, for decades after the war, many couples continued to practice what one black veteran's widow aptly called the "old constitution": an informal system of marriage that had originated in slavery.[19] Many former slaves did not take the important step of having a new marriage ceremony performed or registering their union with government authorities, acts associated with an acceptance of formal, legal marriage. They continued an older way of marriage in which a marital union was not created by a ceremony and a license granted by a government but was initiated by the mutual consent of a couple to live together as husband and wife and the acceptance of the local community that the man and woman in question were a married couple.

The experience of Civil War veterans and their families conclusively demonstrates that two systems of marriage coexisted in the black community in the decades following emancipation: a formal, legal system and an informal system rooted in slavery. Before the war, of course, slaves had had no choice but informal marriage. Hence, it is not surprising that many veterans or their widows testified in their pension applications about legalizing their slave marriages during the war or soon thereafter. However, despite the availability of legal marriage, the pension files of other black veterans and their wives suggest that a substantial percentage of former slaves continued their informal marriages. In short, whereas some ex-soldiers eagerly embraced the new system of marriage, others came to it slowly, if at all, clinging to older ways with their roots in bondage.[20]

Former slaves later described the old constitution as having several basic characteristics.[21] Generally, a man asked the consent of his owner to marry, as well as the consent of his intended's master or mistress if she were owned by someone else. With permission given, the couple "took up" or started living with each other. No ceremony was necessary to establish a slave marriage, although many slaves had one. A white minister might marry favored slaves in their owner's home; other couples "jumped over the broomstick," and some simply set up housekeeping together. With or without a ceremony, however, a slave marriage lacked legal existence, and owners could dissolve such unions at any time.

Consequently, legal marriage, perhaps to the extent of no other institution, symbolized freedom for a portion of the postwar black community. With legal marriages, African Americans gained the assurance—initially from the federal government and later from state governments in the South—that their unions would be respected and protected by law, and that they would never be involuntarily separated from their loved ones again. As a black soldier in a Virginia regiment told his comrades at a religious service in 1866, "The Marriage Covenant is at the foundation of all our rights."[22] By this, he meant that the integrity of marriage—and, by implication, the integrity of the black family—constituted the most important gain for African Americans from the Civil War. However, the soldier also meant that some people in the black community wished to use legal marriage as a precedent for obtaining additional rights, for if black men were granted this most basic right, why should they be denied other critical rights such as suffrage? Hence, for some veterans, legal marriage proved central to the assertion of their manhood.[23] To be a real man was to be a legally married man, asserting the most basic of manhood rights—the authority of a household head—as a first step to asserting other manhood rights.

However, despite the importance that many African Americans attached to legal marriage in terms of racial advancement, not all black veterans and their wives rushed to embrace it. Some ex-soldiers waited many years or even decades to discard the old constitution and continued to cohabit with their wives based on their slave marriages. Kitt Mitchell, a South Carolina veteran, and his wife, who had lived together since 1859, did not undergo a legal marriage ceremony until 1888, nearly thirty years and thirteen children later.[24] Garret Beckley and his wife, married as slaves in Kentucky in 1861, did not register their slave marriage, as required by state law, until 1904.[25] Some veterans who had married as slaves never had new ceremonies performed after emancipation or registered their marriages, as required by law.[26]

Whereas one group of veterans was merely slow to ratify pre-emancipation marriages with new ceremonies or by registration, other ex-soldiers who established marital unions after the war did so in much the same way as antebellum slave marriages. Dispensing with a marriage license and often with a ceremony, they simply "took up" with women, just as before the war.[27] The only difference between these postwar common-law unions and prewar slave marriages was that an owner's permission was no longer needed. A couple's belief that they were married and the community's acceptance of the arrangement cemented a marital union.[28]

The case of Phillip and Josephine Bellfield, who lived in Claiborne County, Mississippi, south of Vicksburg, illustrates the tie between postwar common-law marriage and slave marriage customs. Bellfield joined the Union army in November 1863 as a forty-five-year-old private. After his death in 1890, Josephine applied to the federal government for a widow's pension. Witnesses testified that the couple had begun cohabiting in 1880, well after the death of Bellfield's first wife in 1876. Two of their neighbors, Morgan Black and Glen Willis, stated in an affidavit, "The fact is that he was not legally married to the claimant, but simply married her as was formerly prevalent among slaves. He took her to his house and gave notice to all his friends & acquaintances that she was his wife. Every body, white & black, who knew them, regarded them as man & wife. . . . the claimant was his wife—socially and morally—if not legally."[29]

In cases in which the acceptance of either the couple or their community that they were husband and wife was lacking, no informal marriage existed—even if the couple lived together for a long time and had children. For instance, Rose Baptiste cohabited with a New Orleans veteran, Octave Jessie, for nearly two decades but told a federal pension investigator in 1893, "I lived with him as his wife, but I never went by his name. I would not go by his name as I was not married to him." Although the local community wanted to believe that they were married, Baptiste clearly did not consider Jessie her husband. "The people used to call me by his name," she informed the investigator, "but I would always correct them and tell them that my name was not Rose Jessie."[30]

The influence and persistence of slave marriage customs extended to the dissolution of marriages as well as their formation. Slave divorce, like marriage, was informal in the antebellum South. Only an owner's consent was necessary for slaves to divorce. Some owners readily gave such permission, while others did not. The experience of black veterans suggests that informal divorce survived among former slaves after the Civil War. For those who practiced it, the end of cohabitation rather than a legal decree constituted the end of a marriage. Of seventy-six marriages of black Civil War veterans ending in separation documented in Civil War pension files, only twenty-one of the couples went on to obtain a legal divorce. That is, more than 70 percent of these ex-soldiers who separated from their wives never got a formal divorce.[31]

The case of Tony Alston, a Georgia veteran, illustrates the phenomenon of remarriage without divorce. He had wed "Katie" during slavery, and the couple separated around the time of the Civil War. In December 1866, Alston married Elsie Summers. They moved from Savannah, Georgia, to Goldsboro, North Carolina, and split up about a year later. Alston moved back to Savannah and in August 1868, without obtaining a divorce from Summers, married Diana Cooper. Their marriage did not last much longer than Alston's previous unions. The couple repeatedly separated and reconciled before permanently parting three or four years later. Shortly before his death in 1895, Alston again remarried without obtaining a divorce from Cooper.[32] Alston's marital pattern was not uncommon. Other ex-soldiers remarried after separating from slave wives and women they had married in the postwar period.[33]

The behavior of these veterans and their wives suggests that just as former slaves wrested the power of marital consent from slaveholders when emancipation came, they also granted themselves the prerogative of choosing when and how to end their marriages. Many former slaves apparently did not recognize a substitution of governmental authority for slaveholders' in the process of ending their marriages, and once they had separated from a spouse, they considered themselves, as in the antebellum period, free to marry again.

White Southerners were aware of the persistence of slave marriage customs in their midst. Mary Conti, the employer of Matilda Johnson, who was the slave wife of Levi Johnson, a Mississippi veteran, touched on this phenomenon in 1903 when she testified that the couple had separated several years after the end of the Civil War and Matilda had eventually remarried. "The reason she married another man while Johnson was living is because Johnson left her," Conti stated, trying to explain her employee's behavior. "Being ignorant, she did not think that she was doing anything wrong."[34] Charles G. Townsend, a federal pension examiner who worked in Kentucky, put it more concretely. "It is well known in this state," he reported in 1919, "that follwing [*sic*] Freedom of slaves there was for a time among them a continuance of the same old customs relative to marriage."[35] Even the U.S. Census Bureau indirectly alluded to the phenomenon in 1909, when it speculated that the divorce statistics of white and black Southerners were not strictly comparable because in many black-majority counties there was a "general disregard" among African Americans for marriage laws.[36]

So what is to be made of the survival of the old constitution among African Americans after the Civil War in terms of comprehending the place of veterans and other men in the postwar black family? To begin with, it must be understood that informal marriage was under attack from the earliest days after emancipation. As Townsend's statement implies, slave marriage customs persisted in the black community, but these practices did not last indefinitely. Even before the end of the war, forces were at work encouraging former slaves to adopt the new system of marriage.

Certainly, black soldiers were prompted to abandon the old constitution earlier and more intensively than most other African Americans in the South by chaplains and other white officers in black regiments. However, after the war, pressure came from other quarters as well. Some Southern state governments in the immediate postwar years also insisted that ex-slaves legalize their antebellum marriages. Kentucky, for instance, passed a law requiring freedmen and freedwomen to register their slave marriages with local authorities. Florida was particularly harsh, giving ex-slaves nine months after the passage of its January 1866 law to have a legal ceremony performed and stating that violators would be prosecuted for "fornication and adultery." Evidently, Florida's legislature, dominated by white Southerners in the immediate postwar period, did not trust either black men or black woman to take care of their families and saw legal marriage as a weapon to force them to fulfill their family responsibilities.[37] The illegality of common-law marriage in most of the Upper South and Louisiana after the war no doubt helped discourage informal postwar unions.[38]

However, the most potent influence on African-American veterans and their wives to abandon the old constitution after the Civil War came from within the black community itself. Pension files demonstrate that local black churches were the most effective influence in terms of persuading men and women with informal prewar and postwar marriages to formalize them. Many ministers and congregations disapproved of these unions, seeing the couples as living outside the bounds of religious propriety.[39] They came to see informal marriage as no marriage at all and considered the people who lived in them to be sinners. For instance, Hannah Whittington, the widow of Lewis Booth, a Mississippi soldier who died in 1863, took up with a man named Jerry Turner after the war. Cornelius McCray, a local black minister, later testified to a pension examiner, "Although they appeared to live [as if they were married] . . . there was some talk of expelling . . . [Whittington] from the church on account of her living with this man in adultery."[40] Sometimes black churches made good on the expulsion threat. Mollie Fry, the widow of Philip Fry, an ex-soldier from Kentucky, testified in 1911, "Philip had been a Baptist, but they turned him out of the church because he was living with me without being married." However, if couples gave in and submitted to a religious ceremony, black congregations proved forgiving. For instance, after a minister married Philip and Mollie Fry, the Baptist church in Danville, Kentucky, accepted him back into their fellowship.[41] Sometimes the threat of expulsion was enough to convince a wayward couple to submit to a marriage ceremony. Rosa Farrow, the widow of Volsin Farrow, testified in 1922 that the Mount Olive Baptist Church in Iberville Parish, Louisiana, "compelled us to marry. We were both members of the church and they took up in church that we were living together that way, and Volsin and I got married rather than be put out of the church."[42]

It must be pointed out, however, that the emphasis of black churches was on marriage in the sight of God, rather than legal marriage per se. A church wedding was not always a legal marriage, because either the couple did not obtain a license or the minister did not report the ceremony to the government. Indeed, the lack of a marriage license hurt the pension applications of widows in states such as Louisiana, which absolutely required a government license to validate a ceremonial marriage. For instance, the federal government rejected the application of Emma Barrett, the widow of William B. Barrett, a New Orleans veteran (and prominent Reconstruction politician), because the couple never obtained a license to legalize their 1875 church marriage. It took a special act of Congress to get Emma Barrett on the pension rolls.[43] Still, despite their concentration on religious rather than legal marriage, black churches ultimately made the biggest contribution to the decline of the old constitution.

Yet, for all the forces striving to eliminate them, slave marriage customs survived for many decades after the Civil War. Although informal marriage had been the only option during slavery, former slaves voluntarily continued the practice in the postwar period for a variety of reasons.

Economic factors, which encouraged common-law marriage among working-class people throughout the Western world in the nineteenth century, played an important role in the persistence of the old constitution.[44] Some black veterans and their wives found the costs of legal marriage and divorce to be prohibitive. Assuming that a marriage license represents the minimum price of a legal marriage, in the postwar South, it cost anywhere from 50 cents (Tennessee) to $3.50 (Delaware).[45] Either sum was beyond the means of some cash-poor sharecroppers and day laborers. Divorce was even more expensive. In the post–Civil War period, "no-fault" divorce did not exist, which meant that courts had to find fault with one spouse to justify a divorce. Common grounds included adultery, abandonment, mental and physical abuse, and alcoholism.[46] Hiring an attorney to help prove fault and paying court costs could be an expensive proposition. It was easier and cheaper for poor persons to simply leave their errant spouses.[47]

Hence, economic standing seems to have played a notable role in determining who supported and opposed the old constitution within the postwar black community. Informal marriage appears to have survived most strongly among poor and rural African Americans, while formal marriage was most strongly accepted by the black middle class and those with middle-class aspirations, who embraced legal marriage as leverage for obtaining additional citizenship rights and as a way to prove African-American rectitude to skeptical white people. As Laura Edwards wrote, "many middle-class blacks trumpeted the virtues of legal marriage as a way to elevate the race."[48] In the estimation of the black middle class, uplifting the race required African Americans to abandon this morally questionable relic of the past. Informal marriage had been tolerable during slavery, when there had been no other choice. But once black people had the option, proponents of the new covenant believed that African Americans should choose legal marriage, and if they did not, the community ought to pressure practitioners of the old constitution to do the right thing.

Disagreement over the basis of marriage in the African-American community should also be considered in the context of the larger debate in the United States in the nineteenth century about the legitimacy of common-law marriage. Common-law marriages existed among poor whites as well as poor blacks during this period, and white Americans had become increasingly tolerant of marital informality in the early nineteenth century. As Michael Grossberg has shown, judges in the early 1800s created the concept of common-law marriage to bring informal unions within the law, so as not to deny informally married women inheritance and other widows' rights, as well as to free Americans from the tight regulation of marriage found under the British system during the colonial era. However, by the late nineteenth century, the legal pendulum had swung against common-law marriage, as critics argued that it was "misguided and pernicious, and charged it as well with spawning social anarchy and untrammeled individualism."[49]

It is likely that the growing intolerance of informal unions among white Americans in the late nineteenth century found its way into the postwar black community, especially among middle-class African Americans aspiring to Victorian respectability and those who were apprehensive about their claim to other citizenship rights if their community did not wholeheartedly embrace the institution of legal marriage. No doubt a big part of the concern over "social anarchy" also stemmed from the worry that informal marriage would undermine male authority in the black family. Without legal marriage, it was feared that men and women would not know their proper places in the free black family. Like Union officers during the war, white Americans were afraid that informal unions were encouraging African-American women to be entirely too independent of men.

Still, it is important to note that the growing hostility toward common-law marriage in the United States did not spread uniformly. Some Southern states, especially in the Lower South (except for Louisiana), continued to recognize common-law marriages long after the Civil War. In fact, many of these states automatically legalized slave unions after the war and, rather than requiring new ceremonies or registration, simply declared all black couples residing together on a given day to be legally married thereafter. The inconsistent manner in which Southern states legalized slave marriages and recognized common-law marriage no doubt created confusion among former slaves about whether their marriages were legal.[50]

Likewise, informally married couples clearly rejected the notion that the lack of a marriage license might create confusion about proper gender roles within the black family. Yet, based on certain attitudes about the relationship between husbands and wives, it is clear why advocates of legal marriage in African-American society were uncomfortable with the survival of the old constitution. Testimony from pension files suggests that at least some informally married couples believed in unions of mutual responsibility in which neither partner dominated the other. When asked about Wilson and Eliza Fitchett's lack of a legal marriage, their friend Airey Young reported to a Pension Bureau investigator, "They passed as man and wife, 'he owned her and she owned him.'"[51] In other words, Eliza was not Wilson's de facto property, as might have been the case in a union in which the husband ruled formally as the head of the household. The account of Emma Frederick, discussing her informal marriage to Clement Frederick, also stressed reciprocal obligations and the lack of preponderant power by one marital partner over the other. "We lived together happily and he was good to me," Emma stated in 1903. She added, "I called him 'papa' and he called me 'mama.'" During the examination, the federal investigator asked her, "What agreement did you make with [Clement] when you first began living with him?" Emma replied, "I told him that if he would take me for his bosom wife that I would not allow any man to come between him and me . . . and he promised he would not have any other woman than me."[52] Emma Frederick's testimony also highlighted the close, companionate bonds of her union with Clement, including their sexual fidelity to each other. Likewise, the aforementioned case of Phillip and Josephine Bellfield demonstrates that couples practicing informal marriage believed their unions to be perfectly respectable because they enjoyed the recognition of the community where they lived. They were accepted by their neighbors as husband and wife and did not need governmental authority or patriarchy to undergird their union.

Indeed, for some ex-soldiers and their wives, dropping the old constitution was motivated less by the seeming sanctity of a legal marriage and the attendant claim on manhood and citizenship rights, and more by the fear that a slave or postwar common-law marriage would be treated as invalid by governmental authorities. Lucinda Sibley, the widow of Solomon Sibley, a soldier from Arkansas, stated in 1893, "There was a general impression that our old slave marriages were not valid & we were advised to marry again under the United States regulations."[53] Kizzie Sexton, seconding Sibley's opinion, testified that she and her husband Henry had legally married in 1869 because "this second marriage was advised by friends as a protection to myself and the children."[54] Thomasine Stephens, the widow of Peter Stephens, who lived in New Orleans after the war, told a Pension Bureau investigator in 1913 that she and her husband had legalized their nearly forty-year-old common-law marriage in 1907 "to ratify our former relations & for no other reason."[55]

The Sibley, Sexton, and Stephens widows suggest that they embraced legal marriage for the security it afforded them. Each of these farsighted women realized that in order to get federal pensions, inherit property, and cultivate middle-class respectability, it would be helpful to prove that she was her husband's legal wife.

Yet in adopting the new system of marriage, they gave up the advantages of the old, especially its convenience and economy. Under the old constitution, a wife with an errant husband need not spend an inordinate amount of money proving his fault in a court of law in order to obtain a divorce; she could simply leave the offending spouse and take up with another man at a later date if she wished. Indeed, pension files show that women, like veterans, used informal means to leave marriages they found disagreeable.[56] As Noralee Frankel suggested, the ability of black women to leave marriages without the trouble and expense of a divorce by "quitting" their husbands undercut the power of black men within the African-American family. Black men in the post–Civil War era simply did not enjoy the same economic or legal tools that white men had to undergird a truly patriarchal family. It was simply much easier for their wives to leave them than it was for white women to leave their husbands during this period.[57] This is not to say that perfect equality existed between informally married couples in the postwar African-American community; however, from the perspective of advocates of legal marriage, the more egalitarian nature of these unions and the greater independence they apparently afforded women seemed to threaten the reputation of the race and its potential for advancement in American society in the wake of emancipation.

It is also significant that Civil War pension files demonstrate that both black men and black women switched between the two systems of marriage when they found one or the other to be more advantageous. Some couples who formalized their slave marriages after the war subsequently separated informally from their spouses and later legally married other people. In short, they married legally to obtain the protections of that system and divorced informally to avoid the costs of dissolving a legal marriage. Hence, economics encouraged former slaves to re-embrace the old constitution in divorce practices. Many African Americans simply could not afford the high cost of a legal divorce. Yet it is also likely that the informality of divorce during the slave era led to a more tolerant culture in the poorer and rural segments of the postwar black community for those who did not obtain formal divorces in court. The connection among legal marriage, citizenship rights, and male power did not have the resonance for them that it had for African Americans who aspired to or had achieved greater things in the years after the war. It was more important to impoverished African Africans that they be able to enter into and depart from marital relationships with the same ease that existed before the war. They also did not see their marriages as any less sacred or hallowed because of the lack of legal imprimatur.

Indeed, it was not only poor African Americans who reverted to the old system when marriages broke down. Marital informality appears in the Civil War pension applications of middle-class and even elite African Americans, albeit much more rarely and circumspectly. The most poignant of these cases involved black ministers. Most African-American clergymen attempted to suppress the old constitution in their congregations, but at least a few ministers themselves lived in such informal marital unions. For instance, Diana Cooper, the third wife of Tony Alston, cohabited outside of marriage with a black Methodist minister after her separation from Alston.[58] In another case, a federal pension investigator, R. K. Doe, was convinced that Silvy Granville, the widow of a South Carolina veteran, had entered into an informal union with a local black minister, M. C. Singleton. Though Granville was ostensibly Singleton's "housekeeper," the pension bureaucrat observed that six people lived in Singleton's house, which had "only two bed[s]." Since four of these six people were children, Doe doubted that the relationship between Singleton and Granville was simply platonic but could not prove anything conclusively, as all their neighbors denied any knowledge that the two were intimate.[59]

This case suggests that although middle-class African Americans occasionally entered into informal unions, they felt it necessary to be discreet about them and use subterfuge to deflect attention from the true nature of the relationship. Other couples in informal relationships also claimed that the woman was merely a housekeeper, even when the presence of children indicated that the relationship had a sexual dimension.[60] Hence, though they found it necessary to abandon respectable marital norms in practice, they were loath to reject the ideals behind them publicly.

It is worth mentioning that informal unions also existed among black veterans who had been free before the Civil War. Yet free people of color were much less likely to describe such relationships as marriages than were former slaves. For instance, Lois Jackson, who cohabited for more than forty years with Lot Lee Barton, a black veteran living in upstate New York, denied being his wife, despite the fact that a legal marriage would have qualified her for a widow's pension. Like middle-class blacks, African Americans from free backgrounds often felt compelled to rationalize their informal unions. In Jackson's case, she explained that she would not marry "a man that drank and spent his money for liquor & dissipation." "It was what I earned during the 41-years I lived & cohabitated with the soldier that kept myself, and the children *from the poor house*," she complained.[61] She was unwilling to marry Barton because he did not support their family like a real man. She deigned to live with him but would not sanctify the relationship by accepting him as her legal husband. He did not deserve the honor because of his open infidelity and his failure to be a true provider—essential qualities of a household head. Lot Lee Barton could not support her or behave in a respectable manner, so why should Lois Jackson formally acknowledge him as her legal husband? It is significant that Jackson put her reasons for not marrying the veteran in gendered terms, justifying their lack of a marriage by her partner's lack of manhood, but it is just as important that she made any excuse at all, something few former slaves felt obliged to do.

Yet the number of couples of free origin in informal unions, like middle-class blacks, was small compared with ex-slaves, and it is not surprising that these housekeepers indicated that they would prefer to be wives. They desired the status and respectability that went along with it. William F. Sampson, a freeborn Maryland veteran from Baltimore, lived with two women, Annie Ross and Charlotte Demby, after the war before eventually marrying a third, Rachel Palmer. His marriage to Palmer emotionally devastated Ross, who complained after Sampson's death, "After he married he came back & lived with me a year. He used to say to me that he would marry me but he never did & I have been obligated to raise all his children." Ross was particularly bitter toward Sampson because one of the children was severely handicapped, adding to her burden.[62] Elizabeth Conway proved more successful than Ross in getting her veteran to marry her. She started living with forty-year-old Henry Vass in about 1880, as his housekeeper. Within a few years, Vass and Conway began a sexual relationship. However, being the veteran's lover was not enough for Conway. "I got tired of living with him in the capacity of a wife without being married to him," she told a pension investigator in 1903. In 1890, she finally convinced Vass to marry her.[63]

Like their slave counterparts, at least some veterans who were freemen before the Civil War broke up with their wives and married other women without first obtaining a legal divorce. Jeremiah Bradley, a black Massachusetts soldier who died shortly after returning home from the army, successively married three women before the war, abandoning each in turn and marrying the next without formally divorcing the previous wife. Several of his wives, however, also had previous living husbands when he married them. Some free black men and women, as did former slaves and other working-class people during the nineteenth century, granted themselves informal divorces from their spouses. John Hall Comick, the pension investigator in the Bradley case, reported that a witness, Arabella Burrell, had told him casually after her deposition, "none of them [i.e., people in Jeremiah Bradley's circle of acquaintances] wasted any time getting divorces."[64] Apparently, a segment of the working-class black population in the antebellum North, like former slaves, saw formal divorce as too expensive and troublesome to obtain—as an unnecessary luxury.

Unlike ex-slaves, however, many free people of color felt compelled to justify remarriage without divorce. One common reason advanced was that the estranged spouse had already remarried, breaking whatever marital bonds remained and freeing the other partner to remarry. The case of John West, a black soldier from Pennsylvania who died in the Civil War, demonstrates this belief in operation. After the war, his widow, Mary, married John Craven, but the couple later separated, and Craven remarried. Confronted with the fact that his subsequent marriage was illegal, Craven explained to a pension investigator, "I was told that [Mary] married some[one] else and then I thought if [she] was married I did not need any divorce and so I then got married."[65] Craven's attitude was not limited to ordinary African Americans but could also be found among the black elite. Henry F. Downing, a businessman, diplomat, writer, and black navy veteran, separated from his wife,

Isadora Jackson, and, without divorcing her, married a white Irish woman, Margarita T. Doyle. After Downing's death in 1928, Doyle had a difficult time establishing that she was a legal widow because of Downing's previous marriage. She appealed for help to W. E. B. Du Bois, then president of the NAACP. Writing in support of the widow's claim, Du Bois questioned whether Downing's first wife's remarriage before he married Doyle was not "presumptive proof of a divorce."[66]

The length of a separation from an estranged spouse was another reason cited to justify remarriage without divorce. Diannah Springsteen, the widow of Thomas Simons, a New York veteran, told a pension investigator that her former husband, Peter Hyatt, had left her many years before she married Simons. Springsteen testified, "Before the minister married me to Simons he went and got some book and looked it up and told me that because Hyatt had been gone from me for 7 years and more that I could remarry, and I did."[67] As Springsteen's case demonstrates, at least a few black clergymen took a flexible and compassionate attitude when it came to the dissolution of marriage. They recognized that some marriages, although they still existed on paper, were in reality long dead and that it was unfair to require poor parishioners to either resurrect those unions or go through the difficult, expensive, and time-consuming process of legally divorcing the old spouse before marrying again. No doubt some black clergymen took this attitude with former slaves as well as free people of color.

Yet it is also likely that the explanations of free people of color about their marital informality were also prompted by the stronger disapproval they encountered when they stepped beyond acceptable Victorian middle-class norms. Whereas pension bureaucrats in the South developed low expectations of African Americans in terms of their acceptance of formal marriage and divorce and refused to make explicit moral judgments, at least in their written reports to their superiors in Washington, D.C., their counterparts working in the North were less apt to excuse marital informality and, on occasion, expressed their disapproval in exceedingly harsh terms. For instance, John Hall Comick, the pension investigator in the Jeremiah Bradley case in Massachusetts, was so disgusted by the practices of Bradley and his friends that he finished his report to the commissioner of pensions by gratuitously stating, "I think all the parties to this case, claimant and witnesses, are a disagreeable lot of barbarians."[68] Besides evincing greater disapproval, white Northerners also proved more likely to act on that knowledge. For instance, a court official invalidated the marriage of John H. A. Stephenson, a Pennsylvania veteran, to Mary Jane Temple when he discovered that the bride had a living husband.[69]

In sum, the cases discussed indicate that whatever ideals some African Americans developed about the connections among legal marriage, manhood, and citizenship, the reality of marriage and family life in the postwar period was messier and more complex than such ideals prescribed. Although some people in the postwar black community pushed for legal marriage to help advance the status of their people, by leveraging manhood rights from marital rights and promoting the authority of men within the family, the realities of black life after the Civil War frustrated them to an extent. Tradition, poverty, convenience, and other factors meant that the old constitution was never quite stamped out among the Civil War generation. Its survival also suggests that some African-American veterans simply did not see legal marriage or male heads of households as essential in validating the manhood of black men. They had more important things to worry about concerning marriage and family than a piece of paper formalizing it in the eyes of the government. However, for other black veterans, especially those who were better off or hoped to be better off, legal marriage and male authority were usually essential elements of their identity as men and of the progress of their race in American society.

In any case, the survival of the old constitution limited the growth of male authority within the African-American family after the Civil War. Yet the experience of black veterans demonstrates that they made considerable progress in this regard. Before the end of the war, African Americans in the Union army were taking control of their families, bolstering their manly status in the process. They took surnames they associated with their fathers for the same reason. Not to be known by your father's last name was not to be a true man in the estimation of many black veterans. Likewise, they and other African Americans fought for legal marriage in the decades after the war, because of its association with citizenship and rising manhood. Some veterans believed legal matrimony to be a key factor in demonstrating the morality of their race and leveraging additional manhood rights, while others cleaved to older ways of marriage that they found sufficiently virtuous and more suitable in coping with the vicissitudes of the postwar years. That the old ways tended to undercut the authority of men within the black family was not particularly important to them. Still, the fact that legal marriage remained available throughout this period was a tremendous victory for black veterans, as it was for other African Americans. Having gained and lost their political rights in the South, these men retained their marital rights and the independence of their families from casual white interference. They and their families would benefit in similar fashion from the unprecedented social welfare system created for Union veterans in the wake of the Civil War.

# 5

# Social Welfare

L IKE OTHER UNION VETERANS, African Americans were beneficiaries of the federal government's generosity after the war. The largess came in three forms: military claims, pensions, and federally supported veterans' homes. Collectively, they amounted to a de facto social welfare system, providing veterans and their dependent survivors with a level of security unavailable to the public at large. Yet the experience of black veterans and their families with post–Civil War social welfare, like the other parts of their story, was problematic. On the one hand, former black soldiers benefited greatly from the government's assistance, using its resources to boost their positions in their families, as well as achieve manly independence and dignity in old age. On the other hand, they and their families did not receive an equal share of the benefits and trod a harder path than white applicants to obtain them. As such, post–Civil War social welfare typifies the situation of black veterans. Theoretically, they had achieved equality, but reality fell short of the ideal. Yet even with de jure equality and de facto inequality, African-American veterans and their families still treasured this instance of inclusion in a time of growing exclusion.

Military claims were not, strictly speaking, a form of social welfare. They arose because of the government's failure to pay wages, bounties, and allowances in a timely manner during the war itself. Some soldiers had not even received all the compensation owed them by the time of their discharge. After the war, Congress set up a system whereby veterans could collect the money due them by petitioning the federal government and presenting evidence of the lack of payment. The government then weighed this information against its own records, and if the proof was sufficient, it would authorize the treasury to pay the veterans.

However, the military claims system soon went beyond merely discharging existing debts to former Union soldiers. The U.S. Congress legislated new ones as well. That is, Congress retroactively extended recruitment bounties, the principal type of military claim, to individuals not originally designated to receive them. Its action was meant to equalize payments retroactively for those men who had enlisted early, when bounties were not offered or were not as high as they became later in the war. Practically speaking, equalization unleashed an immediate flood of "arrears" applications and a continuing stream for years after the war, as former soldiers hastened to collect sums that often amounted to hundreds of dollars. Attorneys and claims agents assisted many of these men by greasing the skids of the federal bureaucracy—for a price (usually a percentage of the money recovered).

African Americans benefited greatly from bounty equalization. Many of these men had not received bounties when they joined the Union army. Because most black recruits were slaves, government authorities initially reasoned that granting them freedom for enlisting was more than equivalent in value to any bounty they might receive. So instead, the money went to the slaves' former owners, if the slaveholders were loyal to the federal government, to compensate them for the loss of their property. Congress had made partial amends to African Americans in June 1864, when it authorized a $100 bounty for free black soldiers and other African Americans who had joined the Union army in response to President Lincoln's draft call of October 1863. This act, however, granted bounties to only a minority of black soldiers. To encourage further enlistment, in July 1864, Congress passed a law that equalized bounties for African-American and white recruits; however, this left former slaves who had enlisted before the law's passage ineligible to collect any bounty money. It was not until March 1873 that Congress fully equalized the bounties of former slaves with those of other Union soldiers.[1] Although formal discrimination occurred in the awarding of bounties, African Americans eventually received equal treatment under the law in terms of eligibility to receive them.

Whether former black soldiers received the full benefit of their bounty money was another matter. Allegations reached Congress in the late 1860s of fraud in Tennessee, specifically, that African-American veterans there had been cheated of part or all their bounty money by personnel of the Freedmen's Bureau and private claims agents. The head office of the bureau in Washington, D.C., under orders from the War Department, appointed a commission that traveled to Nashville and other cities in the state to investigate the charges. Although the commission cleared federal personnel of malfeasance in the handling of bounty claims, it substantiated fraud on the part of a number of claims agents. There were two general types of schemes operating. The more common one was that an agent would advance the former soldier a portion of his claim as a loan, charging such an exorbitant interest rate that when the government finally approved the claim, the full amount of the settlement usually went to the agent. Alternatively, the agent would wait until the claim was paid and then extort money from the client well in excess of the fee for services allowed under the law (10 percent of the claim's value).[2]

Whether African-American veterans in Tennessee were really victims of fraud was hotly contested by the alleged perpetrators. D. W. Glassie, the leading claims agent identified by the Freedmen's Bureau commission, proved utterly unapologetic about his activities. He portrayed his transactions with the former soldiers as mutually advantageous, allowing men quicker access to their bounty money through his loans. Glassie essentially argued to the commission that the money he provided assisted the veterans in their pursuit of economic manhood. The agent would loan them money, he stated in an affidavit, "when they desired to rent a farm, and required teams, seed, &c; when they wished to buy a house, a wagon and team, a cow, or anything of the sort that would assist them in making a living." Glassie also argued that his loans helped the veterans care for their families, giving them the resources to look after sick loved ones, cover funeral expenses for dead relatives, and pay lawyers and court fines so that when they were arrested they could stay out of prison and support their dependents.[3] Although Glassie's testimony was self-serving, it clearly shows how desperate black veterans in Tennessee (and no doubt elsewhere) were to receive bounty money, and it shows that they did not fritter away their windfall but generally used it to better themselves and their families materially. In other words, they used it in ways that augmented their role of manly provider.

Although bounties and other types of military claims were a significant form of government assistance to veterans—providing a lump sum to ease the transition from slavery to freedom and, in some cases, making the purchase of land possible—they were insignificant compared with the federal government's pensions for former soldiers and their families. Initially created in 1862 to compensate Union veterans disabled by their service and the survivors of those killed during the war, the pension system was expanded by the Dependent Pension Act of 1890, which extended pension eligibility to all disabled Union veterans, regardless of the cause of the disability, as well as to the survivors of men who had served. With the expanded disability provision generously interpreted by the U.S. Pension Bureau (the Interior Department unit that administered the program), the number of pensioners soared. By 1910, Theda Skocpol estimates, "about 28 percent of all American men aged 65 or more, more than half a million of them, received federal benefits averaging about $189 a year. Over three-hundred thousand widows, orphans, and other dependents were also receiving regular payments from the federal treasury."[4]

Statistical evidence clearly suggests that African Americans received an inequitable portion of the pension money. A random sample of Civil War pension applicants shows that white veterans and their survivors experienced more success in obtaining pensions than did black applicants (see statistical appendix, table 10).[5] More than 92 percent of white Union veterans sampled made at least one successful application, compared with only about 75 percent of black veterans. Likewise, nearly 84 percent of the white widows managed to receive pensions, but only 61 percent of African-American widows made at least one successful application. However, the biggest differential— nearly 34 percentage points—existed between the success rates of white and black parents applying for a dependent parent's pension. White parents had a success rate of almost 70 percent, but for African Americans, it was only around 36 percent. The only category in which the results were equivalent was the applications of minor children, with 50 percent of both white and black applicants making successful claims.

Clearly, a smaller portion of black applicants than white applicants obtained Civil War pensions. Why did such a disparity in success rates exist when there was no overt discrimination against African Americans in pension legislation? Pension legislation passed by Congress was largely neutral on the issue of race, and when it referred to African Americans specifically, the intent was often to assist their applications. For instance, Congress established an easier standard of proof for African-American widows in terms of proving marriage to a Civil War veteran, accepting the reality that slave marriages were harder to document.[6] Hence, the only way to reconcile the theory of pension law with reality is to examine the application process. Although the language of the law suggested that all pension claims received equitable treatment, African Americans clearly had a more difficult time actually obtaining this benefit than did white people. It is impossible to rank factors in terms of their importance in causing the poorer results of black veterans and their families, but examination of the claims process illuminates more fully how each factor could impede or even completely frustrate a Civil War pension claim.

To begin with, it must be understood that the federal government did not automatically grant Civil War pensions to applicants. In the late-nineteenth-century United States, a pension was still generally seen as a reward for the worthy, rather than a general entitlement. In the case of Civil War veterans and their families, federal pensions provided a belated gratuity for the risks and sacrifices of soldiers and sailors during the war. Although the number of people eligible to collect Civil War pensions from the federal government increased over time, especially after passage of the 1890 pension law, applicants still had to prove their worthiness to receive this money. They were required to go through a formal bureaucratic process to substantiate their eligibility according to laws passed by Congress.[7]

Fewer African Americans than whites ended up receiving pensions in part because the bureaucratic process for proving their worthiness left them at a disadvantage. Due to slavery and racial discrimination, a much higher percentage of black applicants for Civil War pensions were poor and illiterate—factors that made it more difficult for them to complete a successful application.[8] Poverty hampered the application process because pursuing a pension claim cost money. Even though pension attorneys took clients on a contingency basis (meaning that they received their fees from the first government pension check), applicants often had to pay some or all of the expenses associated with the claims process.

Several expenses typically arose in Civil War pension applications. Travel costs could easily become the biggest. Witnesses had to be visited and interviewed, and expenses could escalate significantly if any of those people lived a great distance from the applicant. Former soldiers also had to bear the cost of a trip to the nearest surgical board set up by the Pension Bureau to rate their disabilities.[9] Inevitably, the applicant would have to pay for the services of a notary public or court officer to produce legally acceptable affidavits. Costs were often higher for illiterate applicants because they had to hire someone to fill out forms and draft correspondence. In an era in which the average black family income was about $250 per year, the expenses associated with a pension claim were beyond the means of more African American than white applicants.[10] Consequently, more black than white individuals' pension claims languished because of lack of funds.

In addition to poverty and illiteracy, slavery left African Americans with other problems related to proving their cases. For instance, a greater percentage of black than white veterans had difficulty substantiating that they were the same persons who had served in the Union army. Likewise, survivors of black soldiers and veterans had more trouble showing that the dead men who provided the basis for their claims were the same men who had served in the Civil War.[11] These identity inconsistencies occurred more often in African-American cases for three reasons, each related to slavery. First, many former slaves joined the army under their masters' last names but took other surnames after the war to assert male-line family connections and their identity as freemen (see chapter 4). Ironically, by asserting their manhood and making connections with their male forebears, veterans inadvertently caused confusion over their identities that later came back to haunt them or their survivors. Similarly, because members of the same family sometimes chose to take different surnames after the war, it made the connections of veterans and survivors less obvious. Parents and sons, or even husbands and wives, might have different surnames.[12] Second, because a greater proportion of African-American than white recruits was illiterate, fewer could correct clerks who had misconstrued or misspelled their names—inadvertently creating false identities that they later had to explain when they applied for pensions.[13] Third, some black men had joined the army under false names to escape recapture by their owners, who objected to their enlistment.[14]

Whatever the cause of the surname inconsistency, it created a problem for veterans and their survivors when they finally applied for pensions. As a routine step in the application process, the Pension Bureau verified with the War Department that a record existed for the military service of the person providing the basis for the claim. A clerk checked the muster rolls of the unit with which the soldier had served, and the War Department reported back to the Pension Bureau whether the soldier's name could be found there. If the last name of the applicant differed from that of the soldier's wartime records, authorities delayed approval. Rather than grant a pension to a potentially unworthy individual, the Pension Bureau probed further. In some cases, the applicant merely had to submit an affidavit explaining the nature of the name change and the affidavits of witnesses who could verify that the applicant and the soldier were one and the same person. In other cases, however, the bureau dispatched a field investigator to probe the discrepancy. The verification of names sometimes held up pension applications for months or even years before the bureau was satisfied. Black applicants do not appear to have been treated unfairly by the Pension Bureau in this regard. Identity probes also occurred in white pension cases; however, because of the numerous changes of identity associated with the Civil War and emancipation, African Americans were disproportionately the subjects of these investigations.

Furnishing vital dates also proved more of a problem to black than white pension applicants. Birth dates became particularly important after passage of a 1907 law that qualified veterans for pensions based on age: the older a former soldier, the larger his monthly pension rate.[15] Likewise, birth dates had always mattered in the claims of minor children, because their pensions terminated when they turned sixteen. Consequently, the Pension Bureau was very interested in birth dates—information that African Americans could substantiate much less frequently than white applicants could. In many cases, former slaves could not even provide the Pension Bureau with an exact date of birth, let alone a record of it. Such pension applicants did not know their birth dates either because owners had deliberately kept such knowledge from them or because of their preindustrial view of time. Many former slaves, as in other peasant societies around the world, eschewed calendar dates and related important events in their lives to the agricultural cycle or to a significant event that occurred about the same time, such as a great storm, an epidemic, or even a presidential election. Hence, some African Americans were at a disadvantage in a pension system that preferred precise calendar dates.[16]

Besides the obstacles associated with providing documented information, African Americans also collided against human barriers in the application process. Specifically, black applicants encountered claims agents, witnesses, and pension bureaucrats, each of whom influenced the outcome of a claim. Although such people often proved helpful in pushing forward a case, they could also hurt the efforts of black veterans or their survivors.

For most applicants, black and white, a local agent was the key person in the initial phase of the claims process. Although a few attorneys worked directly with claimants from the inception of a case to its conclusion, most did not. The typical pension applicant dealt directly with a claims agent who served as the intermediary with the attorney. These agents usually represented large law firms (most based in Washington, D.C.) that specialized in Civil War pension applications. Claims agents often were notaries or local attorneys, but they could be just about any enterprising person looking to supplement his or her (there were a few female agents) main source of income. Although many agents involved in black pension claims were white, a large number of African-American agents, often ministers or schoolteachers, also performed this service. Whatever their race, these agents sought veterans or survivors who had what they believed to be potentially successful claims. They helped applicants assemble the necessary evidence and sent the paperwork to the Washington law firm, which moved the claims through the bureaucracy of the U.S. Pension Bureau. In successful cases, the claims agent and the law firm shared the fee, in addition to any expenses they could extract from the client.[17]

Because a majority were illiterate, African Americans relied especially heavily on claims agents.[18] These intermediaries were indispensable not only in drafting affidavits and other legal papers but also in helping the applicant respond to questions from the Pension Bureau and serving as a source of information about the complex, ever-changing application process. Without a claims agent, many African Americans entitled to Civil War pensions, especially illiterate claimants, would have been unable to even apply.

For many African Americans, however, claims agents provided as much hindrance as help. Indeed, some black veterans and their survivors were poorly served by their agents. They complained to the U.S. Pension Bureau about neglected cases, delays caused by mix-ups in paperwork, and incompetence, as well as being given bad advice. However, the greatest disservice that pension agents did to black clients was the pervasive practice of presenting fraudulent evidence.[19] Instead of properly determining the facts of the case and obtaining eyewitness testimony or official documents that might exist, many agents in black pension claims contrived false cases built on what one federal pension investigator aptly described as "'ready made' affidavits."[20] The agent would either bribe witnesses to provide false testimony or fabricate sworn statements, ostensibly from actual individuals who might plausibly know the facts of the case. These fraudulent claims were usually built around the service of a real black soldier, but the claims agent misrepresented, falsified, or concealed facts to get an otherwise ineligible applicant a pension or to secure a larger pension than the claimant deserved.

A number of factors made black pension cases ideal for fraud. Certainly, the ambiguity in their life stories and the lack of documentation appealed to crooked claims agents. Because many African Americans had neither precise knowledge of vital dates in their lives nor the records to verify such information, it was difficult for the Pension Bureau to challenge biographical data supplied in black pension cases. In the racial climate of the postwar South, many black pension applicants likely believed that they had little choice but to cooperate in the schemes of corrupt white claims agents. The communications gap between white pension agents and their black clients also encouraged fraud. It was sometimes easier for an agent to formulate the testimony he thought would win approval of the claim or increase the amount of the pension than actually to work with black witnesses to approximate dates and find alternative sources for information that former slaves were often unable to provide.

Still, the biggest motive behind fraudulent black pension claims—as with any fraudulent claim—was greed. These manufactured cases aimed to obtain money from the government that the client did not legally deserve. A claims agent might exaggerate the disabilities of a veteran to win the ex-soldier a larger pension, or he might conceal a sexual relationship on the part of a widow that would disqualify her. In many cases, however, the aim of the fraud was to generate a lump-sum payment of hundreds or even thousands of dollars to compensate an applicant for a pension that he or she should have been receiving from some date in the past. Arrears applications were made possible by legislation passed in 1879. Prior to this date, an applicant could receive pension payments only from the date of the initial claim. The 1879 law enabled applicants to receive payments retroactive to the date of their initial eligibility. For instance, a former soldier disabled during the war who had never applied for a pension could collect arrears going back to the date he was wounded. The widow of a soldier killed during the war could collect arrears from the date of her husband's death. The 1879 pension law resulted in an unprecedented number of new claims, because applicants could collect not only regular pension payments in the future but also an initial lump sum that might be substantial.[21] The arrears claims of African Americans proved especially enticing to crooked agents. African Americans—particularly elderly widows—were less likely to complain after the agent illegally took part of the lump sum. Hence, even though most black pension cases were genuine, their association with fraud made it more difficult for honest claims to win approval from the U.S. Pension Bureau.[22]

Just as African Americans relied on claims agents, they also depended on eyewitnesses to compensate for their lack of written records, another factor that hurt their success in obtaining pensions. The U.S. Pension Bureau gave documentary evidence, especially that of an official nature, greater weight in proving a claim than the testimony of eyewitnesses. Hence, most black applicants could submit only what amounted to an inferior type of evidence. Adding to the harm caused by the lack of documents from the slave era was the poor and incomplete nature of public record keeping in the post–Civil War South.

Their greater reliance on eyewitnesses hurt African Americans in other ways. Sometimes witnesses could not be found to prove important points, or they could not remember critical events. In addition, the greater reliance on eyewitness testimony made African Americans more vulnerable to grudges that witnesses might hold. For instance, although most former owners readily testified in favor of the pension applications of former slaves, a few ex-slaveholders perjured themselves or withheld evidence in the hope of derailing a claim.[23] In other cases, the black community tried to frustrate a pension application. This fate befell Isaac Hibbett, the father of George Hibbett, a veteran who died shortly after returning home from the war. The elder Hibbett applied to the U.S. Pension Bureau in 1884 for a dependent parent's pension. He could not assemble the necessary proof, however, because his black neighbors in Gallatin, Tennessee, refused to testify for him. They believed that Hibbett was unworthy of their help because he remained too close to his former owner and voted for the Democratic ticket (when most Southern blacks were Republicans).[24]

However, the biggest obstacle faced by African Americans in obtaining Civil War pensions was not claims agents or witnesses but the personnel of the U.S. Pension Bureau. These bureaucrats ultimately decided whether an applicant received a pension, and they constituted the decisive barrier to the aspirations of many a hopeful black veteran or survivor. Although ostensibly they were guided by congressional legislation in determining the outcome of cases, the attitudes of bureau personnel shaped the interpretation and application of that law. Because many pension bureaucrats disliked African Americans—and involvement with black applicants did little to improve their opinion—the Pension Bureau scrutinized African-American cases more intensely than those of white applicants.

The greater scrutiny that African Americans received in Civil War pension applications is no more apparent than in "special examinations." This process occurred when the U.S. Pension Bureau was dissatisfied with the evidence in a claim but believed that the case had sufficient merit to prevent its rejection out of hand. These investigations also resulted when information reached the bureau concerning a possible attempt to defraud the government. In either case, the Pension Bureau would dispatch a field investigator or "special examiner" (as the bureau called them) stationed in the region where the claim originated to locate and question witnesses. The special examiner would take depositions and send a report summarizing his findings to the commissioner of pensions in Washington. A special examination significantly delayed the decision on a pension by many months, because most examiners had a backlog of cases, and priority investigations, particularly those involving allegations of fraud, could sidetrack the field investigator while more routine inquiries languished.

Pension claims by African Americans appear to have received special examination more often than white cases did. An examination of the pension files of fifty white Southerners who joined Union regiments shows that only thirteen of the fifty files (26 percent) involved a special examination.[25] In contrast, among the random sample group of black pension applicants, nearly half the files contain a special examiner's report. The investigations in the black cases also appear to have taken longer and were more in-depth.[26]

In part, black Civil War pension cases received more scrutiny simply because they were more complex and difficult to prove. The working assumption of the U.S. Pension Bureau was that an applicant had a stable identity, knowledge of vital dates, and the ability to document this information with records or unambiguous eyewitness testimony. The bureaucracy had difficulty dealing with people who had changed their names and could offer neither vital dates nor other specific information. The inability of many black applicants to follow the conventional path of proving their worthiness led to frustration and suspicion on the part of pension bureaucrats. This attitude was compounded by the widespread distrust of the affidavits and other legal papers submitted by claims agents in black cases. The Pension Bureau made some attempts to deal affirmatively with the special problems inherent in African-American claims, but these efforts were piecemeal rather than systematic.[27]

The interactions between African Americans, especially those in rural plantation districts, and white special examiners did little to dispel the Pension Bureau's mistrust of black applicants. Both sides had difficulty communicating with the other. In particular, the inability of some black applicants to provide dates enormously frustrated the field investigators. "It is singu-larly *impossible* to *get* a colored person to give the *date* of anything," com-plained examiner Eugene B. Payne from Missouri. He had just spent a difficult session with the widow of a black veteran trying to determine the age of her children.[28] Other examiners shared Payne's feelings, not only about getting dates out of some African Americans but also about securing any sort of pre-cise information. Examiner Charles Whitehead was as displeased as Payne after attempting to obtain a personal description of a long-dead veteran from his widow. The best the woman could come up with was that "he was a fat, chunky black niggah wid big lips, wooly head an big black eyes." Whitehead found the description useless. "When one asks an ignorant black woman— little above animal intelligence, to describe some other Negro she knew 40 or 50 years ago," he commented in his report, "we drop special examination to the plane of absurdity."[29] Hence, when special examiners could not gather specific facts from a black witness, it hurt the credibility of the pension claim in their eyes.

Investigators also were swayed by how closely black applicants and their witnesses adhered to the examiner's beliefs about proper behavior by Afri-can Americans. Witnesses who behaved deferentially and showed evidence of white, middle-class standards of morality and industry received praise in reports, and special examiners gave their testimony more weight. In fact, the investigators developed a code language, using words like "industrious," "re-spectable," "reliable," "steady," and "well regarded" to indicate which Afri-can Americans they believed worthy of pensions.[30] Investigators who found the applicant's and witnesses' behavior less appropriate, in terms of indolence, sexual immorality, or some other objectionable quality, questioned their cred-ibility.[31] The perceived moral lapses and inability of some African Americans to provide specific information led many special examiners to doubt the tes-timony of black witnesses in general. "The reputation for truth of all the wit-nesses who are colored cannot be rated higher than 'fair,'" wrote examiner John Lux in 1887, typifying such attitudes. "As those of that race who can be counted reliable and absolutely truthful, are a rarity indeed."[32]

Although it is difficult to trace the effects of pension bureaucrats' racist attitudes in individual cases, the impact on African Americans as a whole is undeniable. Practically speaking, black veterans and their families had a greater burden of proof than white persons had, despite the formal equality of black and white applicants under the law. In a pension system in which eligibility was predicated on the worthiness of the applicant, black people had to work harder to prove that they were truly deserving. It was as though black pension applicants were running a race in which they not only had to clear more hurdles than white veterans and their families but also had to begin the race well back from the normal starting line. Although pension bureaucrats often overlooked defects in white pension cases, they were less likely to do so for African Americans or to give them any benefit of the doubt. There was probably as much fraud in white cases, but the bureau was more likely to ignore it. How aware black pensioners were of the greater burden placed on them is hard to ascertain. If they perceived the greater level of scrutiny their claims engendered, they probably guarded against admitting their true feelings to the Pension Bureau for fear of harming their applications.

Interestingly, some black pension applicants and their agents cleverly played on white racism to assist applications. When an African American had an especially good reputation among local whites, because of a pleasing and deferential manner, the claim sometimes emphasized this fact. For instance, when special examiner A. H. Sweetser was investigating the pension claim of Richard Breck, a black veteran living in Richmond, Kentucky, Sweetser was visited by several local white politicians who offered their support for Breck's pension application, affirming his good character and calling him "Uncle Dick."[33]

Likewise, African Americans were not above bending the truth or telling outright lies if it might push through a questionable pension claim. In fact, some African Americans impressed special examiners with their skill at lying. Such was the case with Nellie Wold, the widow of Lloyd Thurston. "The claimant is rather an intelligent woman and at first impresses me as being truthful," reported examiner M. Whitehead to his superiors in 1893. "But after I got further into her case I find she is unreliable and yet she can tell untruths in such a way that one thinks she is telling the truth." Evidently, Wold had remarried since Thurston's death in 1867, an act that disqualified her from receiving a widow's pension. She sought to conceal this fact from the Pension Bureau, and she would have succeeded if subsequent witnesses had not informed Whitehead of Wold's actual marital history.[34]

Still, these and other investigations show conclusively that some black pension applicants were active and willing participants in the frauds perpetrated on the U.S. Pension Bureau by claims agents. In other words, black applicants were not always innocent parties in attempts to deceive the government. Another such collaborator was Clementine Chatham, who claimed to be the widow of Henry Eber, a black soldier from Louisiana who had died while in the army. Because Chatham did not file her claim until 1893, twenty-seven years after Eber's death in January 1866, the federal government was understandably suspicious. However, whether Chatham had really been Eber's wife was ignored for more than a decade because of confusion about Eber's identity. When that issue was finally settled and the bureau got around to investigating the merits of Chatham's eligibility as a widow in 1906, her lack of credibility made a strong impression on special examiner M. Whitehead (the same man who investigated Nellie Wold). Whitehead reported that Chatham and her claims agent, John H. Van Horssen, "have gathered together a regular crowd of professional witnesses as are often gotten together, who will swear to any thing to help a case, particularly if there is even a shadowy suggestion of a nice money bonus if the claim is allowed." Whitehead managed to get Chatham to admit in her deposition that she had agreed to pay the witnesses small amounts of money, ranging from $1 to $3, when the pension claim was finally approved.[35] Hence, as Chatham's and Wold's cases show, African Americans were not always passive participants in their claims, and some helped perpetrate pension frauds against the federal government.

Certainly, most black pension applicants pushing through their claims did so honestly. However, the wide disparity in the success rates of white and black applicants suggests that even the determination or scheming of some black applicants was not enough to earn African Americans their fair share of the pension money flowing to Union veterans and their survivors from Washington. Despite their formal equality with white applicants under federal law, in practice, African Americans experienced discrimination when applying for pensions. Whether black veterans were aware of this situation is uncertain. Although it was not unusual for African Americans to complain about the slow adjudication of pension claims and other procedural difficulties, it was virtually unheard of for them to claim that these problems resulted from racial prejudice on the part of Pension Bureau personnel, notwithstanding the clear bias evident in the pension files of many black veterans.

Indeed, to the extent that African Americans commented on pensions at all, it was to commend their usefulness. Civil War veterans and their widows interviewed by employees of the WPA Federal Writers' Project in the 1930s exemplify this attitude. "It was a lucky day when de Yankees got me," remarked William Baltimore, an Arkansas veteran, to a WPA interviewer when asked about his Civil War pension. "I'm setting pretty for de rest of my life." The money from his federal pension kept this old and blind veteran secure, while many people around him went hungry in the midst of the Great Depression.[36] James Spikes, another black veteran from Arkansas, agreed with Baltimore. Referring to his Civil War pension, he told the federal writer, "Yes'm it comes in right nice—it does that."[37]

Although it is possible to dismiss the praise of men like Baltimore and Spikes as the fulsome ramblings of elderly men seeking to please a representative of their benefactor, the federal government, other evidence points to the sincerity of such remarks. For one thing, many black pensioners in the South no doubt came to realize that the pensions they received were substantially higher than the pensions their white neighbors got from the individual Southern states for Confederate service. As Theda Skocpol has noted, citing information gathered by early-twentieth-century scholar William Glasson, state government pensions for Confederate veterans and their survivors were significantly smaller than federal pensions. In the first decade of the twentieth century, for instance, Georgia veterans—in what was the most generous state system in the South—were receiving on average about $60 per year; at the same time, their average Union counterparts drew almost $115 per year.[38]

In the aggregate, then, Civil War pensions funneled an enormous amount of money to black veterans and their survivors. Based on data gathered from the random sample group, and ignoring inflation, the average black veteran and his family collectively received payments amounting to $3,759 over the course of about two decades (this figure represents the average amount paid per pension file). Since the federal government paid pension benefits based on the service of approximately 83,320 black soldiers (the number of African-American pension files with a successful application), a conservative estimate of the total amount paid to African-American pensioners is $313 million. When the millions of dollars paid in Civil War bounties and other military claims is taken into account as well, the total represents a previously little appreciated but sizable infusion of money into the post–Civil War black community.[39]

Given the large amount of money distributed, it is not surprising that the memory of Civil War pension benefits persisted among the families of black veterans long after the former soldiers had died. Pauli Murray, discussing her black veteran grandfather, Robert G. Fitzgerald, stated that as a child she would sometimes accompany him to cash his pension check. "He seemed to walk straighter on those days," Murray wrote. "His check was the government's recognition of honored service and of the disability he had suffered in his country's cause."[40] In other words, the money paid to Fitzgerald made him feel like more of a man. It was a tangible token that, in the eyes of the federal government, he was no different from the white Union veterans receiving pensions. Fitzgerald had helped the government out in its time of crisis, and now it was assisting him when he needed a helping hand.

Indeed, many children of veterans inquired of the government—mostly during the 1920s, 1930s, and 1940s, but some as late as the 1960s—whether they too might receive money because of their fathers' Civil War service. For instance, beginning in the 1930s, Beatrice G. Mickey wrote to the pension authorities regularly, seeking benefits. Despite repeated refusals, as late as 1962 she was still asking for a pension.[41] Prompting such letters was the fact that between World War I and World War II, many of the children of Civil War veterans reached old age themselves. They remembered the regular, dependable income that pension checks had brought their parents and sought the same thing for themselves. Likewise, the paltry wages received by most African Americans in the early twentieth century made it very difficult to save money for retirement. Consequently, many children of black Civil War soldiers were forced to scrounge for possible sources of support. They wondered whether the federal government's gratitude to their parents would extend to them in their time of need. Hence, the Veterans Administration received numerous letters from veterans' children requesting pensions a full century after the Civil War.

Pensions helped African-American Civil War veterans live better and more comfortable lives, particularly if the pension was a supplementary source of income. Consequently, pensions bolstered the manhood of black veterans not only psychologically but also economically, becoming the linchpin of their prosperity and, in some cases, their family authority. Such was the status of Kitt Mitchell, a South Carolina veteran. Mitchell was a landowner and grew cotton, corn, and potatoes with the help of his wife, daughter, and son-in-law. "We do very well when we have a good season," Mitchell told a special examiner in 1903, "and what we make, together with my [Civil War] pension, keeps us going very well."[42] Thus, for veterans who, despite their disabilities, could continue working, pensions improved their standard of living and brought them additional security. Pensions helped them fulfill their role as manly provider by allowing them to take better care of their loved ones and supported them in the role of elderly family head—just like Kitt Mitchell. No doubt the pension had helped him hold on to his land, as well as attracting the labor of his daughter and son-in-law, who probably hoped to inherit the property one day.

For those veterans lucky enough to receive arrears at some point, pensions also gave them the means to achieve greater manhood by helping them purchase land and other productive assets. For instance, George Scott, a Northern black veteran, was the recipient of a large lump-sum payment. Scott's arrears amounted to about $1,200, which he used to buy land in his hometown of Benton Harbor, Michigan.[43] Still, as much as government money helped black Civil War veterans and their families, it could be a mixed blessing, especially for widows. For instance, Nancy Thomas, a widow in Austin, Texas, told a WPA writer in the 1930s that other members of the black community "consider[ed] her a sort of bank." Indeed, Thomas's pension check had just arrived at the time of the interview, and people seeking money interrupted the conversation between the widow and the federal writer on several occasions.[44] Another WPA interviewer in Mississippi wrote that the widow he visited had been beaten and robbed on several occasions for her pension money, and she had also been the target of confidence men, seeking to swindle her.[45]

It was not just widows who became the targets of such exploitation, but veterans as well. This was particularly true of veterans who were unable to continue working while receiving pensions or had failed to win arrears claims. These men often could not subsist on their pensions and fell victim to usurers. Lacking other sources of income, these ex-soldiers ran out of money before their quarterly checks arrived. (Although pension payments accrued at a monthly rate, the Pension Bureau paid them quarterly.) Desperation forced them to borrow money from local usurers, who charged exploitive rates of interest and demanded that the veterans leave their pension certificates as collateral for the loans—a practice prohibited under federal law. These certificates served as acceptable security because they were necessary to collect pension payments. Every quarter, each Civil War pensioner had to execute a voucher in the presence of a government official (usually a local postmaster) and present a certificate as proof of his status as a pensioner before the Pension Bureau would send him a check. Without physical possession of the certificate, the veteran could not get paid. The government had established this elaborate procedure both to safeguard payments to the designated beneficiaries and to guarantee that survivors or other parties could not keep the money flowing after a pensioner had died by not reporting his death. The government outlawed the use of pension certificates as collateral for loans, but as usury cases demonstrate, desperate veterans and greedy moneylenders did not hesitate to violate this statute.[46]

The case of veteran Charles W. Goodrich, a retired carpenter living in Washington, D.C., illustrates how these illegal loans worked in practice. Goodrich was about to be evicted from his lodgings and had no way to pay his rent, so he asked for a loan from a local merchant, Staley. In return for $8, the merchant required Goodrich to sign a note for $10.50 and leave his pension certificate and the copy of his executed voucher with Staley. The merchant also demanded that Goodrich execute his voucher so that the Pension Bureau would mail his check to Staley. When the pension check finally arrived, Staley deducted the money owed him, as well as a fee for cashing the check.[47]

Veterans forced to borrow in anticipation of their coming pension checks got caught up in a vicious circle. Forced to pay exploitive amounts of interest and other fees, they lost the full benefit of their pension checks, ran out of money before they received their next checks, and had to borrow money again. Each quarter, they would need the loan earlier than in the previous three-month period. Indeed, these cases usually came to the attention of the Pension Bureau because some veterans, evidently unable to get their certificates out of hock, applied to the government for new certificates on the pretext of having lost the originals. The facts emerged when the Pension Bureau investigated the circumstances of the alleged losses.[48]

Despite the inadequacy of pensions for some veterans, and despite the unfair share of pension money received by African Americans compared with white veterans and their families, the money was still welcome. There were no statistics available in the late nineteenth and early twentieth centuries showing that blacks received an inequitable portion of the federal government's largess, so they relied on anecdotal evidence in assessing the system. In other words, perception was more important than reality. In that respect, they could see many people in their community collecting these payments, so pensions came to symbolize a form of inclusion for black veterans and other African Americans in an era when exclusion and discrimination were common. It also did not hurt the opinion of the black community that this money gave former soldiers the means to fulfill their family responsibilities and strengthen their position as men. Hence, rather than focusing on the discrimination, African Americans perceived Civil War pensions quite positively.

As with pensions, black veterans were theoretically equally entitled to enter the government "homes" built for Union veterans. Both the federal government and state governments established numerous such institutions after the war. (Less well-funded homes built by state governments or private charities also appeared in the South for Confederate veterans.)[49] The most important homes for Union veterans were part of the National Home for Disabled Volunteer Soldiers (NHDVS), organized by the federal government in the late 1860s. The NHDVS consisted of a network of asylums scattered mostly across the North and supported by the federal government. Their initial purpose was to provide a refuge for disabled soldiers who were unable to earn a living after the war and had no family willing or able to care for them. Over time, however, the NHDVS network and other veterans' homes evolved into retirement facilities for impoverished elderly veterans with no better place to go.

Although black veterans could be found in nearly all the NHDVS homes, they were underrepresented throughout the network. African Americans accounted for about 9 percent of Union soldiers and sailors during the Civil War, yet they constituted only around 1 percent of the residents of NHDVS homes between 1876 and 1905, the years for which exact numbers can be ascertained.[50] Even in the NHDVS home in Hampton, Virginia (the only branch in the South before another one opened in Tennessee in 1904), black veterans never made up more than 7 percent of its population, and for most of the years of its operation, the numbers were closer to the 1 percent that was typical throughout the network. These statistics are astounding, considering that residents of the homes tended to be poor men with limited options for sustenance and care. Hence, given their often impoverished socioeconomic status, the underrepresentation of African Americans in the NHDVS network needs further clarification.

During the early history of the National Home for Disabled Volunteer Soldiers, its inhabitants were overwhelmingly men with severe war-related disabilities, such as missing limbs or other injuries that interfered with their ability to support themselves. Because these injuries had usually been sustained on the battlefield, and because most black soldiers had seen less combat than their white counterparts, fewer of them had sustained the types of injuries that would qualify them for entry into an NHDVS home in the early decades of its existence. Likewise, by the time the NHDVS branches started taking in significant numbers of elderly veterans in the 1880s, demographic realities intervened to keep the relative percentage of African Americans in these government homes low. The simple fact was that, with a life expectancy about ten years less than that of their white counterparts, most black veterans did not live long enough to enter the NHDVS as old men. This reality is apparent from the 1890 census. Whereas African Americans had made up 9 percent of Union recruits during the Civil War, by 1890, only about 2 percent of the Union veterans still alive were black men.

It also seems that many African Americans made a conscious decision to avoid the NHDVS. Disabled and elderly black veterans preferred to be cared for by their families or friends, rather than by strangers in an impersonal government facility. Black men who left the NHDVS homes evinced this attitude. For instance, octogenarian Hezekiah Butler requested a discharge from the NHDVS branch at Danville, Illinois, in 1907, writing, "I desire to live with my relations the balance of my days."[51] Both pension files and NHDVS case files demonstrate the interest that extended-family members took in old veterans and their willingness to help them. Hence, African-American veterans depended more on kin networks than on the government for care when they were disabled by the war or in their old age. Instead, it was foreign-born white veterans who made up a disproportionate percentage of the residents of the NHDVS homes throughout its history. These immigrant veterans often did not have family to care for them, as their relations were back in Europe. In this case, black veterans often had access to a better alternative—family care.

Hence, when they had a choice—and most of them did—black veterans generally opted to live outside soldiers' homes, supported by their pensions and cared for by their families. Although the NHDVS homes guaranteed shelter, food, and medical care for former soldiers, they were often unpleasant. Veterans lived under quasi-military discipline, with their daily activities tightly controlled and their sleeping accommodations in communal barracks. Although they were allowed to leave the premises during the day and most evenings, the homes had curfews and tightly restricted the consumption of alcohol. Many veterans could not cope with the institutional conditions and the strict rules of conduct, and some black veterans had regular run-ins with the authorities of these homes, as documented in their case files.

African-American veterans also might have avoided these homes because they reflected the status of their race in the United States more generally. Segregation was fast becoming a legal as well as a social reality in the United States in the late nineteenth and early twentieth centuries, and the NHDVS was no exception. As Patrick J. Kelley noted in his study of the NHDVS, although white and black veterans shared eating facilities and encountered each other around the grounds of the homes, "black residents . . . lived in segregated quarters, ate their meals at segregated tables, and had their hair cut by separate barbers."[52] Yet the subject of race was studiously ignored both in the official annual reports of the NHDVS to Congress and in the case files of individual black veterans. Indeed, the population statistics of the NHDVS homes indicate that administrators followed an informal policy of distributing African Americans among the homes, rather than allowing significant concentrations to occur in a particular home or group of homes. Hence, preserving racial harmony meant segregating African-American veterans in their use of facilities associated with sociability, such as barracks and public facilities, and keeping their numbers minimal in individual homes to lower the probability that white veterans might object to their presence.

The exact thoughts of black veterans about the NHDVS and their treatment there are hard to ascertain, as their case files are largely silent on the issue of race. Nonetheless, in at least one case—that of Stephen Fountain, a resident of the Hampton, Virginia, home—race came to the fore. Fountain entered the Southern Branch (as the Hampton home was called) in January 1871 but was discharged from the facility a year and a half later in June 1872. When admitted, he had been suffering from a hernia and resulting medical complications, but in February 1872, a surgical board found him fit to earn his own living. Soon after his discharge, however, Fountain applied for readmission. Internal correspondence indicates that the staff was opposed to letting him back in because they believed that Fountain was not worthy. They learned that he had not been a soldier in the army (merely a teamster) and that he suffered from venereal disease. Fountain's request for readmission was rejected, but he tried again in 1878, writing directly to former Union general Benjamin Butler, a prominent member of Congress who also headed the Board of Managers of the NHDVS. Fountain's 1878 letter to Butler is revealing. In it, he directly attributes his removal from the home in 1872 to racial prejudice. He implies that the real reason for his ejection was that a white man coveted his job as barber for the facility. Fountain found his removal from the Hampton home particularly troubling because of his belief that the facility had been established specifically for African-American veterans. "I understood from the Hon. U. L. Bond when he gave me transportation from Balto. [Baltimore] to [the] Southern Branch Home," he wrote to Butler, "that that home was established especially for disabled colored soldiers."[53] Despite Butler's sympathy for African-American veterans (late in the war he had commanded the Army of the James, of which the all-black 25th Corps was a part), he rejected Fountain's plea. Further attempts by Fountain to gain readmission to the home over the next decade also failed.

There is no way to determine definitively the authenticity of Stephen Fountain's allegations concerning racial prejudice at the Southern Branch of the National Home for Disabled Volunteer Soldiers. Certainly, even if Fountain's charges were unfounded, there were many authentic instances of racial prejudice against black veterans in the NHDVS and other soldiers' homes. Yet racial prejudice against African Americans during this period is unremarkable.

What is remarkable is that black veterans were accepted into the same homes as white soldiers at all. Certainly they suffered from some degree of discrimination there, but that was a fact of black life in the late nineteenth and early twentieth centuries. Indeed, some African Americans found comfort in the fact that their elderly male relatives were being cared for in their declining years. As Etta Hatcher wrote to her father, who resided at the Central Branch of the NHDVS in Dayton, Ohio, "You don't know how glad I am to think you are kept warm and clean and have something regular to eat."[54] For Hatcher, as for many African Americans in the era of Jim Crow, the important thing was that black people had some access to public programs and institutions, not that their access be absolutely equal to that of whites. As with pensions, perception was more important than reality.

As with pensions, the black experience with the NHDVS demonstrates that African Americans used the program for their own purposes. For some veterans, the soldiers' homes became a refuge, a place where they could avoid the sufferings associated with unemployment and the disabilities that sometimes prevented them from earning a living. As Stephen Fountain wrote to Benjamin Butler in 1878, "I do not care to stay at the Home all the time, but only when I am not able to live at my business elsewhere."[55] Indeed, it was not uncommon for veterans to keep one foot in the outside world, even after they gained admission into the NHDVS network. Some veterans used these federal homes as a sort of senior citizens' center. They would take their meals at the soldiers' home and socialize with other veterans by day, then leave the center after the evening meal for nearby residences, where they would spend the evening and sleep with their wives. In short, the National Home for Disabled Volunteer Soldiers and other soldiers' homes gave ex-soldiers an option at the end of their lives not enjoyed by other African Americans. Although relatively few black veterans took advantage of it, preferring to be cared for by their families, it preserved a modicum of manly dignity for those veterans without better choices.

It was not unheard of for African-American veterans who were sick of their marriages to abandon their wives and go to live with other veterans in the old soldiers' homes. The abandonment of wives by elderly veterans, white as well as black, became enough of a problem that in March 1899, Congress passed legislation allowing deserted wives to collect half of their estranged husbands' pensions if they could prove that they were women "of good moral character and in necessitous circumstances." Indeed, if the wife could make a prima facie case in her initial application, the Pension Bureau would cut off half the veteran's pension until federal investigators were satisfied as to the exact facts. If the husband could prove his wife's immorality or lack of financial need, he would receive the withheld sum, but if he could not, the money would go to his wife, plus half of all future pension payments.[56]

Clearly, the law was aimed at veterans who were not discharging their manly responsibility to support their wives, as illustrated by the case of William and Regina Edmund. The couple were former slaves from Arkansas who had migrated to Ohio in the late 1870s. Despite his steady work as a postal employee, Regina swore to the bureau that her husband had never been a reliable provider to her and their eight children. She claimed that his wages were spent on alcohol and other women, stating, "I have washed for many years and brought up the children myself." She further asserted that when her husband had first received his Civil War pension, he had promised to use the money to pay the rent on their apartment but had stopped doing so when he left to live in a state soldiers' home in Sandusky, Ohio. This action put Regina in a bind, because she could not earn enough money doing washing to pay the rent and other living expenses. She needed the money from her husband's pension to get by. William's response to his wife's complaint was to question her morality by accusing her of often being out after dark, to which Regina replied that she was out after dark only infrequently to attend religious meetings.[57]

The pension file of William Edmund is not clear on the final disposition of Regina's claim, nor were cases under the March 1899 law particularly common in the African-American pension files. Hence, it seems reasonably clear that most former soldiers contributed adequately to the support of their families, or at least their wives did not complain about a lack of support. The lack of 1899 cases provides credible evidence that most African-American veterans used their pension money responsibly and for the benefit of their families, fulfilling the role of manly provider and bolstering their own status in the process.

In any case, black veterans enjoyed more manhood than did their nonveteran contemporaries, in part because Civil War social welfare gave them more choices and empowering opportunities. Even though many black veterans opted not to take up residence in the NHDVS asylums because home care by relatives or friends was more compatible with manly independence and self-respect, the option was there. Civil War pensions made such home care more feasible by subsidizing veterans at a point in their lives when they were less capable or completely incapable of self-support. For those veterans who were still able to work, pensions could even be a means of self-advancement, and at the very least, they were a welcome confirmation of the ex-soldiers' value in the eyes of the federal government. Certainly, black veterans did not receive an equitable portion of the federal assistance available to former Union soldiers and their dependent survivors, and the application process forced them to struggle harder for the benefits they did receive. Racism and many other disadvantages prevented them from fully utilizing Civil War social welfare. Nonetheless, in an era that offered little hope for their race, they grasped at all chances of inclusion, however much reality fell short of the ideal. Reality falling short of the ideal would also come to characterize the experience with Civil War comradeship and the Grand Army of the Republic.

# 6

# Comradeship

**A**FTER THE CIVIL WAR, black veterans worked hard to maintain the bonds of wartime comradeship. Doing so became important to their manhood. They had demanded inclusion in the Union army and equal treatment as their manly due during the war. Afterward, a noteworthy measure of manhood became acceptance in the Union veterans' fraternity, especially its main organizational manifestation, the Grand Army of the Republic (GAR). Black veterans proved quite successful, gaining not only membership in the GAR but also a surprising degree of respect in the group, at a time when African Americans could find increasingly little acceptance or esteem in mainstream American society. Yet inequality was still a fact of life in the GAR, as many white veterans could not live up to the lofty racial ideals of the group. Not surprisingly, then, black ex-soldiers also organized on their own in the years after the war, as well as enjoying informal comradeship outside of organized veterans' groups. In such settings, African-American veterans found that they could sustain and enhance their manhood in ways impossible within the GAR. Still, they never severed their ties with the Grand Army, as inclusion there became important to their sense of self-worth as men.

The Grand Army of the Republic was an unusual group in the late nineteenth century. This period was the golden age of fraternal organizations in the United States, but rigid racial separation was also the rule of the day.[1] Consequently, African Americans generally faced exclusion from white-controlled organizations, so if they wanted to participate in fraternal societies, they had to organize their own. The Grand Army was a notable exception. In its early years, the GAR adopted a membership policy that did not exclude African Americans—in fact, it was formally color-blind. Theoretically, any honorably discharged Union veteran was eligible for membership, regardless of his race.[2] Under this policy, small numbers of black veterans in the North and Upper South made their way into the organization in the 1860s and 1870s.

The formal equality of African Americans in the GAR had its origins in the group's early political connections. With its ties to the radical faction of the Republican party, it should not be surprising that the organization tried to forge a race-neutral policy. Radicals in the GAR, such as its iconic leader John A. Logan, fought for the equality of African Americans during Reconstruction and worked for the same goal within the Grand Army. To Logan and like-minded white Union veterans, wartime loyalty and service, not race, were the critical criteria for GAR membership. This position survived the end of Reconstruction and Logan's death in 1886, and the organization never adopted a formal color line. Black men were able to join the GAR throughout its existence.

Still, despite the GAR's color-blind membership policy, African Americans encountered prejudice from the earliest days of the organization. Such bigotry was first experienced by black ex-soldiers in the North who attempted to join the Grand Army in the wake of the war. They discovered that even white veterans who accepted equality in theory could act quite differently in practice. Such was the case at the George H. Ward Post No. 10 in Worcester, Massachusetts. By 1870, the Ward post had at least one black member, Amos Webber.[3] In May of that year, a second black veteran, Bassill C. Barker, attempted to join. In a GAR post, applicants were accepted or rejected by a vote of the existing members, and only a small minority of votes cast against a candidate—as little as one out of ten—was necessary to reject him.[4] In the case of Barker, the Ward post voted him down at its June 2 meeting. According to Post No. 10's historian, Franklin D. Tappan, quoting from the minutes, "The question being raised, why was he rejected? One comrade vouchsafed the reply that it was because he was a '*nigger.*' Upon motion a new ballot was ordered, and he was again rejected." The failure to elect Barker despite two attempts was an acute embarrassment to the post's leaders, who had sponsored him. They scheduled a third ballot on Barker's application for the next meeting. Word of what had taken place on June 2 spread around Worcester, and when the members of Post No. 10 reassembled on June 9, the hall was packed. The post leaders attempted to remind the membership of the GAR's nondiscriminatory policy by sponsoring a resolution that stated, "no inquiry as to race, color or nationality of any applicant should, or by right ought to be made, either by any Committee or by this Post." The resolution, according to Tappan, passed without "great opposition." Still, when the leadership presented Barker's application a third time, the membership rejected him again, prompting three officers to resign from the post in protest.[5]

The fate of Bassill C. Barker was commonplace for black Union veterans trying to join predominantly white posts in the North, although many African Americans did manage to get in. Indeed, racial discrimination in the GAR remained largely an unofficial phenomenon until the 1880s, when the organization's growing presence in the South threatened to introduce the color line officially. Attempts to plant the GAR in the Lower South soon after the war had generally failed. White Southerners associated the organization with Radical Reconstruction, and the GAR maintained a tenuous foothold in the region only with great difficulty. However, as an increasing number of white Union veterans migrated south following the end of Reconstruction, it became possible to form more GAR posts in the Deep South. The existence of the Grand Army in this region advanced the issue of race to the fore, because it brought the racially progressive membership policy of the organization into direct confrontation with the growing reality of racial segregation in the South.

Black veterans in the Lower South initially found themselves barred from the GAR there. Nowhere did this exclusion become more controversial an issue than in Louisiana and Mississippi. When transplanted white Northerners finally established a viable department (the state- or regional-level unit of the GAR) there in the 1880s, they decided to deny charters to African Americans trying to form posts. That policy ran afoul of the opinions of many white veterans outside of the Lower South, who believed that the doors of the organization should be open to all former Union soldiers, regardless of race. These GAR men challenged the exclusion of African Americans in the Department of Louisiana and Mississippi at the 1887 national "encampment," or annual convention, of the Grand Army held in St. Louis. Philip Cheek Jr., a Wisconsin veteran, proposed to amend the GAR rules to permit African Americans who were denied charters by their departments to apply directly to the national commander of the Grand Army for authority to form new posts. Despite the objection of white delegates from the Lower South, the encampment, dominated by like-minded Northern veterans, approved Cheek's proposal. Still, no black posts were chartered in Louisiana or Mississippi in the wake of the 1887 encampment, as cautious national leaders refused to act.[6]

In fact, African-American veterans in Louisiana and Mississippi finally broke into the GAR not as a result of an initiative from the national organization but because of an internal dispute between the white members in their home region. In 1889, the department commander there, Jacob Gray, served as a pallbearer at the funeral of Jefferson Davis, the former president of the Confederacy. He had intended to make a gesture of sectional reconciliation, but instead, he gravely offended many Union veterans, including a significant number in his department who, despite their residence in the Lower South, still harbored feelings of hostility toward the Confederacy, especially its former supreme leader. Realizing that his position as commander was in jeopardy, Gray sought new supporters to ensure his reelection at the next departmental encampment by hurriedly organizing nine black posts. This action led to a complete schism in the department. Gray's opponents, led by George T. Hodges, who cobbled together the backing of the majority of the department's white membership, insisted that Gray lacked the authority to organize the new posts, carefully avoiding any objection to the black posts on the grounds of race. The adjutant general of the GAR national organization, who attempted to settle the dispute, followed their example. His ruling supported the refusal of the white delegates to seat representatives from the black posts at the department encampment on the technical grounds that the posts had been organized too soon before the meeting.[7]

The African-American posts in Louisiana and Mississippi suffered in limbo for over a year, refused recognition by the department, which was now led by Hodges. Hodges and his followers, realizing that total exclusion was no longer practical, given the sentiments of white GAR men outside the Lower South, appealed to the national organization during the summer of 1890 for permission to establish two separate departments in Louisiana and Mississippi, one for white Union veterans and the other for African Americans. The issue was not taken up until the following August at the 1891 national encampment in Detroit. Arguing the case of the Hodges faction before the delegates at the 1891 meeting was Andrew S. Graham, the department's judge advocate. He first justified separate departments for white and black members on social grounds. Overcoming the hostility of white Southerners, winning acceptance, and securing the future of their offspring, he believed, meant adopting the racial customs of the South. "Our children are growing up there," contended Graham, "They marry. It is right that we should conform to the social laws and rules that surround us." In other words, Graham and other white GAR men in Louisiana and Mississippi feared the disapprobation of white Southerners, and perhaps even violence, if they mixed socially with black Union veterans there. As he bluntly put it, "We are living among enemies."[8]

African-American veterans caused Graham and other white men like him to fear something else. It was clear from the speed with which Gray had organized the nine new black posts in January 1890 that if black and white veterans were put in the same department in Louisiana and Mississippi, African Americans might soon assume control of the organization by virtue of their substantially greater numbers. The prospect of black leaders taking over the Department of Louisiana and Mississippi was too much for Graham and many other white veterans to stomach. He pleaded with his Northern comrades that the larger number of African-American veterans in the region relative to white veterans made separate departments imperative. Graham worried that whites would become a powerless minority in Louisiana and Mississippi if they were forced to organize with black veterans.[9]

It is significant that most former soldiers outside the Lower South did not share Graham's fears. The record of the debate at Detroit in 1891 suggests that white veterans not only in the North but also in the Upper South opposed allowing separate departments in Louisiana and Mississippi for white and black members of the GAR. For these men, wartime loyalty was more important than Southern social customs. To them, a Grand Army man did not associate with another because he belonged to a particular race, but because he had been faithful to the Union. And African Americans generally proved highly qualified on the question of wartime loyalty in the eyes of most white GAR members.

As William Warner, a Union veteran from Missouri, put it, "if you lay wounded, if you were surrounded by the enemy as thick as a swarm of bees, at any moment you were liable to see a black crawling up to you, and when he came you knew he was your friend." Warner then went on to chastise his comrades in the Lower South, saying that friends had advised him against accepting African Americans into the Department of Missouri because white members would desert the organization. However, Warner claimed that rather than losing membership, the organization had increased its membership in the state and become one of the strongest departments in the nation. He finished dressing down his white comrades in the Lower

South by telling them to "go home, I do not think you will be disturbed by these colored posts."[10]

Black veterans who spoke in Detroit also opposed allowing the GAR department in Louisiana and Mississippi to split racially. Edward A. Richey, a black veteran from Kentucky, put forward their position simply but forcefully. "Some people want to know whether the colored comrades desire this division," stated Richey. "Comrades, they do not." Alluding to the spread of disfranchisement and Jim Crow laws and to the rising incidence of violence against African Americans in the South, Richey pleaded with the delegates not "to turn their backs on us in this time of trouble." He also feared that the segregation of black veterans into a separate department would be the first step toward their exclusion from the GAR. With separate departments, he asserted, it was likely that sooner or later "the colored man will be ostracized and put out of the Grand Army of the Republic."[11]

Although Richey's position seems to indicate that black veterans unanimously opposed separating the Department of Louisiana and Mississippi along racial lines, other evidence suggests that this was not the case. The commander in chief of the GAR at the Detroit encampment, Wheelock Veazy, reported that he had received correspondence from six of the nine black posts supporting the idea of creating parallel departments.[12] The apparent split between the African-American veterans in the Gulf region is understandable. Excluded from the existing departmental structure by the followers of Hodges, some black veterans apparently decided that a separate department was preferable to total exclusion from the Grand Army. These men did not share the fears of other black veterans that a separate department was the first step to barring African Americans from the Grand Army altogether. Instead, they perceived that separate departments were their door into the GAR. Certainly not all African-American veterans in Louisiana and Mississippi felt this way, and some sent letters to Veazy protesting the proposal for racially segregated departments. In fact, this disagreement between the two black factions was one more example of the larger debate among African Americans in the late nineteenth century about whether to acquiesce to segregation or resist it.[13]

Leaping on the agreement of some black GAR men in the Gulf region to accept segregation, Commander in Chief Veazy recommended to the Detroit encampment that the Department of Louisiana and Mississippi be separated along racial lines. However, in a step that cheered the hearts of black veterans and the African-American press, the delegates to the 1891 Detroit encampment rejected that proposal and demanded that the black posts be formally incorporated into the department. Their decision obligated Veazy's successor, John Palmer, to force Hodges and his supporters to accept the black posts organized by Gray. Not surprisingly, Hodges and many other white GAR men resisted. Palmer had to remove Hodges from his position as department commander and replace most of his subordinates with men who would carry out Palmer's orders. Five of the eight existing white posts withdrew from the GAR, and white membership in the department plummeted.[14] At the beginning of 1891, before the Detroit encampment, the Department of Louisiana and Mississippi had 345 white members; by 1892, after Palmer's purge, only 114 remained.[15] It was left to the residual white membership and the newly legitimated black posts to rebuild the department.

Palmer's willingness to sacrifice large numbers of white members in order to integrate the black posts in the department was extraordinary, as was the fortitude of the Grand Army rank and file at the Detroit encampment. That the GAR accepted black members was unusual enough in the Gilded Age. However, the fact that many white members, even in the Upper South, opposed separate departments for white and black Union veterans in the Lower South was even more remarkable. It demonstrated the genuine regard that many white veterans had for the African Americans who had donned the Union blue, even decades after the war. Black men had helped save the Union, and the debt owed them was hard to forget. A group of delegates eloquently stated the ideal of interracial comradeship at the 1891 Detroit encampment. "A man who is good enough to stand between the flag and those who would destroy it when the fate of the nation was trembling in the balance," they stated, "is good enough to be a comrade in . . . the Grand Army of the Republic."[16]

Subsequent events in the Department of Louisiana and Mississippi vindicated this position. In a rebuttal to the fear of men like George T. Hodges and Andrew S. Graham, interracial comradeship proved workable even in the Lower South. Certainly, black men quickly became the vast majority of the membership. By 1892, 83 percent of the Grand Army men there were African Americans. However, white membership also rebounded in the five years that followed. The remnant of 114 white members in 1892 more than doubled to 249 by 1897. Apparently, many of the white members who had left gradually returned. Even Hodges, who had led the drive for racially segregated departments in the early 1890s, eventually applied for reinstatement. In the end, the

Department of Louisiana and Mississippi was able to reconstitute all but one of the white posts that had withdrawn.[17]

Yet the controversy over separate departments at the 1891 Detroit encampment was, to a certain extent, merely pretense. During the 1890s, the GAR was inconsistent in its determination to maintain integrated departments in the Lower South. For one thing, although the national press extensively covered the situation in Louisiana and Mississippi, it ignored similar developments within the Grand Army elsewhere in the Lower South around the same time. For example, while the national commander—with newspaper reporters looking over his shoulder—forced the GAR in Louisiana and Mississippi to accept black posts in the department, elsewhere in the region, white members who were unwilling to accept African-American posts seeking charters were able to reject them, as long as they did so quietly. In 1891, for example, as John Palmer was purging the GAR leadership in the Department of Louisiana and Mississippi, an attempt to found a black post in Mobile, Alabama, was successfully scuttled by white Union veterans who feared driving predominantly white posts from the department in that state. It also helped when GAR department leaders in the Lower South could find an ostensibly nonracial reason for not chartering black posts. Beginning in 1892, black men trying to obtain charters for posts in Texas were repeatedly rejected by department leaders on technical grounds, for incorrectly filled out paperwork. The African Americans complained to the national leadership of the GAR, which sent out an investigator in 1896 to study the allegations. His report supported the department leadership in Texas in rejecting the black applicants, effectively settling the issue for the national GAR leadership, especially as the newspapers did not publicize the allegations nationally, as they had in the controversy over the Department of Louisiana and Mississippi.[18]

In any case, the battle over exclusion and segregated departments ignored the reality that effective segregation already existed in the GAR. Although departments might be integrated, it hardly mattered, because most regular activity in the Grand Army took place at local posts, and most African-American members attended segregated posts with an exclusively black membership.

Likewise, the genuine gratitude that many white Union veterans felt toward their black GAR comrades for their wartime service did not entirely eliminate their personal racism. One of the most incisive examples in this regard came from the commander of the Department of California, Edward

S. Salomon. Speaking against the exclusion of African Americans from the GAR in the Lower South at the St. Louis encampment in 1887, he captured in one sentence the incongruous opinion that many white Union veterans had about their black counterparts. He said, "I would rather shake hands with the blackest nigger in the land if he was a true and honest man, than with a traitor."[19] On one level, he expressed the sincere sentiment of respect and appreciation that most white GAR men felt toward African-American veterans. Yet on another level, his statement revealed the ambivalence of many white Grand Army men toward their black comrades. Salomon's biting language hardly bespoke a full acceptance of African Americans as equals. Only their loyalty to the Union and white Southerners' treason had reordered racial etiquette—temporarily and incompletely.

The prejudice toward African Americans in the GAR was, understandably, most apparent in the Southern departments. There, white comrades often treated African Americans in the GAR in a patronizingly racist manner. At best, such attitudes arose from a benign concern for the success of black posts and the welfare of their membership, but they also stemmed from the belief of many white members that African Americans were not competent to run their own posts. William A. Rhegness, a white Union veteran living in the South, typified this feeling. "I was the Adjutant General for the Department of Tennessee, G.A.R.," he said, testifying in the pension application of a black veteran, "and as such it became necessary for me to take [an] interest in the post of colored folks . . . as they were not capable of managing it themselves."[20] Rhegness echoed the sentiments of William J. Ramage, a GAR delegate to the 1887 encampment at St. Louis. "It is utterly impossible in our Department [of Tennessee and Georgia] to find comrades of color who have the ability or the knowledge requisite to keep up their posts," he told the encampment.[21]

It also appears that segregation occurred at most, if not all, Grand Army ceremonies conducted in the Lower South. This practice is not surprising, given that such occasions represented the organization's most prominent manifestation in the region. Although the GAR there survived the forced introduction of black posts, practically speaking, veterans of the two races had minimal interaction. They might encounter each other at department encampments, during visits between white and black posts, and sometimes at department leadership meetings, but these events (with a partial exception for encampments) were private. Public parades and ceremonies were a different matter. There, it was important that white Union veterans, for the sake of peace with their ex-Confederate neighbors, keep themselves apart from their ostensible former comrades at arms. A recent study, emphasizing research in Southern newspapers, found approving accounts of segregation at Memorial Day exercises by Union veterans in the Lower South in the 1890s. It is unknown whether all such public ceremonies of the GAR in that area were segregated, but existing evidence suggests that this pattern was normal by the end of the nineteenth century.[22]

When they did not experience condescension or segregation during public exercises, black veterans were often ignored in the Southern departments. The minutes of GAR encampments in that region say surprisingly little about African Americans, even where they were a significant percentage of the membership. In the Department of Missouri, which kept the most complete accounts of annual meetings of any Southern department and had many black posts, racial issues were never discussed. No hint exists that African Americans were even members of the department, except in the reports of comrades who had died in the preceding year, which included veterans of black units. Although such silence showed the GAR's tendency to avoid the issue of race, it also meant that the organization did not address issues that were important to black members, such as suffrage, and the national organization took no stand against the spread of disfranchisement and Jim Crow in the wake of Reconstruction.[23] Only occasionally did a white GAR leader call other members to task for neglecting their black comrades, such as A. H. Soekland, a department commander in Arkansas. Referring to his predecessors, Soekland complained that they had been interested in black veterans only for the revenue they could generate for the department and had given them little, if anything, in return for their dues. "Permission would be granted to comrades, colored ones in particular, to get together, send in charter fees, and whatever they could get for supplies," indicated Soekland, "and then [they] let the poor fellows get along as best they could."[24]

Black GAR men in the North generally enjoyed a better relationship with their white comrades. A recent study of the Grand Army in the state of Pennsylvania, for instance, found a high degree of interaction between white and black veterans.[25] Most notably, the records of the Robert G. Shaw Post No. 206, an African-American post in Pittsburgh, reveal numerous friendly encounters between black and white veterans there. White GAR men regularly visited the Shaw post, not only in formal capacities but informally as well. Likewise, black men from Post No. 206 showed up as visitors at white posts in Pittsburgh, where they were often invited to speak and even serve as department inspectors, ensuring the adherence of local posts to the national standards of the organization.[26] Such interaction occurred not only in the burgeoning steel city but also throughout the state. Evidence shows the participation of black GAR men in white-run parades and other predominantly white public events associated with patriotism or explicitly commemorating the war.[27]

In fact, some black GAR men in the North fought for the integration of local posts rather than merely at the departmental level. As the early experience of Worcester shows, despite persistent blackballing, African Americans in many places had a realistic chance of being accepted into predominantly white posts. It is difficult to generalize about which black men in the North successfully joined the Grand Army and which black men were rejected. The reception of African-American veterans by Northern Grand Army posts was dependent, at least in part, on the number of black veterans in a given locality. In areas where few black veterans resided, they had a much better chance of being accepted into a local post. For instance, Robert Anderson, a Kentucky-born veteran, was the only black member of a Grand Army post in Hemingford, Nebraska (see fig. 6). Indeed, Anderson likely found himself welcomed in his post because few Union veterans, white or black, lived in Hemingford, which in the late nineteenth century was a tiny community in the sparsely populated western section of the state. The special 1890 census of Civil War veterans recorded only twenty-one men with a Hemingford post office address. White GAR men in such underpopulated locales were probably more ready to overlook skin color in order to maintain a viable post.[28]

The reputation and associations of an African-American veteran also made a difference in whether he was accepted for membership in a Northern GAR post. Black men who were well known and respected by local white veterans appear to have had a much greater chance of getting into the Grand Army. For example, Amos Webber may have been accepted into the Ward post in Worcester, Massachusetts, and Bassill Barker rejected because the white veterans there knew Webber better. Webber worked at a wire mill, where he became a familiar and well-regarded figure to white veterans who were also employed there; Barker, who worked for a black barber, had less contact with the local white Union veterans.[29]

Black men who had the reputation for racially deferential behavior also stood a much better chance of getting into a Northern GAR post. White veterans generally expected blacks who joined their Grand Army posts to be seen but not heard. The attitude of white GAR men was that African Americans in their posts should be grateful for their membership and should not attempt to take a very active role in the organization or seek any real power. Consequently, few black veterans served as officers in the predominantly white Grand Army posts of the North.

Andrew S. Graham summed up the characteristics of an acceptable black veteran in a Northern GAR post during the 1891 debate over a segregated department in Louisiana and Mississippi. With an outsider's observant eye, he told the national encampment: "[In Northern posts, you] . . . may have three or four colored men, nice men, respectable men, whom you all know and speak to every day on the street. They come into your post and you treat them well. They are respectful to you. They take no part in the arrangements; they do not elect the officers. You do all the business and everything of the kind."[30]

Despite the acceptability of African-American members in some Northern posts, the color line was often drawn, especially in cities where racially separate posts were most feasible. Black veterans and the African-American community at large were well aware of that fact. "Here in the North," stated an unattributed article in the *Cleveland Gazette* (the city's black newspaper), "while they [white GAR members] do not object to formation of colored Posts, many do object to and prevent colored ex-soldiers from joining Posts made up of whites."[31]

Like their Southern comrades in Louisiana and Mississippi, who had been torn over whether to acquiesce to a separate department, existing evidence suggests that black veterans in the North were divided over whether to accept segregated posts. Some veterans apparently saw it as their way into the GAR and accepted separate posts, as they had accepted segregated units during the war. For instance, J. W. Simpson, a former commander of the all-black Post No. 27 in Philadelphia, presented a petition to the state encampment in 1885 protesting the rejection of a black man who had tried to join Post No. 116, a predominantly white post in Harrisburg. "That application has in proper form been made," he stated, "but it has been virtually set aside and a withdrawal of it forced by the announcement of the fact that the application would be rejected simply on account of the color of the applicant."[32] Yet Simpson's solution was not to ask Pennsylvania's veterans to force Post No. 116 to open its doors to the black veteran in question but to ask the delegates to authorize an all-black GAR post for the city. (Eventually, an all-black post was organized in Harrisburg.)[33]

An eloquent opponent of racially segregated posts in the North was Robert A. Pinn, a black attorney from Ohio and a Medal of Honor winner. He strenuously resisted an attempt to organize an all-black post in Cleveland in the mid-1880s. To establish a separate black post, he wrote to the *Cleveland Gazette,* was to go against the ideals of the GAR. "The Grand Army of the Republic is indeed what its name implies," he wrote, "it is a grand institution. It knows no creed, race, color nor politics." Further, he contended that a separate black post for Cleveland was unnecessary—and counterproductive. The city had half a dozen GAR posts already, several of them with black members, "Why set up a 'side show'?" he opined. He feared that by organizing a separate black post, African-American veterans would be "drawing a color line for themselves." It was bad enough, in Pinn's opinion, when whites initiated segregation, but when African Americans took that step, they were encouraging whites to build up the ramparts of racial separation even further. Finally, for Pinn, integrated posts were a matter of manly honor. Having achieved equality on the battlefield, it would be an insult to their manhood to accept inequality in the GAR. He wrote: "We fought side by side with our white comrades; our blood mingled and drenched the Southern soil; our united efforts saved our common country for the abode of freemen, and in this sublime time of peace we should not be the first to say we will have no part with our white comrades in perpetuating and enjoying that which is our common heritage. It is an insult to our comrades, and a slander upon our Grand Army."[34]

Despite the segregation and discrimination they faced in the North as well as the South, black veterans still had sound reasons for wanting to join the Grand Army of the Republic. As Pinn's rhetoric makes clear, the GAR's formal belief in the essential equality of black and white Union soldiers, symbolized by its apparently nonracial membership criteria, appealed to African-American veterans. Much as they had hungered for manly respect and equality as soldiers during the war, they still hungered for it afterward. As one historian has suggested, just as fraternal societies during the late nineteenth century helped middle-class young men in their passage to mature manhood, the ideology of the GAR offered many black veterans a shortcut to gaining equal manhood with a significant and influential group of white Americans.[35] The question then becomes, why did they stay in the organization when they came to understand—as all but the most self-deluding must have—that the reality of the organization in terms of race did not quite measure up to its ideals?

First, the GAR could be of significant value to African-American veterans in their Civil War pension applications. Many examples exist to show the usefulness of being a Grand Army man in the pension process. Charles Davis, who had lost his discharge papers, used his GAR membership certificate to substantiate his wartime service with the U.S. Pension Bureau.[36] At a GAR encampment, Abraham I. J. Wright became reacquainted with an old comrade who was able to clear up the discrepancy between Wright's postwar and wartime identities. Unlike many other black veterans who merely changed their last names, Wright had adopted a totally new identity, utterly casting off the slave name under which he had served in the army, Jacob Hutchinson (see fig. 20). The old comrade confirmed to federal bureaucrats that Abraham I. J. Wright and Jacob Hutchinson were one and the same man.[37] GAR affiliations also softened the attitude of some federal officials toward black pension applicants. Will Auter, a special examiner for the Pension Bureau, gave Oscar Johnson, a black Tennessee veteran, the benefit of the doubt in a dubious service-related injury claim because they were both Grand Army members. Auter recommended the approval of the application, even after witnessing Johnson's attorney coach him during his deposition.[38] GAR membership also proved valuable to black veterans in completing the paperwork for their pension claims. Robert H. Isabelle, a black post commander and former officer in the Louisiana Native Guards, wrote the pension application for an illiterate New Orleans veteran, John Spencer.[39]

Indeed, statistical evidence indicates that African-American veterans affiliated with the GAR had greater success in obtaining pensions than did black veterans in general. Nearly 97 percent of the members of the O. P. Morton post in Washington, D.C., succeeded in obtaining Civil War pensions, compared with 83 percent of veterans in the random sample group (or 75 percent of black veterans in the comparison sample with white veterans).[40] Likewise, nearly 93 percent of the veterans in an 1894 roster of the GAR's Department of Georgia got on the pension rolls, eliminating any significant possibility that the greater success of the Morton veterans could be explained by their proximity to pension attorneys, who were found mostly in the nation's capital.[41]

Benefits of GAR membership to African-American veterans went beyond help with pension applications. Posts generally guaranteed a proper burial for all members in good standing, and such men could expect to be laid to rest with the honor of a special Grand Army funeral ceremony.[42] GAR posts also looked after members in need through the post relief fund and provided assistance to the widows and orphans of their members.[43] They sometimes extended assistance to black veterans and their families who were not even affiliated with the organization. In one such case, Philip Lee, commander of the Matt Starr Post No. 378 in Jacksonville, Illinois, tracked down Hanna Brown, the widow of a dead black soldier from Missouri, to inform her of the existence of government bonds that her late husband had purchased while he was in the army and left in the care of a local bank.[44]

The benefits of Grand Army membership were not merely tangible. Although the implementation of racial equality in the GAR left something to be desired, the organization was much better in this regard than most other American social institutions in the late nineteenth century. This truth was captured quite elegantly by Robert Johnson, a black minister from Washington, D.C. As a delegate to the 1891 national encampment in Detroit, he forcefully and succinctly expressed the psychic benefit of GAR membership to the manhood of black Union veterans. "Of all the institutions we belong to," declared Johnson, "no other has brought us so near together as the Grand Army of the Republic."[45] In other words, in a society where they were increasingly segregated and demeaned, many black ex-soldiers greatly valued this rare instance of inclusion in rhetoric and sometimes in reality. Within the Grand Army, at least in principle, black and white men were united in the equality of comradeship. Hence, because equality for black veterans was at the heart of how they judged their progress as men, they valued the ideal of racial equality espoused by the GAR, even if the reality did not always measure up. In most institutions of society, especially in the South, by the late nineteenth century, not even the rhetoric of racial equality was honored. In the GAR, it was respected and, to a surprising extent for the time, actually implemented.

It is also true that despite the fact that few black men achieved leadership roles in a mixed racial context—that is, in integrated posts or at the departmental level—some exceptions can be found. The most notable case in the North was none other than Robert A. Pinn. In 1886, he was elected commander of the Hart Post No. 134, a predominantly white post in his hometown of Massillion, Ohio.[46] Two years later, the overwhelmingly white GAR membership in Ohio elected him junior vice commander of that department.[47] Nor was he the only black veteran to rise to a position of leadership over white veterans in the North. William H. Dupree, a federal civil servant and prominent black veteran of the 55th Massachusetts, became commander of the Benjamin A. Stone post in Boston in December 1894.[48] Although Pinn and Dupree were exceptions to the rule that relegated most black members of predominantly white GAR posts to the sidelines or to purely ceremonial positions, they demonstrated that in some cases the Grand Army allowed exceptional black men into positions of authority.

The rise of black men into true leadership positions can be found not only in the North but in the Southern GAR as well. For example, after George T. Hodges was removed from command of the Department of Louisiana and Mississippi at the behest of the delegates to the 1891 national encampment, black membership in the GAR increased there, and African Americans gradually began to make their way into the department leadership. Although the position of commander and posts such as senior vice commander, adjutant general, quartermaster general, and inspector remained mostly in white hands between 1891 and 1903 (years for which department encampment records exist), black veterans appeared regularly during these years as junior vice commander, chaplain, judge advocate, and chief mustering officer. These positions gave African-American members of the GAR in Louisiana and Mississippi a remarkable degree of influence, not only in terms of the typical state of affairs in the GAR but also in the context of the Lower South, where Jim Crow was entrenching itself.[49] It is also worth noting that at least two black veterans, Felix Antoine and Paul Bruce, served as commander of the Department of Louisiana and Mississippi. Indeed, black veterans became more numerous as department leaders in the latter years of the 1891–1903 period.[50]

Hence, even though black veterans were often second-class members of the GAR, some of these men managed to gain noteworthy status within the organization. Yet even for the vast majority of African Americans who, unlike Pinn, Dupree, Bruce, and Antoine, did not rise to prominence, many still prized their membership in the Grand Army. By allowing African Americans into the organization on a formally equal basis, white veterans implicitly accepted the parity of black service in the Civil War to their own. As has been seen, equality in the Grand Army was more an ideal than a reality, but it was one of the few organizations of the period that even bothered to pay lip service to the concept and actually offered some tangible examples of equality in operation. They usually spent most of their time at separate posts, but white

and black veterans did rub shoulders at the national and departmental encampments and in a number of integrated posts in the North.

The Grand Army of the Republic did not constitute the totality of black Civil
War veteranhood. As hard as they fought to maintain and advance their position within the GAR, African Americans also organized separately outside
of it. The reality was that they usually were a distinct minority in the Grand
Army, and, as indicated earlier, white Union veterans tended to neglect issues important to African Americans. Consequently, it was necessary for black
former soldiers to organize on their own to address their concerns and attempt to bring them to wider attention.

Indeed, given the discrimination and subordination they often faced in
the GAR, it is surprising that black veterans organized themselves outside the
GAR so rarely, and then only temporarily. Significantly, on none of these
occasions did African-American veterans explicitly protest their treatment
in the Grand Army. Instead, they came together to celebrate the special nature of their wartime experience and to defend what they saw as the legacy of
their service: equality and manhood. Few things were more important to black
Civil War veterans in relation to equality and manhood than suffrage, especially when state legislatures and the U.S. Congress proved slow to guarantee
black men the right to vote. Having performed the most burdensome duty
of citizenship—military service—these men felt a strong entitlement to a
citizen's most basic rights.

The response of African-American veterans to the denial of voting rights
to black men was to form the Colored Soldiers and Sailors' League in 1866
(see chapter 3). The league was in no sense a rival to the GAR, which was itself just getting started at that time. The purpose of the Colored Soldiers and
Sailors' League was to create a national group to focus the efforts of African-
American veterans in favor of black suffrage.

After the collapse of the Colored Soldiers and Sailors' League, black veterans initially focused their energy on organizing within the GAR. Black veterans did not move to establish their own national veterans' organization after
the war because they associated acceptance into the GAR with equality in the
fraternity of Union veterans. They demanded inclusion in the organization
that they felt represented all Union veterans and that promised to gain pensions and benefits for all veterans regardless of their color.

However, the GAR's neglect of black concerns led to renewed independent activity by African-American veterans in the North and Upper South by the mid-1880s. Most of these men had been poor before entering military service and returned to poverty after their discharge. This problem was compounded by the fact that many black soldiers had lost their discharge papers, which made it difficult for them to obtain enlistment bounties and pensions or gain entry into government-funded soldiers' homes if they were disabled and had no family to care for them. The widows, orphans, and aged parents of dead black soldiers faced even greater travails in obtaining the government aid to which they were entitled. Such problems, when combined with the Grand Army's inattention to black concerns, forced black veterans to organize outside of the GAR. In 1884, for instance, a call went out to African-American veterans in Ohio to:

> meet in a convention for the purpose of considering and laying before Congress our needs and those of the widows and orphans of our deceased comrades in the award of pensions and bounties, and employment in the service of the General Government, and to form a mutual aid society to seek government aid in setting upon the public lands in colonies, for the establishment of a military and industrial school for the heirs of those who served in the Union army during the late rebellion, and for the distribution of half a million of dollars now in the United States Treasury belonging to colored soldiers as unclaimed bounty.[51]

The call in Ohio was part of a larger effort during the 1880s to organize a national reunion of black soldiers and sailors. State and regional reunion organizations arose in different places throughout the North and Upper South. (Black veterans in the Lower South were, for the most part, too busy trying to get into the GAR to get involved.) For example, black veterans in New England met in Worcester, Massachusetts, in October 1885 to organize the Colored Veterans' Association.[52] Lack of documentation makes it impossible to track all regional manifestations of the black veterans' reunion movement of the 1880s, but its leaders represented regiments originating in Massachusetts, Michigan, Ohio, Iowa, and Kentucky. They met in Dayton, Ohio, in January 1886 to form the Negro Ex-Soldiers' and Sailors' National Reunion Association.[53]

The reunion movement did not emerge as a competitor to black activity in the Grand Army of the Republic. Leading members of the movement remained active in the GAR. For instance, Amos Webber was a leader of the

Colored Veterans' Association in New England while still participating in his local Grand Army post in Worcester, Massachusetts. African Americans also continued to agitate for their goals within the GAR.

Nor did the reunion movement express any hostility toward white Union veterans. On the contrary, white former officers were prominent participants in the meetings of the New England reunion organization. Norwood P. Hallowell, former commander of the all-black 55th Massachusetts, was the keynote speaker at the inaugural meeting of the Colored Veterans' Association. Hallowell's involvement is not surprising. Ties remained close between former officers and soldiers of Massachusetts's black regiments, much more so than in other units. The state had been an important center of antislavery activity before the war, and abolitionists and their sons volunteered for service as officers in the state's black regiments. Many of the former officers displayed a continuing interest in the postwar activities of the African Americans who had served under them.

The reunion movement also called for tightening bonds between black and white Union veterans. In fact, the founders of the Negro Ex-Soldiers' and Sailors' National Reunion Association put closer relations with their white comrades at the top of their agenda—even ahead of mutual assistance and defense of African-American equality. They stated as their top priority: "The object of this society shall be to strengthen and preserve those kind and fraternal feelings which should bind together the desires and sympathies of all soldiers, sailors and marines who united to suppress the rebellion and the Negro soldiers, sailors and marines especially, who united with the double purpose of crushing the rebellion and to more perfectly establish his own freedom, justice, and equal privileges before the law."[54]

The culmination of the reunion movement was a national two-day meeting of black Civil War veterans held in Boston's Tremont Temple in August 1887. It attracted more than 300 veterans and was the largest known assembly of black former soldiers and sailors after the Civil War. Although the meeting was primarily a Massachusetts affair, especially in terms of its leadership, some of the attendees came from regiments raised in other Northern states and in the South. The president of the reunion was none other than William Monroe Trotter, then serving as the recorder of deeds in the District of Columbia (a significant and lucrative federal patronage post). The men present at the convention listened to speeches by Trotter, William Carney (a veteran of the 54th Massachusetts and a hero of the assault on Fort Wagner), and leading white officers of the black Massachusetts regiments. They also paraded through the streets of Boston and capped off the meeting with a boat trip to nearby Higham, Massachusetts, to visit the grave of John A. Andrew, the wartime governor of the state and champion of black troops.[55]

Like the Colored Soldiers and Sailors' League in the 1860s, the Boston reunion of 1887 was rooted in present realities. Although the veterans and their ex-officers commemorated their continuing bonds of comradeship and remembered the special experience of black soldiers in the Civil War, the deteriorating position of African Americans in the aftermath of Reconstruction dominated the business meeting held on the second day. A resolution passed at the reunion called attention to the sorry truth that, by the late 1880s, the gains made possible by black soldiers' service were in jeopardy. It complained "that American citizens of African descent . . . are today in a large portion of this great nation denied justice in the courts, deprived of the exercise of the elective franchise, the victims of mob violence, an unprotected and outraged people."[56]

Yet black Civil War veterans did much more than simply express their fears about escalating discrimination and its effects through black-centered comradeship. They also exhibited a veterans' identity distinct from that of white Union veterans. Part of this separate identity had to do with the development of historical memory of the war divergent from that of their white counterparts in the Grand Army of the Republic (see chapter 7). More relevant to the present discussion is how African Americans came to characterize veteranhood differently from white Union veterans.

The definition of who was a Civil War veteran was broader among blacks than among whites. The experience of the Morton post in Washington, D.C., illuminates this more expansive sense of veteranhood among African Americans. For many years, it was the most important black GAR post in the nation's capital. But the relationship between the post and the Department of the Potomac, of which it was a part, was a troubled one. It came into conflict with the department repeatedly in the late 1890s and early 1900s. The issues of contention included alleged malfeasance, incompetence, and a lack of diligence in enforcing rules on the part of the post's leadership. Despite the fact that the post included men from Washington's black elite and its membership was relatively prosperous, it suffered from chronic financial problems that prevented the post from paying its assessments to the department in a timely way. (Departments and the national leadership of the GAR supported their operations by charging a "tax" on each post.) In 1900, these difficulties prompted a general investigation to determine whether the post's charter should be revoked. Investigators chosen by the departmental leadership reported that they had substantiated most of the long-standing complaints against the Morton post but had discovered something even more troubling—that the post had admitted men to membership who were not Civil War veterans. Some of the men in question had served in the postwar army and navy, but others were civilians with no military experience. The white members of the Grand Army in the Department of the Potomac were not the only ones to complain about what they saw as the African Americans' laxity in terms of admitting men who were not "true" veterans.[57] A. S. Badger, commander of the Department of Louisiana and Mississippi, made a similar complaint in 1893, although he did not pursue the matter to the extent the Department of the Potomac did. The latter department revoked the charter of the Morton post at the conclusion of its investigation.[58]

Still, it is apparent from these complaints and investigations that the definition of veteranhood among African-American veterans was broader and more inclusive than that among white veterans. This inclusiveness was in part merely practical. As the case of the Morton post suggests, the relative poverty of black posts did not permit them to thoroughly investigate the backgrounds of the men who applied for membership. Likewise, many African Americans had a more difficult time substantiating their service in the Union army than did white veterans because of the greater incidence of identity changes connected with emancipation. Yet the broader definition of veteranhood among African Americans also reflected the reality of the black contribution to the Union cause during the Civil War. Many black men had spent months or years as laborers, servants, or teamsters or in other support capacities. Because some of them had come under fire, and because of the value of their wartime efforts to the Union victory and the liberation of their race, these men craved the same recognition accorded to Union army and navy veterans (see chapter 2). Existing evidence from the Morton post and the Department of Louisiana and Mississippi suggests that at least some black posts stretched the rules to accommodate men who had directly served the Union cause but not formally as soldiers or sailors. In doing so, African Americans in the GAR created a broader veterans' identity than existed among white Union veterans. This identity was not limited to men who had served under arms in the Civil War; it included some persons outside the stricter definition of veteranhood favored by white Union veterans. African Americans were more willing to acknowledge contributions to the Union cause that were not strictly of a martial nature but had been just as important to the ultimate triumph of the North. Similarly, they were willing to draw into the Civil War veterans' fraternity the buffalo soldiers, men who had made their race proud by demonstrating in the postwar army that the ability and prowess of black men in the Civil War were not accidental or isolated occurrences. In short, African Americans did not automatically accept white definitions of veteranhood but created their own definitions that served their own needs.[59]

Sometimes those needs took veterans outside of the organized veterans' community. That is, besides reunions and veterans' groups, black ex-soldiers preserved their wartime connections in other ways. As has been seen, groups of black veterans attempted to form colonies after the war in the quest to buy land and for mutual self-protection. None of these colonies appears to have survived long, and in many cases, they never got beyond the planning stages (see chapter 1). Black veterans proved more successful in maintaining informal ties with wartime comrades. The Union army raised many black units consisting of men from the same locale. They joined the army at the same time, served side by side, and then returned home together. Their Civil War service deepened these prewar associations, and their common wartime experience continued to draw them together, despite the forces of postwar mobility and mortality that tore them apart.

One group of men who had their prewar ties strengthened by the conflict were the members of the Brigade Band No. 1, a black army band. Already existent as a group of slave musicians in Maryland before the war, the band's members were recruited by the Union army to play music under the command of Col. William Birney, the officer in charge of recruiting black soldiers in the state. After it finished its recruiting duty, the small unit served in the Virginia theater until the close of the war and then in Texas.[60] Following their discharge, the band members returned to their homes in Hagerstown, a town in western Maryland, and kept in regular contact with one another. Relations were closest among the band's core members, which consisted of brothers Robert, Joseph, and Perry Moxley, as well as James Hill and Thomas Henry. The close postwar ties among these five men came out in the testimony they provided for one another's pension applications. They knew what jobs the others held, whom they had married, their children's names, and myriad other details suggesting regular personal contact. They also explicitly claimed to have kept in touch after the war. James Hill spoke of his prewar ties with Joseph Moxley and their postwar friendship. "I knew the late Joseph Moxley for 4 or 5 years prior to this enlistment," he stated. "And after service I was intimately acquainted with him during the balance of his lifetime."[61] Thomas Henry told a federal pension investigator in 1889 that he had seen Joseph Moxley "almost every day from the time we were discharged until the time he died."[62] Robert Moxley stated, "Thomas Henry I remember as well as I do my brother."[63]

Still, the realities of postwar life made maintaining wartime friendships difficult, even for men as close as the Brigade Band No. 1. Some band members migrated from Hagerstown soon after the war. Those men not in the inner circle of the band were the first to leave. Nelson Coon left for Washington, D.C., soon after the group mustered out. Solomon Sims and Thomas Cyrus headed north into Pennsylvania in the 1870s. Yet even the five men with the closest ties were not immune from the urge to relocate. Robert Moxley, the founder and leader of the band, left Hagerstown for Detroit in the 1880s. Death inevitably took its toll. Joseph Moxley died in 1884, James Hill in 1892, Thomas Henry in 1895, Perry Moxley in 1900, and Robert Moxley in 1904.[64] As long as they lived, however, the men kept in touch. Even separated by considerable distance from his surviving comrades in Hagerstown, Robert Moxley seemed quite knowledgeable about their activities in his pension testimony. He and Thomas Henry saw each other at the GAR national encampment in 1892 held in Washington, D.C., and afterward, Moxley visited his other surviving comrades in Hagerstown on his way back to Detroit.[65]

Other soldiers did not have the advantages of Brigade Band No. 1 in maintaining contact. Consequently, many African-American soldiers lost track of old comrades. This phenomenon was particularly common in the North, where recruitment of black Civil War regiments occurred throughout the region. After mustering out, even close comrades scattered widely to different towns, counties, and even states. Men who had joined units recruited outside their native regions easily lost contact with those they had served with during the war.

High rates of illiteracy and poverty among black veterans also made it difficult for them to correspond with former comrades. Yet, as the case of Andrew J. Smith shows, such correspondence was possible.[66] After serving in the 55th Massachusetts Infantry during the war, Smith returned to his birth state of Kentucky, eventually settling in the western part of the state along the Cumberland River. He farmed and, despite his inability to read or write, exchanged letters with other veterans of his regiment. Among Smith's correspondents was William H. Dupree. Dupree wrote to Smith in July 1890, responding to the Kentucky veteran's letter asking if the 55th was having a reunion that year. Dupree replied that it was not, but that the GAR was holding its annual national encampment in Boston, so many former members of the regiment would be there.[67] In April 1914, Smith got a letter from David Lee, another veteran of the 55th Massachusetts living in Xenia, Ohio. Smith had previously written to Lee, asking if he could provide first-hand testimony that Smith had saved the regimental colors at the battle of Honey Hill. Lee apologetically said that he could not remember Smith's heroism, but indicated that another member of the regiment who lived in Xenia might be able to help.[68] Smith also received two letters in 1915 from another veteran of the 55th, George S. Walker. The first letter in August invited Smith to the GAR national encampment in Washington, D.C. Walker added, "Bring as many of the 55th Boys as you can find as I would like to have a Reunion."[69] In October, Smith received another letter from his old comrade. Walker had visited with some veterans of the 55th Massachusetts at the Washington encampment. He gave Smith the news of who was still alive and who had died, and Walker provided Smith with the addresses of half a dozen former comrades.[70]

However, Smith's most faithful correspondent was not a black veteran but a white officer of the 55th Massachusetts, Burt G. Wilder, the regimental surgeon. Smith had known Wilder in the army and had worked for him as an orderly before being reassigned to combat duties. After nearly fifty years, in 1913, Smith contacted Wilder, by then a retired medical professor, and the *Mayflower* descendant and former Kentucky slave renewed their acquaintance by mail, exchanging letters and postcards for the next five years.

Wilder was working on a history of the 55th Massachusetts based on his wartime letters and eagerly solicited Smith's memories. He asked Smith for his recollection of the important engagements of the 55th, but Wilder proved particularly interested in the battle of Honey Hill, where Smith had saved the regimental colors after the Confederates had killed the 55th's flag bearer. The illiterate Smith complied with Wilder's requests for information by dictating his responses to his nephew.

Although Wilder always addressed Smith formally in his typewritten correspondence, he evinced genuine admiration for the black ex-soldier. Wilder told the black veteran that he had frequently mentioned him in his wartime correspondence, and "always with commendation." When Smith indicated that he had found other veterans who would verify his answers to Wilder's questions about the history of the 55th Massachusetts, the retired professor wrote back, saying, "I do not understand why you got others to vouch for you; I would trust you as much as any other man."[71] His regard for Smith prompted Wilder to try to secure a belated Medal of Honor for the black veteran for his bravery at the battle of Honey Hill, an effort that was unsuccessful.[72]

Besides his memory of wartime events, Wilder also took an interest in the black veteran's prewar history and what he had done since leaving the army. He asked Smith to tell him about his parents and family, querying, "How far back can you ascertain as to your family?" Wilder wanted to know if Smith had married, and if so, about his wife and children. The former officer asked how Smith had earned a living since the war and where he had lived.[73] Perhaps realizing that this was a rare opportunity to question a black man directly about conditions for African Americans in the South, Wilder asked Smith in a subsequent letter, "Please tell me how much land you own; whether you employ other men; whether you have money in the bank; do you vote, and for how many years?"[74]

Wilder was not the only white officer who took an interest in his former soldiers after the war. Capt. Wallace A. Barlett of the 19th USCI, a Maryland regiment, donated land he owned in Prince Georges County, Maryland, for freed people to settle on, in honor of the valor of his black soldiers.[75] Thomas Wentworth Higginson, a colonel of black South Carolina troops during the Civil War, went south a decade later to investigate their condition personally.[76] George Thompson Garrison, son of the prominent abolitionist William Lloyd Garrison and an officer in the 55th Massachusetts Infantry during the war, kept a scrapbook of newspaper clippings on the activities of black ex-soldiers in his regiment.[77] As the reunion movement shows, white officers participated in black veterans' organizations.[78] Many former officers of black regiments also responded to other Civil War veterans who unfairly criticized the performance of black soldiers during the war. Their honor and manhood had become tied up with that of their African-American troops, and they defended it in the face of indifference and hostility from other white Americans (see chapter 7).

Yet time and distance strained the bonds between black soldiers and their white officers, as well as other white Union veterans. Although some ex-soldiers found their former officers friendly and eager to be of assistance, such as occurred with Andrew J. Smith, others received a cold shoulder. Henry Taylor, a Missouri veteran, encountered both attitudes when he wrote to former officers of his regiment, the 102d USCI, seeking testimony to support his claim for a Civil War pension based on service-related injuries. W. W. Spiers, the former surgeon of the regiment, wrote to Taylor in May 1892 from his home in Kansas; although Spiers did not remember Taylor's case, he suggested the names of several other officers who might. Spiers also advised the black veteran to give up his service-related claim because it would be easier to get a pension under the 1890 law, which did not require veterans to prove a war-related disability to get benefits. However, Edward Cahill, one of the officers that Spiers suggested Taylor write to, replied that he did not remember Taylor or his injury and coolly wrote, "If you have been lame ever since [the Civil War] . . . you ought to have applied for your pension earlier when it might have been possible for the officers of your company to aid you."[79]

As the exchange between Cahill and Taylor suggests, relations between black and white Union veterans often had something of an edge to them. Although many white veterans genuinely admired their black counterparts, racism always remained lurking just beneath the surface, and with certain notable exceptions, white Union veterans treated African-American veterans as second-class comrades at best. Certainly, it is imperative to give the Grand Army of the Republic credit for being one of the most progressive organizations of its day in terms of race relations. Otherwise, it would not have attracted so many black members and would-be members. That African Americans were able to participate with white men in one of the leading fraternal organizations of late-nineteenth-century America is certainly worth noting and celebrating. It testifies to how the manhood shown by black soldiers during the Civil War could soften hearts and change minds. But despite the considerable interaction and comradeship expressed, a gulf persisted between the two groups that was never quite bridged. This gap between white and black Union veterans was not only a matter of a willingness to associate; it went much deeper to the way both groups remembered the war.

# Memory

L IKE ALL VETERANS, African Americans carried the memory of the Civil War in their minds. Although their written discourse concerning the war was nowhere near as extensive as that of white soldiers, they nonetheless managed to articulate a distinct vision of the war and their place in it. At the center of their memory was emancipation. For them, freedom for the slaves was the central outcome of the war, and they considered themselves the manly liberators of their people. Not surprisingly, then, black soldiers were proud of their military service and wanted it to be remembered. Yet increasingly, African-American veterans were forced to fight against the defamation and trivialization of their service in the collective national memory. Not only did white Americans grow more forgetful of black service as the years passed, but also the national interpretation of the war became increasingly dominated by white Southerners. Hence, to the extent that black veterans were recollected, too often those memories were dismissive or pejorative in nature. Such attitudes offended the manhood of black veterans, especially well-educated men of the black elite. In response, these former soldiers vigorously defended what they saw as their heroic wartime service, even as their words fell ever more on deaf, indifferent, or unfriendly ears.

The way black veterans remembered the Civil War developed within the context of the memory created by white Union veterans. With the Grand Army of the Republic taking the lead, white veterans emphasized the preservation of the Union and the consolidation of national authority as the central accomplishment of the war. In their view, Union soldiers had heroically put down a revolt against the nation's duly elected government, settling for good the federal government's preeminence over the states. Consequently, they described the conflict not as the "Civil War" but as the "War of the Rebellion." That title emphasized to them the war's central purpose: the suppression of treason. Although freedom for the slaves was also an agreeable outcome for most white Union veterans, it was not as significant to them as keeping the Union intact.[1]

For black veterans, the emphasis was exactly the opposite. They saw the preservation of the Union as something good, but only because it became synonymous with freeing the slaves. In their view, emancipation had made the United States worth preserving. It was by far the more important legacy of the war. Hence, rather than seeing themselves as saviors of the Union, they remembered themselves as warriors in an army of liberation. Yet in fighting for freedom, they had done an invaluable service not only to their own people but also to the entire American nation. That is, African-American veterans believed that by their manly sacrifice they had helped create a much better nation than had existed before the war.

George M. Arnold, an ex-slave and prominent veteran of the 4th USCI, eloquently articulated this view. As some white members of the GAR questioned the value of black participation in the Union army at their 1887 encampment in St. Louis, he issued a forthright reminder of what African-American soldiers believed they had accomplished, and its significance. For Arnold, there was no doubt that emancipation was the central outcome of the war. However, he went further. Rather than being a gift of the government, freedom was something that black soldiers had earned for themselves and their people. In earning this freedom, according to Arnold, black troops had helped bring American reality closer to the American ideal of freedom. "They washed the blood scars of slavery out of the American flag, and painted freedom there; they snatched the black lies out of every false star upon its folds and set in their stead the diadem of liberty," insisted Arnold. "They tore the Dred Scott decision from the statutes and wrote there, 'All men are equal before God.'"[2]

For Arnold, saving the Union was noteworthy, but principally as evidence of the forbearance of black soldiers—showing their willingness to rescue an undeserving nation that had previously considered them of little significance. He commented, "They helped to save from dismemberment a union of States, a country that only recognized them as property. . . . They served as soldiers and seamen, in the army of a country that accepted the fiat Negroes have no rights that white men need respect." By their selflessness and sacrifice, Arnold suggested, black soldiers had won freedom for themselves and other African Americans, proved their manliness, and showed that they were worthy of manly respect and deserved the same rights accorded white men.[3]

Besides having a different perspective on the war's significance, black veterans also came away from the war with a different set of heroes. The names African Americans chose for Grand Army posts illustrates this point. White Union veterans tended to name their posts after major war figures, such as Ulysses S. Grant and William Tecumseh Sherman, or GAR luminaries such as John A. Logan. Black veterans sometimes named their posts after such men, but they more often named them after their own particular icons. For instance, black veterans named posts after white officers of African-American units who had gained heroic stature in their eyes. Hence, numerous Robert G. Shaw posts appeared, commemorating the fallen colonel of the 54th Massachusetts Infantry.[4] Black veterans in the GAR honored prominent abolitionists, expressing comradely connections with the men who had also battled to end slavery in the decades before the Civil War. Consequently, there were William Lloyd Garrison and Wendell Phillips posts in New York City.[5] Black ex-soldiers named their GAR posts for wartime governors who pushed for African-American recruitment, such as John A. Andrew of Massachusetts and Oliver P. Morton of Indiana.[6] They recognized prominent Radicals with Thaddeus Stevens and Charles Sumner posts.[7] Black veterans also named posts after heroes in their own community. Frederick Douglass and Martin R. Delany posts appeared.[8] Finally, countless African-American posts were named after black Civil War heroes, some of whose brave deeds were known only to their comrades. Louisiana's veterans had an André Cailloux post, named for a black officer killed at Port Hudson in May 1863, and an Anselmas Planciamos post, honoring another African American who gave his life at the same battle.[9]

Decoration Day (later called Memorial Day) was an important date on the calendars of African-American veterans. The spring holiday was a solemn occasion on which to remember, in the words of one black minister, those who "were now sleeping the sleep that knows no waking."[10] Black veterans decorated the graves of black soldiers and GAR comrades with flowers. However, they did not limit their decoration activities to those two groups. In 1885, black veterans of the Thaddeus Stevens and William Lloyd Garrison posts in New York City decorated the Lincoln monument in Union Square.[11] In 1886, Boston veterans sent delegations to decorate the grave of William Lloyd Garrison, the prominent abolitionist, and Crispus Attucks, the black martyr of the 1770s Boston Massacre. Later, they decorated Garrison's statue on Commonwealth Avenue and visited the Robert G. Shaw monument and the tomb of Edward N. Hallowell, Shaw's successor as commander of the 54th Massachusetts Infantry. The last stop was the grave of Charles Sumner, champion of African Americans as a U.S. senator from Massachusetts during the Civil War and Reconstruction.[12]

Ceremonies like the ones just described were more important for black veterans than for white ex-soldiers, Northern and Southern. Because a considerably higher percentage of the African-American population was illiterate compared with white Americans, former soldiers' vision of the conflict manifested itself in terms of public celebration rather than the written word. Some of these men certainly put their thoughts about the Civil War to paper. However, because so many of them could not read or write, public events reached former soldiers and other members of the African-American community more readily than writing could. As one scholar put it, a "robust celebratory culture that flourished during the late-nineteenth century ensured that the black sense of the past was something more than a rhetorical discourse accessible principally to literate, elite African Americans."[13] Black veterans played an important role in this culture as it pertained to memory of the Civil War and emancipation. They helped put together such celebrations and served as prominent participants or as the objects of commemoration. As such, they played critical roles in formulating how the African-American population nationwide came to view the war.[14]

Consistent with their wartime memory's emphasis on emancipation, one critical aspect of the conflict that the black Grand Army celebrated in ritual was the coming of freedom to the slaves. In 1886, for example, Robert G. Shaw Post No. 206 in Pittsburgh appointed a committee to organize a commemoration of emancipation by the membership.[15] In December 1897, the Shaw post in Pittsburgh received an invitation to attend a religious service on the evening of New Year's Day 1898, commemorating the thirty-fifth anniversary of the Emancipation Proclamation.[16] Likewise, in New York City in 1887, members of the John A. Andrew and Thaddeus Stevens posts escorted Cuban Americans celebrating the recent liberation of the slaves on that island (Spanish authorities had freed its last slaves the year before, and Brazil would emancipate the last slaves in the Western Hemisphere in 1888).[17] No doubt, African-American veterans participated in many other celebrations of emancipation that occurred over the years for which no records survive.

With their heroes and acts of commemoration, black veterans showed a vision of the Civil War broader than the conflict itself. The persons they honored demonstrated that, for them, the conflict was merely an important chapter in a struggle that had begun before the war and continued after it: the battle for the freedom and equality of black people in American society. With Attucks, they called attention to the manly sacrifice African Americans had made for American freedom in earlier wars (and, by implication, strengthened their own claims to suffrage and citizenship). They honored Garrison for his uncompromising stand favoring the immediate abolition of slavery during the antebellum years; Shaw and Hallowell for their leadership of and advocacy for black troops during the war (and Shaw in particular for his martyrdom at Fort Wagner). In decorating Sumner's grave, the ex-soldiers remembered his steadfast support for their people, especially during Reconstruction. Finally, in joining the Cuban emancipation celebration, they showed that their conception of the Civil War extended beyond the borders of United States. Some veterans evidently believed that the struggle involved more than merely their own freedom or that of people of African descent in the United States; it encompassed the plight of those in bondage throughout the entire African diaspora in the Americas.

The impressively broad perspective exhibited by African-American veterans was not unique to them. Black historians writing the history of their race of the late nineteenth and early twentieth centuries also tended to contextualize the Civil War and black military participation in that conflict in the same sprawling historic and geographic terms.[18] Likewise, African-American authors, though uniformly praising the men of their race who had served the Union, did not inordinately single them out.[19] Nearly two centuries of struggle against bondage had produced many heroic men of their race that African Americans could admire. What black soldiers had done during the war was quite praiseworthy, and they were manly heroes in the black community in the United States, but they were not the only people worthy of high regard in the struggle for freedom and equality. Such heroes could be found far back in the past and well beyond the nation's borders.

Although their own people spoke well of black veterans, such was not the case with another group living in close proximity. Among white Southerners, African Americans who had served in the Union army were anything but heroic or manly. The attitude of many former Confederates toward black veterans was often one of unremitting hostility immediately after the war.

Both black soldiers and veterans often found themselves the targets of violence during this period. These attacks were prompted by the anger of white Southerners over the supposed disloyalty of African Americans who had joined the Union army, the fear of armed black men in their midst, and the importance of black troops as symbols of the antebellum Southern world turned upside down (see chapter 1). Such attacks eventually died down, however, partly for practical reasons. In some parts of the postwar South, especially the border states, the Mississippi Valley, and coastal areas of the Atlantic seaboard, many of the able-bodied black men were veterans of the Union army. And as much as white Southerners may have hated these former Union soldiers in their midst, they needed their labor. But white Southerners never forgot or forgave what they had done.

The attacks against black veterans also ended soon after the war because white Southerners relocated much of their hostility to the white Northerners responsible for the African Americans' recruitment. Foreshadowing the popular image of African Americans that would be most fully articulated by the Dunning school of Reconstruction historiography, white Southern writers in the aftermath of the war portrayed black men in the Union army as simpleton dupes of white Northerners bent on pillaging and tyrannizing the South. Edward A. Pollard, in his *Southern History of the War* (1866), set the tone for the dismissive manner in which many white Southerners treated the black men who had fought in the Civil War. Pollard, the editor of the *Richmond Examiner*, mentioned African-American soldiers only once in his massive polemic history of the conflict. In this brief discussion of their service, he could not conceive of them as intelligent individuals with the ability to make rational choices. Instead, black Union troops were dim-witted pawns of the Yankees. Pollard placed the blame for black military service on what he described as "the anti-Slavery party in the North," not on the soldiers themselves. To him, the use of African-American troops constituted a war crime committed by vindictive white Northerners—"a savage atrocity inflicted on the South," as he put it.[20] Interestingly, Pollard looked on the enlistment of African Americans as a crime against the black troops, as well as against the white South. He held that the military service of African Americans was an offense against the black men because it took them away from the peaceful plantation labor for which they were best qualified, exposing them to the dangers of military service, for which they were neither suited nor trainable. To Pollard's way of thinking, the hands of white Northerners were red with the blood of gullible black cannon fodder. (He conveniently neglected to mention that late in the war, the Confederate government had decided to use black troops in a last, desperate attempt to stave off defeat.)

Confederate veterans echoed Pollard's approach to black Civil War soldiers as they defined their memory in their literature of the war, especially in the pages of the *Confederate Veteran,* a publication of the United Confederate Veterans, the largest organization of former Confederate soldiers and counterpart of the Grand Army of the Republic. Black Union soldiers were mentioned rarely in the pages of the *Confederate Veteran,* and then usually only as part of the scenery of the war or as stooges of the Yankees fit to be slandered. For instance, Confederate veterans claimed that the black soldiers at Fort Pillow, where Southern forces massacred African-American prisoners of war, had been intoxicated, as though the alleged drunkenness of their victims justified killing them.[21] And even though former Confederate H. D. Twiggs grudgingly praised the courage of the 54th Massachusetts Infantry, which had assaulted Fort Wagner, South Carolina, in July 1863, he never mentioned that the regiment was black.[22]

The black "veterans" that white Southerners deigned to praise were their "faithful negroes." These were the body servants and other African Americans who had remained loyal to white Southerners during the Civil War and had willingly assisted the Confederate war effort.[23] Although their exact numbers can never be ascertained, there is little doubt that they were a rather small minority compared with the vast majority of black Southerners who sided with the Union. Yet former Confederates played up their existence, even as they ignored or disparaged the much more numerous black Union veterans around them. The *Confederate Veteran* periodically published profiles of faithful Negroes, and such persons received a warm welcome at Confederate veterans' reunions and other white Southern ceremonies associated with remembrance.[24] They helped white Southerners maintain the illusion that African Americans had been happier under slavery and that they willingly accepted the segregation and disfranchisement of the post-Reconstruction period.

Like the Confederate veterans who inhabited the old soldiers' homes of the South, these faithful Negroes played a role assigned to them in the white Southern memory of the war. If Confederate veterans in such homes were living monuments to the virtues that white Southerners associated with their Civil War soldiers, the faithful Negroes were living monuments to the characteristics that white Southerners believed more African Americans should display—loyalty and subservience.[25] They helped white Southerners ignore the very real progress black men had made in achieving the attributes of manhood during the Civil War and Reconstruction, as well as the efforts of black leaders—including many former soldiers—to preserve those gains (see chapter 3).

The African Americans who joined the Confederate postwar celebration did so for their own reasons, not the least of which was gaining the favor of the rulers of the post-Reconstruction South. During the Jim Crow era, in which white Southerners quite literally held the power of life and death over them, some black men evidently decided that it was prudent to cater to the myth of the Lost Cause, as the view of the war espoused by former Confederates came to be known. Financial incentives also prompted this choice. In the early decades of the twentieth century, Confederate veterans in some Southern states successfully pushed for pensions for African Americans who had rendered steadfast service to the Confederacy during the war.[26] The economic need of numerous elderly former body servants, laborers, teamsters, and other black men who had worked for the Confederate army no doubt prompted them to apply for these small pensions and identify themselves as faithful Negroes. Likewise, there were more informal rewards for African Americans attending Confederate veterans' reunions in the South. For instance, when interviewed by representatives of the WPA in 1930s, the family of Tuck Spight, a Mississippi man and the former body servant of a Confederate officer, informed the interviewer that after the war, Spight had become a member of the local "Confederate Veterans Camp." After returning from a Confederate reunion in Little Rock, Arkansas, with more money than he had left home with, the old black man had explained "that he had made a talk for the people and they gave him money."[27] Spight was not the only former Confederate servant to exploit the sentimentality of white Southerners to see him through his declining years. Another Mississippi man, identified by the WPA interviewer only as "Uncle Army Jack," was cared for in his old age by the family of the Confederate officer he had served during the war as a body servant.[28] In the case of both Spight and Uncle Army Jack, the veterans had already passed on, and the WPA interviews were conducted with informants who had known the men in life. Members of the white family that had taken care of Uncle Army Jack went out of their way to tell the interviewer that "he loved to recount his war experiences and loved to dwell on the period he served his master in the War between the States, and seemed to feel that war service gave him special prestige, as most negroes at that time felt. They took pride in the fact they were loyal to the South, and justly so."[29]

In short, even decades after the war, some white Southerners felt the need to believe that "good" African Americans had taken their side during the war and that the Yankees had lured away the rest, but because they were an inferior people, they were not fully responsible for their actions. For their own reasons—the attention they received, the praise, the state government pensions, money given to them at Confederate reunions, and care in their declining year—some elderly black men were willing to become living monuments to the loyal Negroes who had genuinely existed during the Civil War, but whose numbers had become overblown in white Southerners' quest to justify the system of racial oppression in the Old South, slavery, and the new system of racial oppression, Jim Crow, that emerged in the years following the end of Reconstruction.[30]

While one group of whites—former Confederates—largely ignored the existence of black Union veterans, another smaller group celebrated their existence—the former officers of black regiments. This is not surprising, since the fortunes of these men had become inseparably tied to the reputation of their soldiers. When history treated black soldiers well, their former officers looked good. When history treated black soldiers badly, their former officers looked bad. Hence, ex-officers of African-American regiments took a role in trying to shape a positive image for their former soldiers and themselves in the postwar debates among Union veterans and in publications meant for broader consumption.

Not surprisingly, the former officers of African-American troops in the Union army were almost uniform in praising their men. Their approach is understandable, given the disparagement many white officers were subjected to as a result of their association with African Americans during the war.[31] Consequently, ex-officers of black regiments sought to bolster their image by reminding other Union veterans and the Northern public of their positive contribution to the war effort, as well as that of the African-American troops they had led. Over the decades, then, the admiration they showed for the manly virtues of their former soldiers was consistent. In 1880, for instance, Garth W. James, a former captain in the 54th Massachusetts Infantry, praised black soldiers as being every bit as brave as their white counterparts. He said that they "made a brave fight against an unfair foe and fought as well as we [white Union soldiers] did."[32] A decade later, William Eliot Furness, a former officer in both the 3d and 45th USCI, praised black soldiers not only for their valor but also for their manly restraint in not making war on slaveholders, despite centuries of exploitation and abuse, until given official sanction. "Not till the muskets of the Federal Government were placed in their hands," Furness wrote, "did they presume to meet their rebellious masters in war; but then they shrank not from any duty which a brave soldier should perform."[33] Perhaps the strongest praise for black troops from a white former officer in the U.S. Colored Troops (USCT) came from James H. Rickard, who had served with the 19th USCI, a Maryland regiment that had fought in the trenches before Petersburg. In his personal experience, Rickard believed that the black soldiers were the bravest he had encountered. "For deeds of personal daring and heroism . . . I saw none that excelled what I saw among the colored troops."[34] In other words, white officers largely accepted the manly vision African-American veterans had of themselves, attributing to them such masculine characteristics as self-control, audacity, and personal courage.

For all the approbation that former USCT officers heaped on African-American soldiers, it is apparent that they never totally understood the men they had led in the war. That is, their assessments of black troops were replete with not only sincere praise but also racist stereotypes. Indeed, it is fair to say that many of these ex-USCT officers adopted a tone of respectful racism in assessing their former underlings.[35] Like white veterans in the Grand Army of the Republic, they demonstrated that although African Americans' wartime service had softened and ameliorated their bigotry toward the black men who had worn the Union blue, it never entirely eliminated it—even for those who had served most closely with African Americans and had fought and died with them. In other words, if Civil War service could have eliminated racism, this certainly should have been the case for white officers of black troops, but even many of them could never totally overcome their prejudices.

Despite the persistence of a racist mind-set, the writings of white officers show that they never forgot nor lost admiration for their black soldiers, however colored their feelings were by residual prejudices. The same cannot be said of the general histories of the war written before the end of the nineteenth century. Admittedly, some of these histories spoke highly of African-American soldiers. Perhaps the most vociferous in its praise was William A. Crafts's *The Southern Rebellion* (1870). Crafts lauded the manly courage of black troops at various engagements throughout the war. Largely ignoring Port Hudson, the first major appearance by African Americans on the battlefield, he concentrated instead on their subsequent appearance at Milliken's Bend. Crafts believed that this battle had settled the question of whether black men would fight and their value as soldiers. "The engagement at Milliken's Bend was important," he wrote, "because it established the fact that the negro possessed courage and endurance." Crafts concluded, "The valor of [black troops] . . . dispelled the idea the negro would not fight."[36] Other authors of general war histories, such as Henry Stacke, Rossiter Johnson, and John A. Logan, also praised the black soldiers' courage and their contributions to Union victory.[37] Logan was particularly fulsome in his admiration for African-American troops, which was not surprising, given his Radical Republican affiliations. "Through the war," he wrote, "at Wilson's Wharf, in the many bloody charges at Petersburg, at Deep Bottom, at Chapin's Farm, Fair Oaks, and numerous other battle-fields, in Virginia and elsewhere, right down to Appomattox—the African soldier fought courageously, fully vindicating the War-wisdom of Abraham Lincoln in emancipating and arming the Race."[38]

Yet in general histories of the Civil War published before 1900, the experience of black soldiers tended to get lost in the larger story of the conflict. Some authors of early histories mentioned a few salient facts about African-American troops, but nothing more substantial, and they certainly did not offer enough information or analysis for readers to get even a minimal sense of the experience of black soldiers. Thomas P. Kettell set the pattern early in his *History of the Great Rebellion* (1865), in which he briefly mentioned the assault of the 54th Massachusetts Infantry on Fort Wagner, South Carolina, and the equalization of black soldiers' pay with that of their white counterparts, but he wrote nothing else about African Americans in the Union army.[39] John William Draper, in *History of the American Civil War* (1870), offered some brief positive comments about black enlistment in the Union army and criticized the activities of Northern recruiters in the South who tried to satisfy enlistment quotas for their states by enlisting black men, but he had nothing else to offer on African-American soldiers.[40] Other authors seem to have deliberately downplayed the role of black troops, mentioning engagements in which they participated but minimizing or ignoring their presence. An example of the former was George B. Herbert's *The Popular History of the Civil War in America* (1884).[41] Herbert briefly mentioned the Fort Pillow massacre but downplayed the fact that black troops were the main victims in this incident. An example of the latter was Theodore Ayrault Dodge's *A Bird's-Eye View of Our Civil War* (1883).[42] Dodge devoted considerable space in his book to engagements such as Port Hudson in 1863 and the battle of the Crater in 1864, in which African Americans played an important part. Yet by his account, an uninformed reader would not know that black soldiers had even been there, let alone been significant participants. In short, from the earliest days after the war, some authors marginalized or expurgated African-American troops from the pages of the history of the Civil War.

Black veterans were acutely aware of how white Americans, through acts of omission and commission, were erasing their presence in the history of the war or maliciously misrepresenting it. Consequently, it is not surprising that a few elite black veterans sought to present their interpretation of African-American troops in the Civil War, not only in the black community but also in the larger American society.

Perhaps the most ambitious effort of a black Civil War veteran in the battle for memory came from the pen of George W. Williams. Williams was a prolific author and an enigmatic man. Born free in 1849, he joined the Union army as a teenager in 1865 under an assumed name. Williams spent the last days of the war in Virginia and then served garrison duty in Texas. After leaving the army, he went south to Mexico, where he joined the republican forces battling to free the country from French interventionists and their native collaborators. Shortly before the republican victory in Mexico, the young adventurer returned to the United States and enlisted in the 10th U.S. Cavalry in August 1867. Williams's service in the 10th was uneventful until May 1868, when he received a gunshot wound in the lung. The exact circumstances of the shooting are unclear, but army records indicate that it was not service related. In any case, the army discharged Williams because of his injury in September 1868. After leaving military service, the young veteran (he was only nineteen) went to St. Louis and then settled for a short time in Quincy, Illinois, farther upstream on the Mississippi River, where he developed an interest in becoming a minister. Knowing that he would need further education to fulfill this ambition, Williams applied to and was accepted by Howard University in Washington, D.C. However, he did not stay long at Howard and moved from there to the Newton Theological Institution in Boston. After graduating from Newton in 1874, he entered the ministry as a Baptist. He rose rapidly, becoming minister of the prestigious Twelfth Baptist Church in Boston in 1875. Despite his success, the ministry palled quickly, and within fourteen months, Williams had resigned and moved back to Washington, where he tried to establish a black-oriented political journal, *The Commoner*. This venture quickly failed, and Williams worked a short time for the post office before accepting a position at the Union Baptist Church in Cincinnati, Ohio. Continuing to find politics more interesting than the ministry, Williams ran for state office in 1877 and lost, but he won a seat in the Ohio House of Representatives two years later. He served for one term and did not run for reelection, turning to the writing of history instead. Williams had been collecting material for a history of black people in America since the 1876 centennial. In 1883, he published *History of the Negro Race in America from 1619–1880*. It was a massive two-volume work that received generally favorable reviews and established Williams as a pioneering historian of the African-American experience. Equally impressive was his study of black soldiers in the Civil War, which appeared five years later.[43]

George W. Williams's *A History of the Negro Troops in the War of the Rebellion* (1888) was a product of the reunion movement among black Civil War veterans in the 1880s, which sought to remind the nation of the wartime contributions and accomplishments of African-American soldiers as a way of fighting the deteriorating position of the black community in the wake of Reconstruction. It began out of the veteran's efforts at GAR campfires to share the experience of African-American troops with white ex-soldiers, many of whom had little knowledge or appreciation of the contribution of colored regiments to the Union victory. Not surprisingly, then, Williams spent much of this book substantiating the worth of black soldiers to the Union cause and their valor in battle. With the activities of black soldiers often ignored or belittled in many general war histories written by white authors, he had little choice.

After a lengthy discussion of the historical background of black fighting men going all the way back to ancient Egypt, including a description of black soldiers' contributions in earlier American wars, he finally described their service during the Civil War itself. His story of the dramatic rise of African Americans from despised servitude to manly warriors has become the staple of Civil War history, but it was not commonly known in the 1880s by the postwar generation. Although sympathetic white authors had sketched the broad outlines of black heroism in the Civil War, Williams fleshed out this story by providing numerous detailed examples. His narrative was also quite mindful of the dramatic quality of the Civil War service of African Americans, particularly the rapid change that military service brought to their lives, especially the opportunities for expanded manhood. As Williams poetically wrote, "from clanking chains to clashing arms; from passive submission to the cruel curse of slavery to the brilliant aggressiveness of a free soldier; from a chattel to a person; from the shame of degradation to the glory of military exaltation."[44]

Yet in writing the history of black soldiers in the Civil War, Williams felt obliged to prove points that would have seemed superfluous in any discussion of white troops. Especially significant in this respect was the issue of the federal government's legal authority to recruit black soldiers. "The legal status of the Negro soldier ought never to have been a mooted question," complained Williams, but he then spent the better part of a chapter demonstrating the validity of that exact point.[45] He also felt a need to prove that men of African descent were especially well suited physically to serve as soldiers and that slavery had not destroyed either their mental or physical capacity for military service.[46] Williams then went on to answer the classic questions about the Union's black troops, which were still being asked in the late 1880s. Did African Americans make good soldiers? Would they fight as bravely and as fiercely as white soldiers? Williams answered affirmatively to both questions and then demonstrated the soldierly qualities of African-American troops in various theaters of the war. "Testimony to the martial valor of the Negro soldier comes from the lips of friend and foe alike," he concluded. "There is no testimony offered in rebuttal; there is but one opinion—'*The Colored Troops fought nobly.*'"[47] Still, Williams found it necessary to argue this point at considerable length, because even after the Civil War, the bravery and manhood of black troops were not taken for granted, as they were for white soldiers.

The defensiveness apparent in Williams's *A History of Negro Troops* also permeated Joseph T. Wilson's *The Black Phalanx* (1887). Unlike Williams, Wilson was Southern born, although he had spent much of the prewar period in the North. He was also unusual among black soldiers, in that he entered the army a well-traveled man, having worked on New England whaling ships before the war. In September 1862, in Union-occupied New Orleans, he enlisted in the 2d Louisiana Native Guards. Wilson was discharged from that unit in September 1863 for poor eyesight but managed to reenlist three months later in the 54th Massachusetts Infantry. His service in the 54th Massachusetts was short, as he was wounded at the battle of Olustee two months

after joining the regiment and received a medical discharge in May 1864. After
the war, Wilson settled in Norfolk, Virginia, where he launched a career as a
newspaper editor and politician. He was active in the postwar suffrage movement in Virginia and gained several federal appointments during Reconstruction and afterward, a product of his deep involvement in the Republican party.
By the time of his death in 1891, Wilson had moved from journalism into the
insurance business.[48]

Like Williams, Wilson began his book not with the Civil War but earlier.
He did not go back as far as ancient Egypt, but only to the American Revolution. Likewise, the story he told displayed the same defensiveness. Wilson felt
compelled to prove that black men had played an active and manly role in
the Revolution and the War of 1812. "It seemed proper," he wrote, "that the
memory of our forefathers not be allowed to remain longer in obscurity; that
it was fitting to recall *their* deeds of heroism, that all might know the sacrifices they made for the freedom their descendants were so long denied from
enjoying."[49] This was something that few, if any, white authors of a Civil War
history would have felt obligated to do. Wilson then spent the remainder of
the book discussing the dramatic transformation of public opinion in the
North from opposition to black recruitment to support for it, the enlistment
and organization of African-American troops, and their performance in
different theaters of the war. Wilson proved no less strident than Williams in
defending the worth of black soldiers to the Union cause. "The laurels won
by the Phalanx [the term Wilson used to collectively refer to black Union
soldiers] in the Southern States," he stated, "was proof of its devotion to the
cause of liberty and the old flag, which . . . within a short period had been
but a symbol of oppression to the black man."[50]

Other African-American authors who had not served in the war also
exhibited defensiveness in describing the military participation of black men
in the Civil War. William Wells Brown set the pattern in his groundbreaking
book *The Negro in the American Rebellion: His Heroism and His Fidelity* (1867).
Brown's coverage of African-American soldiers in the conflict was predict-
ably laudatory but consisted almost entirely of verbatim extracts from Northern newspapers praising the performance of black troops. Although such
large-scale borrowing was not unusual in nineteenth-century writing (Wilson did the same thing in *The Black Phalanx*), it is significant that Brown chose
not to describe the military performance of African Americans in his own
words but leaned on the crutch of white sources. Evidently, he felt that his

words or words from other African Americans would not have the same cred-ibility.[51] Other black historians in the late nineteenth and early twentieth cen-turies shared Brown's defensive attitude. Each considered it necessary to defend the value of black soldiers to the Union cause. It was not enough merely to recount what black soldiers had done in the war; they felt a need to prove the worth of African-American troops as well.[52]

Between the lines of these accounts of black Civil War soldiers, written by both veterans and nonveterans in the African-American community, was also a defensiveness about black men as men. That is, black authors felt ob-ligated not only to vindicate the performance of black men as soldiers but also to demonstrate repeatedly that they had fought like men. This insecu-rity manifested itself in passages that were replete with gushing descriptions of the manly behavior of African-American soldiers on the battlefield and elsewhere. The purpose of such passages was to leave the reader with no doubt that black soldiers had exhibited all the requisite masculine virtues of warriors. *A History of the Negro Troops* provides a typical, if more elo-quent than average, example of the language of manliness employed by contemporary African-American authors in characterizing black soldiers. Williams wrote:

> He [the black soldier] disappointed his enemies and surprised his friends. He was not only impulsive in the onset, but cool and stub-born in repelling an assault. He exhibited the highest qualities of soldiership at Port Hudson in repeatedly assaulting the enemy in strong works with great physical obstructions to contend with. It was true he had the inspiration and poetry of numbers to incite him to deeds of valor; but at Milliken's Bend he was a raw recruit, and yet he did his fighting with the bayonet, often dying with his antagonist's steel in his body. Often he transfixed the enemy, and showed him-self possessed of great personal courage when every semblance of order and organization had melted in the heat of battle. At Olustee and Honey Hill, at Poison Springs and Chaffin's Farm, he proved that he was endowed with that military intelligence of unit that make the concrete strength of an army. The Negro was a soldier in every sense of the word.[53]

To be fair to Williams and other black authors, white Americans certainly gave them ample cause for their defensive approach. As has been seen, many general histories of the war often belittled the role of black soldiers. Yet it was not merely history that signaled the disdain of some white Americans. From the earliest days after the war, black veterans were slighted. They were excluded from the Grand Review of the Union Army through Washington, D.C., in May 1865, although some black military laborers were allowed to march for the amusement of the spectators.[54] Physiological information gathered by the U.S. Sanitary Commission on African-American troops was used soon after the war to explain away their satisfactory wartime performance and provide a "scientific" explanation for the general inferiority of African Americans. Poorly trained operatives measured the height, weight, and other physical characteristics of nearly 2,900 black soldiers as part of a larger study of 16,000 Union troops. Analysis of the data supported many popular racist beliefs of the day, including notions that African Americans were more apelike than whites, that racial mixing made mulattos less hardy than "full-blooded" Africans, and that black men's brains were smaller than those of white men.[55] Thus, black Civil War veterans displayed such defensiveness in their memory of the war because the slights they received had wounded their manhood to such an extent that it was virtually impossible for them to respond in any other way. They felt obliged to defend their manly honor.

This insecurity displayed by black veterans stands in stark contrast to the aggressive manhood of African-American troops immediately after the war. At that time, anything had seemed possible, but by the late nineteenth century, the limits to their manhood had become readily apparent to African-American veterans and to other men of their race. Attacks on their manly status were appearing virtually everywhere they turned, whether through segregation laws, the denial of the ballot box, or histories of the Civil War that slandered African-American troops.

However, perhaps more bothersome to black veterans was the forgetfulness that many white Americans manifested about their military exploits. This growing amnesia troubled black ex-soldiers greatly. They were proud of their Civil War service. Recruited under dangerous circumstances, facing the distinct possibility of death or re-enslavement if captured, discriminated against by an army that had promised them equal treatment, black soldiers had fought and died as bravely as white troops had. They had proved their manhood in the most definitive fashion, on the field of battle, yet many in white America seemed unaware of their accomplishments.

On occasion, black Civil War veterans lashed out against this forgetfulness and the way that it aggravated their sense of wounded manhood.

This feeling of exclusion from Civil War memory explains the 1895 lament of Christian A. Fleetwood that, "after each war, of 1776, of 1812, and of 1861, history repeats itself in the absolute effacement of remembrance of the gallant deeds done for the country by its brave black defenders and their relegation to outer darkness."[56] Fleetwood was not alone in his lament. At the end of his book on the Civil War, Williams also condemned the neglect of black soldiers in mainstream commemorations of the conflict. "The deathless deeds of the white soldier's valor are not only embalmed in song and story, but carved in marble and bronze."[57] But black men had received no such acknowledgment.

To correct this injustice, some black veterans pushed for a memorial to their wartime service. During the late nineteenth century, numerous monuments were being erected in commemoration of white Civil War soldiers, both Union and Confederate. Yet none of these monuments honored black soldiers. African Americans simply lacked the resources to build impressive monuments, and the lack of such monuments put them at a serious disadvantage in the battle for memory. As one scholar put it, "Blacks could never anchor their memory of the Civil War in . . . public spaces . . . in the same manner that whites could."[58] If monuments to black soldiers were to be built, the money would have to come from sources outside the African-American community. George W. Williams, for instance, proposed that the federal government build a monument to black Civil War soldiers near Howard University in Washington, D.C. He provided a detailed plan for a monument that would acknowledge the roles played by African Americans in the Union army and navy, the prominent battles in which they had fought, and the number of men who had served and died.[59] Williams certainly was not the first former soldier to call for a monument to honor the contributions of himself and his comrades. In December 1884, Charles Sumner Post No. 9 in Washington, D.C., organized a meeting of African-American veterans to begin pushing for the construction of a national monument to black soldiers. Despite the prominent participants, which included Robert Smalls (who was then a member of the U.S. House of Representatives) and Blanche K. Bruce, the first black man to serve a full term in the U.S. Senate, nothing appears to have come of the gathering, since no monument to black soldiers was ever built in the nation's capital during the lifetimes of the men who had fought in the war.[60] They simply could not convince the federal government to fund the project, nor could they raise the money from within the impoverished black community.

African-American soldiers did not go entirely uncommemorated among the numerous structures built to honor the men who had fought on both sides in the war. Indeed, one of the most impressive and enduring Civil War monuments was Augustus Saint-Gaudens's bas-relief of Robert Gould Shaw and the 54th Massachusetts Infantry, unveiled on the Boston Commons in 1897 (see fig. 10). Saint-Gaudens depicted a dignified but determined Colonel Shaw on horseback in the midst of his regiment on the march. The sculpture lavished considerable attention on each soldier, resulting in individual portraits of the anonymous mass of black troops. With true artistic genius, he created a timeless monument that did not become garish as artistic tastes changed, a fate suffered by many of its counterparts across the country honoring white soldiers and sailors.[61]

Although Saint-Gaudens's masterpiece was welcomed by African-American veterans nationwide, it was not a true monument to all black Civil War soldiers. It commemorated a particular regiment, the 54th Massachusetts, rather than the mass of African Americans who had served in the United States Colored Troops or the Union navy. The monument also subordinated the black soldiers to Colonel Shaw. Shaw is on horseback, while his men march on foot, mirroring in art the racial hierarchy prevalent in the United States in the late nineteenth century. In addition, the Shaw memorial was located in Boston, which, although a major East Coast city, could not showcase the monument in the national consciousness as prominently as if it had been located in Washington, D.C., or New York City. Hence, although Saint-Gaudens's sculpture was an impressive exception to the growing amnesia concerning black service in the Civil War in the late nineteenth century, Christian Fleetwood's outrage over African Americans' absence from mainstream memory of the war was more indicative of the turn-of-the-century reality.

The problem of Civil War memory for black veterans was not limited to historical amnesia. Having sacrificed much on the battlefield to obtain freedom and equality for African Americans, these men were also worried about the deteriorating situation of their race in the South. The promise of freedom wrought by the war was in eclipse by the late 1880s. The passage of segregation laws and disfranchisement began to extend across the South, the exploitation of black farmers intensified, and lynching and other violence directed at African Americans increased and went unpunished. Unless black veterans acted to reawaken the public conscience, their wartime sacrifice would be in vain. How could they be warriors and manly victors if what they had fought for was overturned?

In that moment of crisis, African-American veterans found many white Americans indifferent to their concerns, including many of their comrades in the Grand Army of the Republic. Northern white veterans might occasionally invite a prominent black Civil War figure, such as Frederick Douglass, to address them at the annual encampment of the GAR, but they paid little attention to the cause he represented. Likewise, they paid little attention to preserving suffrage and equal citizenship rights for black Americans, a cause being pushed by African-American veterans.

In part, white Union veterans did not join their black counterparts in the quest for black manhood rights because of their vision of the nation at the end of the nineteenth century. As Stuart McConnell pointed out, the GAR's lack of response to the rise of Jim Crow, disfranchisement, lynching, and the crop lien system was a product of their outmoded worldview. According to McConnell, that worldview "embraced an antebellum form of liberal capitalism rather than a linguistic-cultural prescription, emphasized republic preservation rather than dynamic change, and treated the Civil War as an unassailable monument rather than an unequivocal triumph. It was peculiar because it described the United States of 1860 better than it described the United States of 1890."[62] In other words, many white Northern veterans continued to hold an idealized vision of the United States as it had been before the Civil War. African Americans fit awkwardly, if at all, into this picture, so black people were largely ignored. For African Americans, the war had been primarily a war of liberation, but for white veterans, it remained first and foremost a war to save the Union. Northern white soldiers cheered the end of slavery, which they saw as incompatible with the free labor system that was an integral part of their liberal-capitalist ideology, but to them, the important outcome of the war remained the preservation of the Union. For such white veterans, emancipation did not necessarily translate into support for black suffrage and citizenship rights.

Indeed, some white Union veterans who happened to learn about their black counterparts' interpretation of the war were troubled by what they heard. Typical in this respect was Andrew S. Graham, judge advocate of the

GAR in Louisiana and Mississippi before the national organization forced that department to accept African-American posts. Living in Louisiana, he encountered African-American veterans at Chalmette, the federal military cemetery near New Orleans. Like his white Southern neighbors, he could not conceive of black soldiers having been active players in the war. In Graham's mind, the liberation of slaves was the result of the sacrifice of white Union soldiers. "The colored man was not a factor at all," he confidently told the white veterans at the 1891 Detroit encampment of the GAR. "It was for him you were working. He has benefited by it all, by your sacrifices, and yet he doesn't recognize it." Consequently, it bothered him to hear black veterans at Chalmette boast of liberating themselves. As Graham put it, "I heard not three months ago in the same cemetery a colored man say that he had nothing to thank the United States for, it was by their own right brawny arms that they won their freedom."[63]

Although not every white Union veteran had the occasion to be offended like Graham, it is fair to say that by the end of the nineteenth century, differing memories of the Civil War made a meaningful postwar alliance between white and black Union veterans a doubtful proposition. To white veterans, all that mattered about the war was that the Union had been saved (even if, in reality, industrialization, immigration, and other changes meant that the nation they had saved was fast disappearing). They might to varying degrees suspect ex-Confederates of continued disloyalty and respond when politicians raised its specter, if only to insist that the politicians remember to vote for more generous pensions for veterans, but few white Northern veterans harbored any illusions about a new Southern rebellion. For most white veterans, the war was over, Northern dominance was secured, and nothing more needed to be done but to preserve the status quo.

Another reason why black Civil War veterans found their white counterparts lukewarm to notions of equal rights for African Americans was the gradual rapprochement between white Union veterans and their Confederate counterparts that gained momentum in the 1890s. Blue-Gray reunions proliferated in that decade and the decades that followed. As the antipathies of the war subsided, reconciliation occurred based on a mutual respect for the courage and the authenticity of each side's convictions. Although white Northern veterans continued to believe that the Confederates had erred in rebelling against the Union, they accepted their former enemies as men who had made an honorable mistake. The peacemaking between white Union veterans and former Confederate soldiers shunted memories of blacks' wartime service and their postwar concerns aside. The growing regard of white Grand Army men for their counterparts in the United Confederate Veterans left their black comrades in the GAR increasingly in the shadows. The reconciliation of white Northern and Southern veterans also made it easier for the former group to accept the rise of the Jim Crow South by making their black former comrades seem less like real men, not worthy of their respect or equal citizenship. Although not all white Union veterans were comfortable with the repressive Jim Crow system, their reconciliation with Confederate veterans was an implicit sign that they did not intend to actively resist it either.[64]

The reconciliation of white Union and Confederate veterans was indicative of the increasing success white Southerners had in selling their version of the war to a national audience. Black veterans and other African Americans encountered ignorance of and indifference to their emancipationist view of the war because, in an era of virulent racism, the Lost Cause had an appeal to mainstream America. Although many Union veterans were not ready to buy into the view that the South's wartime aims had been noble and that the Confederacy had been defeated only by superior numbers, many accepted the ideology of white supremacy at its foundation. As their bitterness toward their former enemies receded and their gratitude to black veterans evaporated in the racist atmosphere of the late nineteenth and early twentieth centuries, they could grow to respect ex-Confederates. Likewise, racist ideology made it increasingly easy not to take the manhood of black veterans seriously. Hence, as white Union veterans gravitated toward what David Blight in his recent study of the Civil War described as a "reconciliationist vision," they abandoned whatever support they had had for the equality and citizenship rights of black veterans and other African Americans.[65] Although racism was not an explicit part of this reconciliationist vision, as it was with the Lost Cause, it was implicit.

Black veterans were clearly bothered by the way some of their white Union counterparts were abandoning them and insulting the manhood they believed they had proved so definitively in the war. Their reaction no doubt accounts for the bewilderment of Robert Johnson in 1891 when he told his white GAR comrades in Detroit, "If you turn your back upon us whom shall we look to, where shall we go?"[66] African-American veterans had hoped that white veterans would side with them in the battle to preserve their gains from the war, but by the early 1890s, they realized that Union veterans were more interested in sectional reconciliation than in racial justice. Even a few former Confederates could not help but feel a small bit of sympathy for the cold shoulder black veterans were beginning to receive from their erstwhile allies. As one black veteran, William Murrell Jr., poignantly described it, "Those who loved to shake hands with the gray refused to decorate at Chalmette on Memorial Day, and we did it while they stood around, and the rebels said to us, 'You boys have our sympathies. Don't you see how your old friends treat you?'" It must have been especially galling to Murrell's manly pride to be reminded by Confederate veterans, of all people, how wide the chasm had become between black Civil War veterans and their white comrades.[67]

In the face of such growing alienation, black veterans could do little but vainly try to redirect the attention of white Union veterans to the past in a bid to revive the wartime alliance. Black veterans consistently, and usually gently, reminded white veterans of the assistance they had rendered them during the war. As one African-American veteran put it to his white comrades at the national encampment of the GAR in 1891, "Remember that in the dark days when you . . . were struggling to maintain this country, it was the black man that came to your assistance and stood by until the last enemy was gone."[68] Now was the time for white veterans to discharge that manly debt of honor. The problem was that few white Union veterans felt that they owed such a debt; because of their racist sentiments, many of them increasingly doubted that their black former comrades were fully men.

African Americans also tried to revive the wartime alliance by celebrating as heroes those white Northerners who had supported their cause during the war. In particular, they singled out Robert Gould Shaw. In his history of black troops in the Civil War, George W. Williams proved particularly obsequious in his treatment of the martyred colonel. In proposing a black veterans' memorial in Washington, D.C., Williams suggested naming the park in which the monument would stand for Shaw rather than for a heroic black soldier. He thought that naming the park for Shaw was "eminently proper." "He came from a noble race of men," Williams wrote. "He was pure as he was just, beautiful as he was good, patriotic as he was brave." Also important, Williams continued, was Shaw's particular service at the head of black troops. "It would quicken the pulse of national patriotism, it would elevate the feelings of the Negro, it would inform the Present, instruct the Future, and bind the friends of freedom to the generous heart of the nation," he wrote.[69] Through Shaw and other heroic white friends to the black race, African-American veterans like Williams tried to create connections of memory with white Union veterans. Revered among both white and black veterans in the GAR, Shaw would be the means to link their memories of the Civil War. However, many white Union veterans did not share this admiration for Shaw, a man whose sacrifice they increasingly forgot about as the years went by, if they had ever been aware of him at all.

Increasingly neglected and condescended to, black Civil War veterans threw themselves on the mercy of their white comrades in the GAR. Realizing their relative powerlessness within the Union veterans' fraternity, some black veterans' masculine pride was not above self-abasement. For example, at the 1891 Detroit encampment, Robert Johnson, after expressing his fear that the rise of Jim Crow might lead to segregated departments or, even worse, to the expulsion of African Americans from the GAR, ended his statement on a conciliatory note. Although he feared the worst from his white comrades, Johnson expressed the hope that they would uphold the principle of racial equality in the Grand Army instead of accepting formal segregation in the organization. "I see too many honest faces here for that," Johnson told the encampment. "I see principle here. I see charity here and I see loyalty."[70] With diplomatic words, he explicitly appealed to their generosity and implicitly appealed to the memories of shared cause and shared sacrifice in an attempt to shore up the status of African Americans in the GAR and preserve the fraying and increasingly illusory ties between white and black Union veterans.

As Johnson's approach demonstrates, there was little else but words that black veterans could employ to persuade white veterans and other Americans. However, their efforts were more and more for naught as they struggled against the ideological current of the nation. Although many of their ex-officers and other white Americans who had embraced the emancipationist vision never forgot their manly service, in the half century between the end of the Civil War and U.S. entry into World War I, the rest of the nation grew increasingly forgetful, apathetic, or even hostile to their accomplishments in the atmosphere of virulent racism that permeated the United States by the early twentieth century. Yet even in such an unfavorable environment, former soldiers did not give up their efforts to sway white America. Elite men such as George W. Williams and Joseph T. Wilson energetically and, in the case of Williams, eloquently reminded the nation how they had helped liberate themselves and their people as Union soldiers and sailors. Certainly, their efforts were not totally in vain, for the African-American community continued to pay homage to them throughout this period as they took their places of honor in its public celebrations, even as their ranks grew thinner with each passing year. But their failure to win the battle of memory, as well as other defeats they suffered during the postwar period, meant that black Civil War veterans could claim at best only an incomplete success in their quest for manhood. They knew that they were men, they had proved that they were men, but they could not force white Americans with racist notions to accept that fact.

# Epilogue

S O HOW DID BLACK VETERANS fare in their quest for manhood? The post-war period was at best a mixed success for these men. On the one hand, the Civil War left a significant positive legacy for the black soldiers who survived the conflict, one that validated their manhood. They enjoyed a privileged position compared with other African Americans in the post-war period. The 1890 census found a disproportionate percentage of them in the North and in the growing urban centers of the South, and as a group, they enjoyed more prosperity than other African Americans did. Veterans were widely admired in the black community, and their contribution to the Union victory helped soften the attitude of many white Northerners toward them as well, especially former soldiers. African-American veterans also benefited from the largess of the federal government toward Union veterans and their families, particularly in the form of military pensions.

On the other hand, the postwar triumphs of black veterans were tempered by the incompleteness and impermanence of some of their gains. Immediately after the Civil War, black occupation troops and returning veterans became the target of widespread violence by white Southerners who were unwilling to recognize them as men and felt dishonored when they tried to exercise their manhood. In later years, black veterans also suffered from belittlement and a growing forgetfulness outside their own community about their wartime accomplishments, and too often, they saw the citizenship rights they had earned through military service taken away. Informal marriage also limited their ability to assert their authority within their families; on the whole, however, freedom increased their standing there at a somewhat faster pace than among their nonveteran contemporaries. Consequently, the experience of former soldiers and sailors in the postwar period was an ambiguous victory, in that their lives were better after the Civil War, but not unequivocally so. They achieved an impressive measure of "Manhood & Equality," but it was in some ways deficient or fleeting.

If longevity was the ultimate test of manhood among black Civil War veterans, then Joseph Clovese was the winner. Except for living to extreme old age, however, there was little remarkable about his life. The descriptive card in his compiled service record at the National Archives in Washington, D.C., indicates that he was born around 1844 in St. Bernard Parish, Louisiana. He grew up there on the plantation of his French-born owner and enlisted in the Union army in 1863. Clovese served just over two years until his discharge at De Valls Bluff, Arkansas, in January 1866. Like many other African-American soldiers in the Mississippi Valley, he never participated in a major battle, just a few skirmishes. He did mostly garrison and fatigue duty. After the war, Clovese worked at the gruesome task of reburying the war dead at Vicksburg and then obtained a job as a civilian employee of the postwar army's quartermaster department. Later, the veteran worked for a decade on steamships and flatboats traveling the Mississippi River before settling in Slidell, Louisiana, where he gardened, farmed, and worked at a lumber-yard for a time.

Indeed, the only thing truly unusual about Joseph Clovese's life was its length. Most black men of his generation did not see their fiftieth birthdays, so it is not surprising that by dying at age 107, he survived not only his children but his grandchildren as well. Clovese was conscious of his incredible longevity and that he had outlived his era. Although he enjoyed such innovations as the radio, the mid-twentieth-century world seemed a scary place to him. "There are more troubles now than I ever remember," he told an interviewer a few years before his death. "It's a bad, bad, bad world. It's just wars and more wars coming."[1] Perhaps his words reflected Clovese's realization that the world had become a more dangerous place since the nineteenth century. The carnage of the Civil War paled in comparison to the slaughter and genocide associated with World Wars I and II. Clovese also lived long enough to witness the advent of atomic warfare, the start of the Cold War, and the prospect of the human race annihilating itself.[2] It is little wonder then that this nineteenth-century man was frightened by the twentieth century.

Time finally caught up to Joseph Clovese in the summer of 1951. A few years before, he had joined the great migration, taken north by his companion and caregiver Valerie Daniels. In March of that year, he appeared at the Veterans Administration (VA) hospital in Dearborn, Michigan, complaining of chest and abdominal pain. Yet his appearance and mental faculties were such that the VA staff had a hard time believing that he was 107 years old.

Clovese stayed at the hospital until late May, when he was released after repeatedly expressing a strong desire to be part of the annual Memorial Day parade in Dearborn and the Fourth of July festivities, if his health held up that long. It apparently did, but barely. He was readmitted to the Dearborn VA hospital in a coma on July 9. Clovese managed to regain consciousness for a short time, but he slipped back into a coma and died on July 13, 1951. With his passing, black Civil War veterans' quest for manhood came to a definitive end.[3]

Or did it? Around the time of Joseph Clovese's death, African Americans began to see encouraging changes made possible by the civil rights movement. Clovese had been there for its first years. He died before the milestone 1954 Supreme Court decision in *Brown v. Board of Education,* which invalidated the separate but equal doctrine of *Plessy v. Ferguson.* But Clovese had lived long enough to hear of President Harry S. Truman's 1948 order desegregating the U.S. armed forces. This development must have seemed wondrous to a man who had come of age in an era when black men had to fight just for the right to fight. Now black men not only had won the right to serve but were deemed by the commander in chief, himself a white Southerner, man enough to serve side by side with whites. Had he lived another decade, Clovese would have seen the Second Reconstruction come in earnest to the South, and he would have witnessed the rights that he and other black soldiers had fought for finally begin to be realized with greater applicability and permanence.

Although Clovese and his comrades did not live to experience the Second Reconstruction, they were beneficiaries of it historically. That is, the civil rights movement led to a resurgence of historical research about black Civil War soldiers. Certainly, literature on these men had never entirely disappeared, but like most African-American history in the first part of the twentieth century, such works were few and could rarely find mainstream publishers in either the commercial or the academic world. There was, for example, no book-length history of black troops in the Civil War published after the late 1880s, and until after World War II, most scholarly articles on the subject appeared in publications such as the *Journal of Negro History.* Like other historical literature on African Americans in the early twentieth century, writing on black Civil War soldiers was segregated in publications that served a mostly black readership and garnered little attention in the larger society. As two bibliographers of black Americans in the U.S. military aptly stated, "The treatment of the Black soldier [in historical writing] was a reflection of the treatment of the larger black population."[4]

When the treatment of black people in the United States began to improve after World War II, so did the coverage of black Civil War veterans and, most importantly, their historical reputation. The rehabilitation was part of a larger reassessment of African Americans in which historians at first wrote more sympathetically about their experience and eventually came to see them as active players in the history of the United States. The trajectory of writing on black Civil War soldiers very much fit this scenario, especially the first post–World War II book on black troops in the Civil War, Dudley Taylor Cornish's *The Sable Arm* (1956). Given the long neglect of his subject in mainstream writing on the Civil War, it is understandable that Cornish's chief aim was to resurrect knowledge of black soldiers serving and fighting in the Union army. In other words, *The Sable Arm* was largely a compassionate narrative of the black struggle to participate meaningfully in the Civil War, or, as the author stated, "to show the gradual emergence of the Negro soldier as a member of the Union army and to assess his contribution to that army and to the outcome of the war."[5]

Yet, as kind as Cornish was to black soldiers, he and other early revisionist authors tended to neglect how these men had actually thought and acted during the conflict. They wrote about these men sympathetically, but still more as objects than as thinking and feeling human beings. In the last few decades, the best scholarship on African-American troops in the Civil War has tried to understand them as real people with ideas, beliefs, and emotions that they acted on and as individuals who had an impact on the world around them, rather than merely as passive figures being acted on. Books such as the Freedmen and Southern Society Project's monumental *The Black Military Experience* (1982) and Joseph T. Glatthaar's *Forged in Battle* (1990) let African-American soldiers tell their own stories and probed their actions and motivations. Far from portraying them as subhuman dupes of the Yankees (as Edward A. Pollard did in 1866), historians writing on black Civil War soldiers since 1980 have generally depicted them as humble men caught up in extraordinary circumstances. Hence, the portrayal of African-American troops has undergone an almost complete reversal since World War II, showing these men to be individuals who, under difficult circumstances, tried to do the best they could for themselves, their families, and the community, within the limits of their background and the restrictions placed on them, which they valiantly resisted when their sense of justice was offended. Though perhaps not as positive as the history that black soldiers themselves articulated back in the nineteenth century, the profile and reputation of these men have improved greatly due to the work of academic historians since World War II, in contrast to the neglect, misunderstanding, and defamation they encountered during their lifetimes.

This improved image eventually moved beyond academia into the realm of popular culture, where African-American soldiers of the Civil War have come to enjoy an even more glowing reputation. The seminal event that allowed them to transcend scholarship and achieve wider acclaim was the release of the film *Glory* (1989). If a picture is worth a thousand words, then this Hollywood film easily exceeded the effects of decades of scholarly writing on black soldiers, at least in terms of its impact on the general public. In two hours, *Glory* successfully captured in cinematic fashion the quest for manhood of the 54th Massachusetts Infantry. Although the film contained some factual inaccuracies, on the whole, it fairly represented the spirit of yearning for manly respect that was at the heart of African-American service for the Union during the Civil War and that continued for the rest of these men's lives. Just as *A Birth of a Nation* (1915) demonized black soldiers and made Confederate soldiers and the Ku Klux Klan seem heroic and even romantic at the beginning of the twentieth century, *Glory* rehabilitated African-American troops at the end of that century. Instead of being depicted as pawns of evil Yankees and as lusting uncontrollably after white women, they were shown as brave men fighting discrimination that insulted their manhood, even as many of them stoically went to their deaths with Colonel Shaw in a courageous but foolhardy assault on Fort Wagner, South Carolina.

*Glory* not only ignited interest in the experience of black Civil War soldiers in the mainstream culture but also led to renewed enthusiasm for these men in the African-American community. For example, before the movie's release, there were few black participants in the Civil War reenactment community, which had been dominated by white men—many with Confederate sympathies. Since the movie's release, according to Cathy Stanton and Stephen Belyea, fifteen black reenactors' organizations have appeared, five based on the 54th Massachusetts and ten patterning themselves on other African-American Civil War regiments. In their quest for authenticity, some of the black reenactment units have even recruited white reenactors to serve as their "officers" (black men still led the companies behind the scenes).[6] The renewed attention prompted by *Glory* was at least partly responsible for the building of a national memorial to black Civil War soldiers and sailors in Washington, D.C., unveiled in July 1998. Located near the entrance to the U Street–Cardozo stop on the Green Line of the Metrorail system, the memorial seeks to fulfill the vision of George W. Williams for a monument to black soldiers and sailors in the nation's capital. Designed and crafted by Ed Hamilton, perhaps the most gifted African-American sculptor working today, the monument honors the black men who served in the Union both individually, with each of their names on its three "Walls of Honor," and collectively, through Hamilton's stunning "Spirit of Freedom" sculpture. Built with private money, the African-American Civil War Memorial also demonstrates the financial progress of the black community in being able to honor its heroes and successfully raise money from outside sources, both of which the Civil War generation was largely unable to do when it came to building physical monuments.[7]

In short, with growing positive attention from both scholars and the general public, African-American veterans have enjoyed an impressive, if posthumous, rehabilitation in Civil War memory since the end of World War II. Although the history of black soldiers did not serve the needs of sectional reconciliation, virulent racism, industrialization, urbanization, and overseas expansion in the early decades of the twentieth century, it did serve the needs of a nation trying to reconcile its ideals with reality in the midst of the Cold War, a mostly ideological conflict that increasingly called on the nation to live up to those principles. Black Civil War soldiers would become an inspiration for the post–World War II generations that renewed the battle for freedom and equality, role models for black men still looking for respect in mainstream society at the end of the twentieth century, and heroes for Americans who embraced racial tolerance and multiculturalism in a world where both seemed increasingly under attack as the twenty-first century approached. That is, they would be one rallying point for the black community as it sought to counteract the propaganda of neo-Confederates that exaggerated the support of the so-called faithful Negroes to the Southern cause, and as they struggled to remove symbols of the Confederacy from places of honor in government institutions and from state flags in the South. Hence, although these men did not win the battle for memory that they fought during their lifetimes, their efforts to articulate their experience ensured that it would be rediscovered and eventually become an important part of the mainstream history of the Civil War and a tool in the ongoing battle over the conflict's memory in present-day culture wars. These developments represent the ultimate triumph of the black veterans, much better than the victory, ambiguous at best, they enjoyed during their lifetimes.

# Statistical Appendix

*After the Glory* is based primarily on information gathered from two study groups: a random sample of 1,044 black Civil War soldiers, and a second group consisting of 204 African-American veterans who engaged in notable activities in the postwar period. The aim of examining these two groups is to understand the lives of both ordinary and extraordinary veterans. Studying ordinary veterans helps uncover the general patterns of their existence, how they fit into the postwar African-American community, and their relations with white veterans of the Civil War, Union and Confederate. Exploration of the careers of notable black veterans is important not only because of their role in postwar politics and as leaders in the black community but also because they most fully articulated the meaning of the Civil War for African-American veterans.

The random sample is drawn from the "Index to Compiled Service Records of Volunteer Union Soldiers Who Served with the United States Colored Troops" (Microfilm No. M589) at the National Archives in Washington, D.C. The selection strategy was to choose just over 1,000 soldiers at even intervals throughout the ninety-eight reels of microfilmed index cards—one for each soldier; the index cards were arranged alphabetically by surname, first name, and middle name and initial, and then in ascending order by regiment and company.

After the subjects for the random sample group were identified, I looked up each subject individually to see if there was a Civil War pension application in that subject's name. Two pension indexes were consulted at the National Archives: "General Index to Pension Files, 1861–1934" (Microfilm No. T288), and "Organization Index to Pension Files of Veterans Who Served between 1861 and 1900" (Microfilm No. T289). Of the 1,044 subjects in the random sample group, 534, or just over half (51.1 percent), appeared in either or both of these pension indexes. This meant that at least one pension application had been filed under his name, either by the veteran personally or by a survivor (widow or parent, or on behalf of a minor child). An examination of each of these files revealed that of the 534 applications, 451 of the black soldiers whose service formed the basis of the application had evidently survived the war. In most of these cases, the veteran himself had applied for a pension, although in some cases he had not lived long enough to do so, and the evidence of survival came from information provided by the family member who eventually applied for a pension.

This indirect method of choosing veterans from among documented survivors of a random sample of African-American soldiers produced a study group whose characteristics were quite similar to the patterns apparent in the population of black Civil War veterans as a whole, as revealed by the 1890 special census. That is, there was a close correspondence between the characteristics of the veterans documented in Civil War pension files and the existing aggregate data on African-American veterans from the special 1890 enumeration. For instance, of the 347 black veterans from the sample group for

# After the Glory

whom a region of residence could be determined from pension files, 22.8 percent resided in the North in 1890, 36.6 percent in the Upper South, 38.6 percent in the Lower South, and 1.2 percent in the West (0.9 percent lived outside of the United States or were in the U.S. Army). By comparison, in 1890, the Census Bureau found 26.8 percent of black veterans resided in the North, 37.2 percent in the Upper South, 34.5 percent in the Lower South, and 1.4 percent in the West. Likewise, there was a close match in the number of veterans living in large cities. About 21.5 percent of black veterans lived in cities with more than 25,000 people in 1890, according to the census. Of the 343 former soldiers in the sample group with urban or rural residence information in their pension files, 22.7 percent lived in cities with populations over 25,000 people. In short, although not perfectly representative of black veterans of the Civil War, the random sample provides a good approximation of the ex-soldiers alive in 1890.

Veterans chosen for the notable group consist primarily, but not exclusively, of black ex-soldiers who held postwar leadership roles. A few notable veterans, however, did not play any leadership roles. Their selection was the result of the availability of unusual research material, such as an autobiography or a manuscript collection. Given the rarity of such materials, it was essential that they be utilized. Most of the subjects in the notable group, however, were culled from the biographical dictionaries of prominent African Americans published since the Civil War.

The notable group is not limited to those persons whose presence in the Union army can be verified; it includes individuals with unconfirmed service claims and men who worked in support capacities in the Union and Confederate forces doing menial labor, spying, scouting, and recruiting. Many of these men who worked as cooks, servants, laborers, teamsters, or in other capacities supporting the military operations of the Union and Confederate armies were veterans of the war in the sense that they experienced military discipline and camp life and came under hostile fire. In addition, the definition of a veteran was broader among African Americans than among whites. There is evidence that some of these support personnel sought to be accepted as veterans in the African-American community, and to some extent, they succeeded (see chapter 6). Hence, *After the Glory* includes these men as source material allows. However, since the lives of soldiers are better documented, they are the principal subjects of this book.

The notable group was culled from the following sources: William J. Simmons, *Men of Mark: Eminent, Progressive, Rising* (1887); H. F. Kletzing and W. H. Crogman, *Progress of a Race: The Remarkable Advancement of the American Negro from the Bondage of Slavery, Ignorance and Poverty to the Freedom of Citizenship, Intelligence, Affluence, Honor and Trust* (1897); Charles Alexander, *One Hundred Distinguished Leaders* (1899); J. L. Nichols and William H. Crogman, *Progress of a Race: The Remarkable Advancement of the American Negro from the Bondage of Slavery, Ignorance and Poverty to the Freedom of Citizenship, Intelligence, Affluence, Honor and Trust*, revised and enlarged (1920); Frank Lincoln Mather, ed., *Who's Who of the Colored Race: A General Biographical Dictionary of Men and Women of Negro Descent* (1915); Clement Richardson et al., eds., *The National Cyclopedia of the Colored Race* (1919); Rayford W. Logan and Michael R. Winston, eds., *Dictionary of American Negro Biography* (1982); Eric Foner, *Freedom's Lawmakers: A Directory of Black Officeholders during Reconstruction* (1993).

*Table 1.* Regional Distribution of African Americans in 1890: Civil War Veterans versus the General Population

|  | Civil War Veterans | | General Population | |
| --- | --- | --- | --- | --- |
|  | No. | % | No. | % |
| Upper South[a] | 20,032 | 37.2 | 2,397,694 | 32.1 |
| Lower South[b] | 18,705 | 34.8 | 4,494,431 | 60.1 |
| North[c] | 14,427 | 26.8 | 543,707 | 7.3 |
| West[d] | 635 | 1.2 | 36,908 | 0.5 |
| Total | 53,799 | | 7,472,740 | |

[a]Delaware, District of Columbia, Kentucky, Maryland, Missouri, North Carolina, Tennessee, Virginia, and West Virginia.
[b]Alabama, Arkansas, Florida, Georgia, Louisiana, Mississippi, Oklahoma, South Carolina, and Texas.
[c]Connecticut, Illinois, Indiana, Iowa, Kansas, Maine, Massachusetts, Michigan, Minnesota, New Hampshire, New Jersey, New York, Ohio, Pennsylvania, Rhode Island, Vermont, and Wisconsin.
[d]Arizona, California, Colorado, Idaho, Montana, Nebraska, Nevada, New Mexico, North Dakota, Oregon, South Dakota, Utah, Washington, and Wyoming.
*Sources:* U.S. Census Bureau, *Report on Population of the United States at the Eleventh Census: 1890, Part II* (Washington, D.C.: GPO, 1897), 803; U.S. Census Bureau, *Compendium of the Eleventh Census: 1890, Part III* (Washington, D.C.: GPO, 1897), 473.

*Table 2.* Sector of Employment: Comparison of Black and White Union Veterans, Confederate Veterans, and Black Nonveterans in 1890

|  | Black Union Veterans | | White Union Veterans | | Confederate Veterans | | Black Nonveterans[a] | |
| --- | --- | --- | --- | --- | --- | --- | --- | --- |
|  | No. | % | No. | % | No. | % | No. | & |
| Unskilled | 26,320 | 49.8 | 194,189 | 21.3 | 36,401 | 9.6 | 176,596 | 40.4 |
| Artisan, skilled | 4,484 | 8.5 | 186,626 | 20.5 | 34,847 | 9.2 | 27,110 | 6.2 |
| Domestic and personal service | 2,541 | 4.8 | 15,074 | 1.7 | 2,795 | 0.7 | 13,476 | 3.1 |
| Business entrepreneurs | 18,089 | 34.2 | 441,559 | 48.4 | 275,062 | 72.6 | 214,059 | 49.0 |
| Professional | 1,408 | 2.7 | 74,357 | 8.2 | 29,791 | 7.9 | 5,349 | 1.2 |
| Total | 52,842 | | 911,805 | | 378,896 | | 436,590 | |

[a]Black men aged forty-five and older in 1890 who had not served in the Civil War.
*Source:* U.S. Census Bureau, *Report on Population of the United States at the Eleventh Census: 1890* (Washington, D.C.: GPO, 1897), 1:402–7, 2:807–10.

# After the Glory

Table 3. Survival Rates: Comparison of Black and White Union Veterans, Confederate Veterans, and Black Nonveterans

|  | White Union Veterans | Confederate Veterans | Black Union Veterans | Black Nonveterans[a] |
|---|---|---|---|---|
| Civil War enlistments (army + navy) | 1,811,429 | 750,000 | 196,975 | — |
| Not enlisted |  |  |  | 647,861 |
| Died in service | 323,375 | 258,000 | 36,847 | — |
| War survivors(%) | 1,488,054(82.1) | 492,000(65.6) | 160,128(81.3) | — |
| Alive in 1890(%) | 980,274(54.1) | 428,747(57.1) | 53,799(27.3) | 340,514(52.6) |

[a]Black men aged forty-five and older in 1890 who had not served in the Civil War.
Sources: Ira Berlin, Joseph P. Reidy, and Leslie S. Rowland, eds., Freedom: A Documentary History of Emancipation, 1861–1867, Series II. The Black Military Experience (Cambridge: Cambridge University Press, 1982), 12; Frederick H. Dyer, A Compendium of the War of Rebellion, vol. 1 (New York: Thomas Yoseloff, 1908), 12; E. B. Long with Barbara Long, The Civil War Day by Day: An Almanac, 1861–1865 (New York: Da Capo Press, 1971), 705–6, 709–12; Joseph P. Reidy, "Black Men in Navy Blue during the Civil War, "Prologue 33 (Fall 2001): 156; U.S. Census Bureau, Report on Population of the United States at the Eleventh Census (Washington, D.C.: GPO, 1897), 1:486, 803–4; 2:3–5.

Table 4. Black Officeholders by State, 1867–1877: Veterans versus Nonveterans

|  | Veterans | | Nonveterans | | Total | |
|---|---|---|---|---|---|---|
|  | No. | % | No. | % | No. | % |
| Louisiana | 46 | 31.3 | 164 | 12.4 | 210 | 14.3 |
| South Carolina | 29 | 19.7 | 285 | 21.5 | 314 | 21.3 |
| Mississippi | 24 | 16.3 | 202 | 15.2 | 226 | 15.4 |
| North Carolina | 17 | 11.6 | 163 | 12.3 | 180 | 12.2 |
| Florida | 7 | 4.8 | 51 | 3.8 | 58 | 3.9 |
| Georgia | 5 | 3.4 | 103 | 7.8 | 108 | 7.3 |
| Virginia | 5 | 3.4 | 80 | 6.0 | 85 | 5.8 |
| Alabama | 4 | 2.7 | 163 | 12.3 | 167 | 11.3 |
| District of Columbia | 3 | 2.0 | 8 | 0.6 | 11 | 0.7 |
| Tennessee | 3 | 2.0 | 17 | 1.3 | 20 | 1.4 |
| Arkansas | 2 | 1.4 | 44 | 3.3 | 46 | 3.1 |
| Missouri | 1 | 0.7 | 0 | 0.0 | 1 | 0.1 |
| Texas | 1 | 0.7 | 45 | 3.4 | 46 | 3.1 |
| Total | 147 |  | 1,325 |  | 1,472 |  |

Source: Eric Foner, Freedom's Lawmakers: A Directory of Black Officeholders during Reconstruction (New York: Oxford University Press, 1993), xiv.

*Table 5.* Antebellum Status of Veteran and
Nonveteran Black Officeholders, 1867–1877

| | Veterans | | Nonveterans | |
| --- | --- | --- | --- | --- |
| | No. | % | No. | % |
| Slave | 40 | 32.0 | 339 | 53.6 |
| Free | 72 | 57.6 | 252 | 39.9 |
| Both | 13 | 10.4 | 41 | 6.5 |
| Subtotal | 125 | 100.0 | 632 | 100.0 |
| Unknown | 19 | | 689 | |
| Total | 144 | | 1,321 | |

*Source:* Eric Foner, *Freedom's Lawmakers: A Directory of
Black Officeholders during Reconstruction* (New York:
Oxford University Press, 1993), xviii.

*Table 6.* Racial Ancestry of Veteran and
Nonveteran Black Officeholders, 1867–1877

| | Veterans | | Nonveterans | |
| --- | --- | --- | --- | --- |
| | No. | % | No. | % |
| Black | 45 | 34.4 | 472 | 48.2 |
| Mixed | 86 | 65.6 | 508 | 51.8 |
| Subtotal | 131 | 100.0 | 980 | 100.0 |
| Unknown | 13 | | 341 | |
| Total | 144 | | 1,321 | |

*Source:* Eric Foner, *Freedom's Lawmakers: A Directory of
Black Officeholders during Reconstruction* (New York:
Oxford University Press, 1993), xvi.

*Table 7.* Literacy Status of Veteran and
Nonveteran Black Officeholders, 1867–1877

| | Veterans | | Nonveterans | |
| --- | --- | --- | --- | --- |
| | No. | % | No. | % |
| Literate | 125 | 96.9 | 808 | 80.9 |
| Illiterate | 4 | 3.1 | 191 | 19.1 |
| Subtotal | 129 | 100.0 | 999 | 100.0 |
| Unknown | 15 | | 322 | |
| Total | 144 | | 1,321 | |

*Source:* Eric Foner, *Freedom's Lawmakers: A Directory of
Black Officeholders during Reconstruction* (New York:
Oxford University Press, 1993), xxiv.

*Table 8.* Occupations of Veteran and Nonveteran Black Officeholders, 1867–1877

|  | Veterans | | Nonveterans | |
|---|---|---|---|---|
|  | No. | % | No. | % |
| Unskilled | 34 | 15.2 | 391 | 26.3 |
| Artisan, skilled | 43 | 19.3 | 320 | 21.5 |
| Domestic and personal service | 2 | 0.9 | 18 | 1.2 |
| Business entrepreneurs | 42 | 18.8 | 273 | 18.4 |
| Professional | 102 | 45.7 | 485 | 32.6 |
| Total | 223[a] | | 1,487[a] | |

[a]Some black officeholders had more than one occupation.
*Source:* Eric Foner, *Freedom's Lawmakers: A Directory of Black Officeholders during Reconstruction* (New York: Oxford University Press, 1993), xxi.

*Table 9.* Property Holdings of Veteran and Nonveteran Black Officeholders, 1867–1877

|  | Veterans | | Nonveterans | |
|---|---|---|---|---|
|  | No. | % | No. | % |
| $0 | 14 | 17.9 | 222 | 26.1 |
| $1–500 | 19 | 24.4 | 250 | 29.4 |
| $501–1,000 | 17 | 21.8 | 66 | 7.8 |
| $1,000+ | 28 | 35.9 | 312 | 36.7 |
| Subtotal | 78 | 100.0 | 850 | 100.0 |
| Unknown | 66 | | 471 | |
| Total | 144 | | 1,321 | |

*Source:* Eric Foner, *Freedom's Lawmakers: A Directory of Black Officeholders during Reconstruction* (New York: Oxford University Press, 1993), xxii.

*Table 10.* Pension Application Success: Comparison of White and Black Civil War Veterans and Their Survivors

|  | No. of Applicants | No. Pensioned | % Pensioned |
|---|---|---|---|
| White (n = 545) |  |  |  |
| Veterans | 419 | 388 | 92.6 |
| Widows | 252 | 211 | 83.7 |
| Children | 52 | 26 | 50.0 |
| Parents | 36 | 25 | 69.4 |
| Black (n = 545) |  |  |  |
| Veterans | 350 | 264 | 75.4 |
| Widows | 298 | 181 | 60.7 |
| Children | 40 | 20 | 50.0 |
| Parents | 45 | 16 | 35.5 |

*Source:* "General Index to Pension Files, 1861–1934" (Microfilm No. T288), National Archives, Washington, D.C.

# Notes

## Introduction

1. Rayford W. Logan and Michael R. Winston, eds., *Dictionary of American Negro Biography* (New York: W. W. Norton, 1982), 833–42.

2. James M. Trotter to Edward W. Kinsley, 2 June 1864, Edward W. Kinsley Papers, Special Collections Library, Duke University, Durham, N.C.

3. In the interest of economy, soldiers and sailors will be referred to collectively by the former word.

4. Kenneth M. Stampp, *The Peculiar Institution: Slavery in the Ante-bellum South* (New York: Knopf, 1956); Stanley Elkins, *Slavery: A Problem in American Institutional and Intellectual Life* (Chicago: University of Chicago Press, 1959).

5. John W. Blassingame, *The Slave Community: Plantation Life in the Antebellum South* (New York: Oxford University Press, 1972), 88.

6. Eugene D. Genovese, *Roll, Jordan, Roll: The World the Slaves Made* (New York: Vintage Books, 1974), 486, 489.

7. Herbert G. Gutman, *The Black Family in Slavery and Freedom, 1750–1925* (New York: Vintage Books, 1976), 190.

8. Deborah Gray White, *Ar'n't I a Woman: Female Slaves in the Plantation South* (New York: W. W. Norton, 1985), 153. See also James Oliver Horton, "Freedom's Yoke: Gender Conventions among Antebellum Free Blacks," *Feminist Studies* 12 (Spring 1986): 55; James Oliver Horton and Lois E. Horton, "Violence, Protest and Identity: Black Manhood in Antebellum," in *Free People of Color: Inside the African American Community*, ed. James Oliver Horton (Washington, D.C.: Smithsonian Institution Press, 1993), 94.

9. Maurice Wallace, "'Are We Men? Prince Hall, Martin Delany, and the Masculine Ideal in Black Freemasonry, 1775–1865," *American Literary History* 9 (Fall 1997): 396–97.

10. Michelle Mitchell, "'The Black Man's Burden': African Americans, Imperialism, and Notions of Racial Manhood: 1890–1910," *International Review of Social History* 44 (1999 Supplement): 80. For other recent studies of black manhood in the nineteenth century, see Daniel P. Black, *Dismantling Black Manhood: An Historical and Literary Analysis of the Legacy of Slavery* (New York: Garland Publishing, 1997), 99–170, and Darlene Clark Hine and Earnestine Jenkins, eds., *A Question of Manhood: A Reader in U.S. Black Men's History and Masculinity*, 2 vols. (Bloomington: University of Indiana Press, 1999–2001).

11. Gail Bederman, *Manliness and Civilization: A Cultural History of Gender and Race in the United States: 1880–1917* (Chicago: University of Chicago Press, 1995), 243 nn. 36, 37.

12. Ibid., 21.

13. Ibid., 11.

14. Ira Berlin, "Time, Space, and the Evolution of Afro-American Society on British North America," *American Historical Review* 85 (February 1980): 44–45.

15. Harry L. Watson, *Liberty and Power: The Politics of Jacksonian America* (New York: Hill and Wang, 1990), 232.

16. Gutman, *Black Family in Slavery and Freedom,* 167–68; Eric Foner, *Reconstruction: America's Unfinished Revolution, 1863–1877* (New York: Harper and Row, 1988), 85–87.

**Prologue**

1. Unlike the army, the Union navy accepted free black men from the beginning of the war (and contraband slaves after September 1861) and integrated African Americans into its regular crews. Having long faced greater manpower shortages than the army, the navy had a well-established tradition of black men serving aboard its vessels by the time of the Civil War. However, with racially integrated crews, it is difficult to compile definitive information on the number of African Americans in the Union navy. The number cited has been as high as 29,511, a rough estimate made by the U.S. Navy early in the twentieth century and widely disseminated by Herbert Aptheker in a 1947 article. Later, David Valuska revised this number down to about 10,000 after examining naval enlistment records. More recently, Joseph P. Reidy and a group from Howard University more systematically reexamined those records and increased the figure of black men who served in the Union navy during the Civil War to around 18,000. See Herbert Aptheker, "The Negro in the Union Navy," *Journal of Negro History* 32 (April 1947): 179; David L. Valuska, *The African American in the Union Navy: 1861–1865* (New York: Garland Publishing, 1993), 9–14, 83; Joseph P. Reidy, "Black Men in Navy Blue during the Civil War," *Prologue* 33 (Fall 2001): 156. See also Steven J. Ramold, *Slaves, Sailors, Citizens: African Americans in the Union Navy* (De Kalb: Northern Illinois University Press, 2002), 55–62.

2. Thomas J. Morgan, "Reminiscences of Service with Colored Troops," in *Personal Narratives of Events in the War of the Rebellion Being Papers Read before the Rhode Island Soldiers and Sailors Historical Society* (Providence, R.I.: Rhode Island Soldiers and Sailors Historical Society, 1885), 14.

3. Charles F. Cooney, ed., "I Was . . . Eager to Become a Soldier," *Manuscripts* 26 (Fall 1974): 281.

4. James Oliver Horton, "Freedom's Yoke: Gender Conventions among Antebellum Free Blacks," *Feminist Studies* 12 (Spring 1986): 55.

5. Reid Mitchell, *The Vacant Chair: The Northern Soldier Leaves Home* (New York: Oxford University Press, 1993), 68.

6. Ira Berlin, Joseph P. Reidy, and Leslie S. Rowland, eds., *Freedom: A Documentary History of Emancipation, 1861–1867,* Series II, *The Black Military Experience* (Cambridge: Cambridge University Press, 1982), 362–405; Joseph T. Glatthaar, *Forged in Battle: The Civil War Alliance of Black Soldiers and White Officers* (New York: Free Press, 1990), 169–76.

7. Quoted in Glatthaar, *Forged in Battle,* 170.

8. Berlin et al., *Black Military Experience,* 365–66.

9. Ibid., 366.

10. Ibid., 303–12.

11. Capt. J. A. et al. to Maj. Gen. N. P. Banks, 19 February 1863, in ibid., 316–17; see also Glatthaar, *Forged in Battle*, 123–35; James G. Hollandsworth Jr., *The Louisiana Native Guards: The Black Military Experience during the Civil War* (Baton Rouge: Louisiana State University Press, 1995), 70–83.

12. Anonymous Black Soldier, 4th USCI, New Berne, N.C., to Edwin M. Stanton, Secretary of War, Washington, D.C., 2 October 1865, in Berlin et al., *Black Military Experience*, 654.

13. Ibid., 483–87.

14. Frederick H. Dyer, *A Compendium of the War of the Rebellion*, vol. 1 (New York: Thomas Yoseloff, 1959), 12; E. B. Long with Barbara Long, *The Civil War Day by Day: An Almanac, 1861–1865* (New York: Da Capo Press, 1971), 710. Long cites 360,222 as the most accurate figure for Union dead in the Civil War, with 224,580 of these men dying of disease. Dyer cites the figure of 36,847 black men dead, with 29,658 dying of disease. Subtracting the black figure from the total leaves 323,375 white men dead, with 194,922 dying of disease. Hence, the percentage of black Union soldiers who died of disease is 80.5 percent, and the corresponding percentage of white Union soldiers is 60.3 percent.

15. Berlin et al., *Black Military Experience*, 633–36.

16. Ella Lonn, *Desertion during the Civil War* (New York: Century Company, 1928), 234–35. The percentages stated are arrived at by the following computations: Lonn, citing congressional statistics, indicates that 278,044 Union soldiers deserted during the Civil War of the approximately 2 million men who served. Of these men, 8,607 were black and about 269,508 were white. With 178,975 black men serving and around 1,821,025 white men, the desertion ratio arrived at is 14.8 percent for white soldiers and 4.8 percent for black soldiers. Lonn's figures were largely confirmed by my random sample of black Civil War soldiers. Of the 1,044 soldiers studied, only 67, or 6.4 percent, deserted.

The number of black men who served in the Union army can be determined much more precisely than the number of white men. Because of their almost total federalization and the lack of reenlistments, data on the number of black men who served are much more exact. For the best estimates of the number of white Union soldiers, see Long, *Civil War Day by Day*, 705.

17. Sgt. John Sweeny, Nashville, Tenn., to Brig. Gen. Fisk, 8 October 1865, in Berlin et al., *Black Military Experience*, 615.

18. Ibid., 611–13; John M. Blassingame, "The Union Army as an Educational Institution for Negroes, 1861–1875," *Journal of Negro Education* 34 (Spring 1965): 156.

19. George R. Sherman, *The Negro as a Soldier* (Providence, R.I.: Rhode Island Soldiers and Sailors Historical Society, 1913), 17–18.

20. Of the 1,044 men in the sample group, 169, or 16.2 percent, held the rank of corporal or above at some point in their military service.

21. Glatthaar, *Forged in Battle*, 248.

22. George P. Rawick, ed., *The American Slave: A Composite Autobiography, Supplement, Series 1*, vol. 9, pt. 4, *Mississippi Narratives* (Westport, Conn.: Greenwood Press, 1977), 1877.

23. A. W. Greely, *Reminiscences of Adventure and Service: A Record of Sixty-five Years* (New York: Charles Scribner's Sons, 1927), 98.

24. Chap. James Peet to Adj. Gen. Lorenzo Thomas, 8 June 1864, Letters Received, Adjutant General, U.S. Army, ser. 12, RG 94 (also Document K-549, FSSP).

25. Chap. C. W. Buckley, 47th USCI, to Lieut. A. R. Mills, Adjutant, 47th USCI, 1 August 1864, Letters Received, Adjutant General, U.S. Army, ser. 12, RG 94 (also Document K-541, FSSP); emphasis in original.

26. Ibid.

27. Chap. Peet to Adj. Gen. Thomas, 1 August 1864, RG 94 (also Document K-549, FSSP); emphasis in original.

28. Rawick, *American Slave: Supplement, Series 1*, vol. 10, pt. 5, 2028.

29. George P. Rawick, ed., *The American Slave: A Composite Autobiography, Supplement, Series 2*, vol. 3, pt. 2, *Texas Narratives* (Westport, Conn.: Greenwood Press, 1979), 558.

30. W. E. B. Du Bois, *Black Reconstruction in America: An Essay toward a History of the Part which Black Folk Played in the Attempt to Reconstruct Democracy in America, 1860–1880* (New York: Harcourt, Brace, and Company, 1935), 110.

## Chapter 1. The Postwar Transition

1. Ira Berlin, Joseph P. Reidy, and Leslie S. Rowland, eds., *Freedom: A Documentary History of Emancipation, 1861–1867*, Series II, *The Black Military Experience* (Cambridge: Cambridge University Press, 1982), 733; Joseph T. Glatthaar, *Forged in Battle: The Civil War Alliance of Black Soldiers and White Officers* (New York: Free Press, 1990), 218.

2. Capt. Edwin O. Latimer to Lieut. Col. A. G. Chamberlain, 27 June 1865, in Berlin et al., *Black Military Experience*, 738.

3. E. G. Baker to Messrs. Irby & Ellis & Mosely, 22 October 1865, in ibid., 748.

4. Ibid.

5. H[enry] M. Turner, Columbus, Ga., to Edwin M. Stanton, Secretary of War, Washington, D.C., 14 February 1866, in ibid., 757.

6. Capt. Fred Mosbach to Capt. W. W. Deane, 8 March 1865, in ibid., 760.

7. Gail Bederman, *Manliness and Civilization: A Cultural History of Gender and Race in the United States, 1880–1917* (Chicago: University of Chicago Press, 1995), 12.

8. Bertram Wyatt-Brown, *Southern Honor: Ethics and Behavior in the Old South* (New York: Oxford University Press, 1982), 436.

9. Berlin et al., *Black Military Experience*, 733–34, 736.

10. Alexander Newton, *Out of the Briars: An Autobiography and Sketch of the Twenty-ninth Regiment Connecticut Volunteers* (Philadelphia: A.M.E. Book Concern, 1910), 69–89.

11. Berlin et al., *Black Military Experience*, 771.

12. Elijah Reeves, Clarksville, Tex., to Zachariah Chandler, U.S. Senator, 14 September 1865, in ibid., 774–75.

13. Anonymous to Gen. Daniel Sickles, 13 January 1866, in ibid., 777.

14. Capt. G. E. Stanford et al., Whites Ranch, Tex., to Pres. Andrew Johnson and Sec. of War Edwin M. Stanton, Washington, D.C., 30 May 1866, in ibid., 780.

15. Bell Irvin Wiley describes this punishment as "suspension by the thumbs from a limb or pole in such a manner as to permit only the toes to touch the ground. When left in position for an hour or more, as was not unusual, the victim suffered extreme pain." He indicates that it was a common punishment for "disorderly or disrespectful" conduct. See Bell Irvin Wiley, *Life of Billy Yank: The Common Soldier of the Union* (Baton Rouge: Louisiana State University Press, 1952), 200.

16. Glatthaar, *Forged in Battle,* 223–24; Court Martial of James Allen, Joseph Grien (alias Green), Joseph Nathaniel, and Thomas Howard, 3d USCI, File No. 00 1477, Court Martial Case Files, RG 153.

17. Berlin et al., *Black Military Experience,* 765; Frederick H. Dyer, *A Compendium of the War of the Rebellion,* vol. 3 (New York: Thomas Yoseloff, 1908), 1739.

18. Berlin et al., *Black Military Experience,* 782–83.

19. Order No. 43, Headquarters, 6th USCC, 16 April 1866, in ibid., 788.

20. Charles A. Watkins, near Centerville, Md., to Gen. O. O. Howard, Commissioner of the Freedmen's Bureau, Washington, D.C., 13 March 1866, in ibid., 805.

21. Ibid., 799–810.

22. Quoted in W. Fitzhugh Brundage, "Race, Memory, and Masculinity: Black Veterans Recall the Civil War," in *The War Was You and Me: Civilians in the American Civil War,* ed. Joan E. Cashin (Princeton, N.J.: Princeton University Press, 2002), 137.

23. Maj. George D. Reynolds to Lieut. Stuart Eldridge, 5 October 1865, Letters Sent, Southern District of Mississippi, ser. 2246, RG 105 (also Document A-9074, FSSP).

24. Capt. J. H. Durkee to Col. T. W. Osborn, 28 February 1866, Letters Received, Florida State Assistant Commissioner, ser. 586, RG 105 (also Document A-1044, FSSP).

25. 1st Lieut. W. L. McCullough to Capt. D. H. Williams, 30 April 1866, Narrative Reports of Operations of Subordinate Officers, ser. 242, RG 105 (also Document A-2453, FSSP).

26. Henry Marrs to Edwin M. Stanton, Secretary of War, Washington, D.C., 14 May 1866, Registered Letters Received, Washington Headquarters, ser. 15, RG 105 (also Document A-6032, FSSP).

27. Nell Irvin Painter, *Exodusters: Black Migration to Kansas after Reconstruction* (New York: Alfred A. Knopf, 1977), 75.

28. Berlin et al., *Black Military Experience,* 742, 754–56.

29. Ibid., 743, 763.

30. Clement Richardson et al., eds., *The National Cyclopedia of the Colored Race* (Montgomery, Ala.: National Publishing Company, 1919), 357.

31. James Gilbert Ryan, "The Memphis Riot of 1866: Terror in the Black Community during Reconstruction," *Journal of Negro History* 62 (July 1977): 244.

32. Altina L. Walker, "Community, Class and Race in the Memphis Riot of 1866," *Journal of Social History* 18 (Winter 1984): 235.

33. Quoted in Bobby L. Lovett, "Memphis Riots: White Reaction to Blacks in Memphis, May 1865–July 1866," *Tennessee Historical Quarterly* 38 (Spring 1979): 11–12.

34. Quoted in Kevin W. Hardwick, "'Your Old Father Abe Lincoln Is Dead and Damned': Black Soldiers and the Memphis Riot of 1866," *Journal of Social History* 27 (Fall 1993): 110.

35. Ibid., 113–15.

36. Ibid., 117–18.

37. U.S. Congress, House, Report of the Select Committee on the Memphis Riots, *Memphis Riots and Massacres*, 39th Cong., 1st sess., 1866, 6–7.

38. Hardwick, "'Your Old Father Able Lincoln,'" 119–20.

39. Ibid., 121–22.

40. Walker, "Community, Class and Race," 240.

41. Larry M. Logue, *To Appomattox and Beyond: The Civil War Soldier in War and Peace* (Chicago: Ivan R. Dee, 1996), 87; emphasis in original.

42. Lieut. S. N. Clark to Brig. Gen. C. H. Howard, 31 March 1866, Letters Received, District of Columbia Assistant Commissioner, ser. 456, RG 105 (also Document A-9775, FSSP); J. S. Griffing to Edwin M. Stanton, Secretary of War, Washington, D.C., 2 July 1866, ibid.

43. Col. J. Durrell Greene to Bvt. Lieut. Col. W. L. M. Burger, 25 February 1866, Letters Sent, May 1865–March 1866, ser. 623, RG 393 (also Document C-1703, FSSP).

44. The literature on black soldiers in the postwar U.S. Army is extensive. See Frank N. Schubert, *On the Trail of the Buffalo Soldier: Biographies of African Americans in the U.S. Army, 1866–1917* (Wilmington, Del.: Scholarly Resources, 1995), 495–505.

45. Civil War Service Records of Joseph Ramour (alias Joe Remo), 80th USCI; Milton Denny (alias Charles Davis), 65th USCI; John Spencer, 77th and 85th USCI and 10th USCHA; Edward (alias Edmund) Story, 80th USCI, RG 94.

46. Civil War Pension Files of John Walker, 31st USCI; Austin Waters, 15th USCI, RG 15.

47. Pension File of Henry Womack (alias Thompson), 40th USCI, RG 15.

48. Pension Files of Milton Denny (alias Charles Davis), 65th USCI; Clement Jones, 72d USCI; Charles Key, 111th USCI; Morris Murrell (alias Smith), 107th USCI; John Spencer, 77th and 85th USCI and 10th USCHA; John Walker, 31st USCI; Austin Waters, 15th USCI; Henry Womack (alias Thompson), 40th USCI, RG 15.

49. Of the 451 black veterans I documented in Civil War pension files, only 9 served in the regular U.S. Army after the war.

50. It is worth noting that a few ex-soldiers maintained contact with the army after the war through employment at the national cemeteries, which were established to provide dignified burials for soldiers killed in the war. Erastus Green, a Virginia veteran, worked from 1867 to 1872 in the greenhouse of Arlington National Cemetery. Despite the disabilities he incurred while a prisoner of war, a sympathetic U.S. army captain gave Albert Kelly a job doing light work at the national cemetery in Murfreesboro, Tennessee. Kelly later moved on to work at the national cemetery in Nashville. Other veterans maintained their ties to the army in less formal ways. For instance, Alexander Porter, a Mississippi veteran, worked after his discharge for a former white officer. See Pension Files of Erastus Green, 1st USCI; Albert Kelly, 111th USCI; Alexander Porter, 58th USCI, RG 15.

51. Berlin et al., *Black Military Experience*, 782–83.

52. Steven Hahn, "'Extravagant Expectations' of Freedom: Rumour, Political Struggle, and the Christmas Insurrection Scare of 1865 in the American South," *Past and Present* 157 (November 1997): 127–28.

53. N. Noyes to J. W. Alvord, 18 May 1866, Letters Received by Rev. J. W. Alvord Relating to the Freedmen's Savings Bank, March 1865–April 1870, ser. 157, RG 105 (also Document A-10590, FSSP).

54. George R. Sherman, *The Negro as a Soldier* (Providence, R.I.: Rhode Island Soldiers and Sailors Historical Society, 1913), 18.

55. See McCullough to Williams, 30 April 1866, ser. 242, RG 105 (also Document A-2453, FSSP).

56. Claude F. Oubre, *Forty Acres and a Mule: The Freedmen's Bureau and Black Land Ownership* (Baton Rouge: Louisiana State University Press, 1978), 29–30.

57. Ibid., 165.

58. George Hitchen to Maj. Gen. O. O. Howard, 4 January 1868, Letters Received, Washington Headquarters, ser. 15, RG 105 (also Document A-9534, FSSP); Oubre, *Forty Acres and a Mule,* 165–66.

## Chapter 2. Life Patterns

1. Evangeline Thurber, "The 1890 Census Records of the Veterans of the Union Army," *National Genealogical Society Quarterly* 34 (March 1946): 7–9.

2. Ibid.; U.S. Census Bureau, *Compendium of the Eleventh Census: 1890, Part III* (Washington, D.C.: GPO, 1897), 473.

3. Ira Berlin, Joseph P. Reidy, and Leslie S. Rowland, eds., *Freedom: A Documentary History of Emancipation, 1861–1867,* Series II, *The Black Military Experience* (Cambridge: Cambridge University Press, 1982), 12; U.S. Census Bureau, *Report on Population of the United States at the Eleventh Census: 1890, Part II* (Washington, D.C.: GPO, 1897), 803.

4. Of the sixty-seven interregional moves by black Civil War veterans in the random sample group documented in the pension files, thirty-nine (58.2 percent) were to the North. The North was the most popular destination for black migrants. Between 1870 and 1910, approximately 940,000 African Americans migrated across state boundaries. The largest part of the exodus was from the Atlantic states, which lost 627,000 black residents. A more modest exodus of 192,000 persons took place from the Upper South and the older cotton states of Alabama, Louisiana, and Mississippi; 122,000 people also left the interior border states of Kentucky, Missouri, and Tennessee between 1870 and 1910. The majority of these migrants went to the North, which experienced its first sizable influx of African Americans during this period—627,000 people. Southern states with relatively little development before the Civil War—Florida, Arkansas, Texas, and Oklahoma—also saw a sizable inflow of migrants, gaining 334,000 African Americans. West Virginia and the District of Columbia together gained 78,000 black residents between 1870 and 1910 as African Americans in Virginia and North Carolina headed west and north. See Hope T. Eldridge and Dorothy Swaine Thomas, *Population Redistribution and Economic Growth: United States, 1870–1950,* Part III, *Demographic Analysis and Interrelations* (Philadelphia:

## After the Glory

American Philosophical Society, 1964), 260; William Cohen, *At Freedom's Edge: Black Mobility and the Southern White Quest for Racial Control, 1861–1915* (Baton Rouge: Louisiana State University Press, 1991), 294–97.

5. Civil War Pension Files of Stephen Baxter, 6th USCC; Basil A. Davis, 102d USCI; Joseph Faro, 28th USCI; Charles Frazier, 100th USCI; Edward Head, 120th USCI and 6th USCC; William Lucas, 109th USCI; Richard Simpson, 120th USCI and 6th USCC; Allen Walker (alias Walkup, alias King), 122d USCI, RG 15.

6. Pension Files of Allen Allis (alias Ellis), 68th USCI; George H. Fisher, 59th USCI; John Calvin McMahan, 18th USCI; John Palmer, 53d USCI; William Smith (alias Fry), 60th USCI; Anderson Taylor, 4th USCHA; Henry Taylor, 102d USCI, RG 15.

7. Pension Files of Isaiah Holt, 72d USCI and 13th USCHA; Jacob Hutchinson (alias Abraham I. J. Wright), 4th USCHA; Henry Taylor, 102d USCI, RG 15.

8. Pension File of George H. Fisher, 59th USCI, RG 15.

9. Pension File of Harry Givens, 8th USCHA, RG 15.

10. Ibid; also see Pension Files of Stephen Astor, 117th USCI; Charles Hall, 55th Massachusetts Infantry; Nelson Jeffies, 125th USCI, RG 15.

11. David M. Katzman, *Before the Ghetto: Black Detroit in the Nineteenth Century* (Urbana: University of Illinois Press, 1973), 105–7; Stephan Thernstrom, *The Other Bostonians: Poverty and Progress in the American Metropolis, 1880–1970* (Cambridge, Mass.: Harvard University Press, 1973), 176–94; David A. Gerber, *Black Ohio and the Color Line: 1860–1915* (Urbana: University of Illinois Press, 1976), 60–61; Kenneth L. Kusmer, *A Ghetto Takes Shape: Black Cleveland, 1870–1930* (Urbana: University of Illinois Press, 1976), 66–69; Elizabeth Hafkin Pleck, *Black Migration and Poverty: Boston, 1865–1900* (New York: Academic Press, 1979), 122; Cohen, *At Freedom's Edge*, 96–105.

12. Rayford W. Logan and Michael R. Winston, eds., *Dictionary of American Negro Biography* (New York: W. W. Norton, 1982), 443, 602; *New York Freeman*, 14 March 1885.

13. Joshua McLancthon Addeman, *Reminiscences of Two Years with the Colored Troops* (Providence, R.I.: N. Bang Williams, 1880), 37.

14. Lewis Latimer's hand-written biographical sketch and Edison Pioneer's obituary, Lewis H. Latimer Papers, Schomburg Center for Research of Black Culture, New York, N.Y.; Logan and Winston, *Dictionary of American Negro Biography*, 385–86.

15. George M. Fredrickson, *The Black Image in the White Mind: The Debate on Afro-American Character and Destiny, 1817–1914* (New York: Harper and Row, 1971), 167–68.

16. Leslie H. Fishel, "Northern Prejudice and Negro Suffrage, 1865–1870," *Journal of Negro History* 39 (January 1954): 8–26.

17. Katzman, *Before the Ghetto*, 196–206; Gerber, *Black Ohio and the Color Line*, 247–70; Kusmer, *A Ghetto Takes Shape*, 53–65.

18. Census Bureau, *Report on Population*, 815–16; *Compendium of the Eleventh Census*, 540–79.

19. Ibid.

20. Urban areas in this context are defined as towns with more than 8,000 people, the common definition used by the U.S. Census Bureau in the late nineteenth century. The estimate of 10 percent urbanization for 1860 assumes that a representative percentage from

the North, Upper South, and Lower South living in urban and rural areas before enlistment was recruited into the Union army. The following percentages of black men lived in towns with 8,000 or more people in 1860: North, 34.2 percent; Upper South, 3.5 percent; Lower South, 1.8 percent. These figures are not explicitly provided in 1860 census tables but can be extrapolated by adding up the population of black men in cities and dividing it by the total population of black men in that region. These percentages were then multiplied by the number of black men recruited into the Union army in these regions—North, 34,454; Upper South, 76,075; Lower South, 67,507—giving an estimate of 17,670 black men recruited from towns of over 8,000 people. A total of 178,036 black men enlisted in the Union army in the North, Upper South, and Lower South. Hence, approximately 9.9 percent of black Civil War recruits (17,670 divided by 178,036) lived in cities of over 8,000 people before the war. No doubt this estimate understates the actual percentage of black men who enlisted from urban areas, since black men in cities had easier access to recruiters, and urban men are overrepresented in pension files, but the error is probably not sufficient to upset the observation that veterans became more urbanized after the war. See U.S. Census Bureau, *Population of the United States in 1860: Compiled from the Original Returns of the Eighth Census* (Washington, D.C.: GPO, 1864), 2–590; Berlin et al., *Black Military Experience*, 12.

21. These figures come from members of the random sample group appearing in the pension files. Of the 310 former soldiers whose residence was known in the 1870s, 79 of them (25.5 percent) lived in cities with over 8,000 people. Of the 343 veterans whose residence was known in the 1890s, 123 of them (35.9 percent) lived in cities with over 8,000 people.

22. Census Bureau, *Report on Population*, 815–16. The comparable urbanization rate for the white population nationwide was 24 percent in 1890.

23. Eric Foner, *Reconstruction: America's Unfinished Revolution, 1863–1877* (New York: Harper and Row, 1988), 81.

24. Howard N. Rabinowitz, *Race Relations in the Urban South, 1865–1890* (New York: Oxford University Press, 1978), 22–24; Kevin W. Hardwick, "'Your Old Father Abe Lincoln Is Dead and Damned': Black Soldiers and the Memphis Riot of 1866," *Journal of Social History* 27 (Fall 1993): 112–13.

25. High-status occupations, as defined by me based on 1890 census job titles, include actors; agents; artificial flower makers, artists, and teachers of art; authors and literary and scientific persons; bakers; bankers and brokers; barbers and hairdressers; basket makers; blacksmiths; bleachers, dyers, and scourers; bone and ivory workers; bookbinders; bookkeepers and accountants; bottlers and mineral and soda water makers; brass workers; brewers and maltsters; brick and tile makers and terra-cotta workers; Britannia workers; brokers; broom and brush makers; builders and contractors; butchers; butter and cheese makers; button makers; cabinet makers; carpenters and joiners; carpet makers; carriage and wagon makers; chemists, assayers, and metallurgists; clergymen; clock and watch makers and repairers; commercial travelers; compositors; confectioners; coopers; copper workers; dentists; designers, draftsmen, and inventors; distillers and rectifiers; door, sash, and blind makers; dressmakers;

electroplaters and stereotypers; engineers and surveyors; engravers; glass workers; gold and silver workers; government officials; goldsmiths, locksmiths, and bell hangers; hair keepers; harness and saddle makers and repairers; hat and cap makers; hotel keepers; journalists; lace and embroidery makers; lawyers; leather curriers, dressers, finishers, and tanners; machinists; manufacturers and officials of manufacturing companies; marble and stone cutters; masons; meat and fruit packers, canners, and preservers; mechanics; merchants and dealers; miscellaneous professional musicians and teachers of music; musical instrument makers; nurses and midwives; officers of the U.S. Army and Navy; painters, glaziers, and varnishers; photographers; physicians and surgeons; piano and organ makers and tuners; pilots; plasterers; plumbers and gas and steam fitters; potters; powder and cartridge makers; printers, lithographers, and pressmen; professors in colleges and universities; publishers of books, maps, and newspapers; restaurant keepers; roofers and slaters; sail, awning, and tent makers; saloon keepers; sewing machine makers; ship and boat builders; tailors and tailoresses; teachers; theatrical managers and showmen; tinners and tinware makers; tool and cutlery makers; trunk, valise, leather-case, and pocketbook makers; umbrella and parasol makers; undertakers; upholsterers; veterinary surgeons; and wheelwrights. See Census Bureau, *Report on Population,* 807–10.

26. See William J. Simmons, *Men of Mark: Eminent, Progressive, Rising* (Cleveland, Ohio: Geo. M. Rewell Co., 1887); H. F. Kletzing and W. H. Crogman, *Progress of a Race: The Remarkable Advancement of the Negro from the Bondage of Slavery, Ignorance and Poverty to the Freedom of Citizenship, Intelligence, Affluence, Honor and Trust* (Atlanta: J. L. Nichols and Co., 1897); Charles Alexander, *One Hundred Distinguished Leaders* (Atlanta: Franklin Printing and Publishing Co., 1899); J. L. Nichols and William H. Crogman, *Progress of a Race: The Remarkable Advancement of the Negro from the Bondage of Slavery, Ignorance and Poverty to the Freedom of Citizenship, Intelligence, Affluence, Honor and Trust* (Naperville, Ill.: J. L. Nichols and Co., 1902); Frank Lincoln Mather, ed., *Who's Who of the Colored Race: A General Biographical Dictionary of Men and Women of Negro Descent* (Chicago: Memento Edition, Half-Century Anniversary of Negro Freedom in the U.S., 1915); Clement Richardson et al., eds., *The National Cyclopedia of the Colored Race* (Montgomery, Ala.: National Publishing Company, 1919).

27. Deposition of Alexander Fuller, 13 March 1888, Pension File of Alexander Fuller, 23d USCI, RG 15.

28. Bvt. Brig. Gen. John Eaton to Rev. E. E. Hale, 13 November 1865, Letters Sent, District of Columbia Asst. Commissioner, ser. 449, RG 105 (also Document A-9918, FSSP).

29. Census Bureau, *Report on Population,* 1:402–7, 2: 807–10.

30. Deposition of James Henry Mabin, 2 January 1894, Pension File of James Henry Gordon (alias James Henry Mabin), 60th USCI, RG 15.

31. Pension File of James Walton, 102d USCI, RG 15.

32. John L. Paine, Special Examiner, St. Louis, Mo., to the Commissioner of Pensions, Washington, D.C., 19 November 1897, Pension File of Henry Taylor, 102d USCI, RG 15.

33. Frederick H. Dyer, *A Compendium of the War of Rebellion,* vol. 1 (New York: Thomas Yoseloff, 1908), 12; E. B. Long with Barbara Long, *The Civil War Day by Day: An Alma-*

*nac, 1861–1865* (New York: Da Capo Press, 1971), 705–6, 709–12; Census Bureau, *Report on Population,* 1:486, 803; 2:3–5.

34. U.S. Census Bureau, *Negro Population, 1790–1915* (Washington, D.C.: GPO, 1918), 298. The pre-1900 mortality data from the census for African Americans are nearly useless due to serious undercounting. For instance, in 1880, the Census Bureau found that in the year preceding the enumeration, 14 per 1,000 whites had died, and 17 per 1,000 African Americans. These figures seemed suspect even to the Census Bureau. In its report on the 1880 census, it confessed that since census returns from the South were the most unreliable in the nation due to poor enumeration, the death rate for black people was no doubt higher than the official figure reported. See U.S. Census Bureau, *Report on the Mortality and Vital Statistics of the United States as Returned at the Tenth Census (June 1, 1880)* (Washington, D.C.: GPO, 1885), xxxiv.

35. Sirag Eldin Hassan Suliman, "Estimation of Levels and Trends of the U.S. Adult Black Mortality during the Period 1870–1900" (Ph.D. diss, University of Pennsylvania, 1983), 170. Suliman estimated the life expectancy of white and black males at age ten, decade by decade: 1870–1880, white men, 49.2, black men, 42.54; 1880–1890, white men, 49.75, black men, 41.0; 1890–1900, white men, 50.31, black men, 40.84.

36. Michael Anthony Cooke, "The Health of Blacks during Reconstruction, 1862–1879" (Ph.D. diss., University of Maryland, College Park, 1983), 102–17.

37. Census Bureau, *Negro Population,* 314; David McBride, *From TB to AIDS: Epidemics among Urban Blacks since 1900* (Albany: State University of New York Press, 1991), 10–12.

38. Of the 451 men in the random sample with postwar information in their pension files, 214 had information there on their cause of death. Of those with known death dates, 60 of these men died before 1890, and 154 died in 1890 or after. Of the men who died before 1890, the three most common causes of death were respiratory diseases (45 percent), circulatory diseases (18.3 percent), and infections/parasitic diseases (20 percent). Hence, respiratory diseases—especially tuberculosis—dominated the documentable causes of death before 1890. After 1890, circulatory diseases (now 29.2 percent of the total) replaced respiratory diseases (24 percent) as the single largest killer. Deaths attributable to infections/parasitic disease declined to 10.4 percent, and urinary/kidney disease rose to become a significant factor for the first time, responsible for 11.7 percent of known deaths.

39. Robert Anderson, *From Slavery to Affluence: Memoirs of Robert Anderson, Ex-Slave* (Hemingford, Nebr.: Hemingford Ledger, 1927), 51.

40. Eric Foner, *Free Soil, Free Labor, Free Men: The Ideology of the Republican Party before the Civil War* (New York: Oxford University Press, 1970), 15–26.

41. Anderson, *From Slavery to Affluence,* 48–50.

42. Ibid., 52–57.

43. Ibid., 51.

44. Ibid., 57. See Mabel Hitchcock to the Veterans Administration, 9 December 1936, Pension File of Robert Ball (alias Anderson), 125th USCI, RG 15. Daisy Anderson lived a long time after the death of her husband, dying on 19 September 1998 at the age of ninety-seven in a Denver, Colorado, care facility. See Jim Kirksey, "Civil War Veteran's Widow

Dies at 97," *Denver Post*, 24 September 1998, A1; Tilley Fong, "Last Surviving Widow of Civil War Soldier, Dies," *Rocky Mountain News* (Denver, Colo.), 24 September 1998, 5A.

45. T[homas] W[entworth] Higginson, "Some War Scenes Revisited," *Atlantic Monthly* 42 (July 1878): 3.

46. Of the 451 veterans documented in pension files who survived the war, at least 50 (11.1 percent) show evidence of having owned real estate.

47. Loren Schweninger, *Black Property Owners in the South, 1790–1915* (Urbana: University of Illinois Press, 1990), 183.

48. Julie Saville, *The Work of Reconstruction: From Slave to Wage Labor in South Carolina, 1860–1870* (Cambridge: Cambridge University Press, 1994), 145–47.

49. W. Fitzhugh Brundage, "Race, Memory, and Masculinity: Black Veterans Recall the Civil War," in *The War Was You and Me: Civilians in the American Civil War*, ed. Joan E. Cashin (Princeton, N.J.: Princeton University Press, 2002), 145–46.

50. *New York Age*, 30 May 1891. Regrettably, the *Age* did not reproduce the text of these sermons or provide any sort of summary.

51. *Advocate* (Leavenworth, Kans.), 4 July 1891; *Appeal* (St. Paul, Minn.), 24 May 1890, 15 and 22 August 1891; *Cleveland Gazette*, 6 March and 12 July 1884, 5 December 1885, 20 January 1886, 22 May 1886, 4 and 11 December 1886, 2 April, 11 June, 16 July, and 13, 20, and 27 August 1887; *New York Freeman*, 20 August 1887 and 2 July 1892.

52. *Afro-American Ledger* (Baltimore, Md.), 6 June 1903. In fairness, it should be noted that the editor of the *Afro-American Ledger* was John H. Murphy, himself a Civil War veteran. However, the tone of this article is not atypical of similar articles reporting on aging veterans in the black press.

53. *Freeman* (Indianapolis, Ind.), 26 May 1906.

54. Ibid., 25 May 1907.

55. Ibid., 30 May 1908.

56. *Washington Bee*, 4 June 1887.

57. Minute Book, December 14, 1881–June 19, 1885, Robert G. Shaw Post No. 206, Records of Miscellaneous Posts, 1861–1940, Grand Army of the Republic, Department of Pennsylvania, Archives of Industrial Society, University of Pittsburgh, Pittsburgh, Pa.

58. Minutes of 17 December 1897 and 7 January 1898, in Minute Book, June 15, 1897–September 17, 1904, ibid.

59. William W. Grimes, *Thirty-three Years Experience of an Itinerant Minister of the A.M.E. Church* (Lancaster, Pa.: Eml. S. Speaker, 1887), 24–25.

60. William Henry Johnson, *Autobiography of William Henry Johnson* (Albany, N.Y.: Argis Company, Printers, 1900), 17.

61. Ibid., 162.

62. For two other excellent examples of accounts similar to William Henry Johnson's, see William H. Robinson, *From Log Cabin to Pulpit: Reminiscences of My Early Life while in Slavery* (Eau Claire, Wis.: James H. Tifft, Publishing Printer, 1913); William Mallory, *Old Plantation Days* (Hamilton, Ontario, Canada: n.p., [1902]).

63. See Simmons, *Men of Mark*, 1133; Civil War Service Record of Caesar C. Antoine, 7th Louisiana Infantry and 10th USCHA, RG 94.

## Chapter 3. Politics

1. Edwin S. Redkey, ed., *A Grand Army of Black Men: Letters from African-American Soldiers in the Union Army, 1861–1865* (Cambridge: Cambridge University Press, 1982), 293–96.

2. Philip S. Foner and George E. Walker, eds., *Proceedings of the Black National and State Conventions, 1865–1900,* vol. 1 (Philadelphia: Temple University Press, 1986), xiii–xxiii, 115–19. The black regiments represented in Nashville in September 1865 included the 13th, 14th, and 15th USCI, the 1st and 3d USCHA, and Battery A, 2d USCLA.

3. Eric Foner, *Freedom's Lawmakers: A Directory of Black Officeholders during Reconstruction* (New York: Oxford University Press, 1993), 114.

4. Ibid., 173, 208.

5. Quoted in Bobby L. Lovett, "Memphis Riots: White Reaction to Blacks in Memphis, May 1865–July 1866," *Tennessee Historical Quarterly* 38 (Spring 1979): 12.

6. Redkey, *Grand Army of Black Men,* 294.

7. Ibid., 294–95.

8. *Christian Recorder,* 5 January 1867, in Foner and Walker, *Proceedings of Black National and State Conventions,* 1:291.

9. Leslie H. Fishel, "Northern Prejudice and Negro Suffrage, 1865–1870," *Journal of Negro History* 39 (January 1954): 8–26.

10. Versalle F. Washington, *Eagles on the Buttons: A Black Infantry Regiment in the Civil War* (Columbia: University of Missouri Press, 1999), 78.

11. Gilles Vandal, "The Origins of the New Orleans Riot of 1866, Revisited," *Louisiana History* 22 (Spring 1981): 139–65.

12. Gilles Vandal, *The New Orleans Riot of 1866: Anatomy of a Tragedy* (Lafayette: Center for Louisiana Studies, University of Southwestern Louisiana, 1983), 183f.

13. Ibid., 174, 183.

14. Ibid., 176–80.

15. Foner, *Freedom's Lawmakers,* 284–85. This figure is probably not precise because some men falsely claimed military service, and others' service did not become known to history.

16. Counting enlistments in both the Union army and navy, 196,975 black men served in the Civil War. Of these, about 40,555 died in service, leaving 156,420 survivors (because there are no separate mortality statistics for black men in the Union navy, it is assumed that the same percentage of black sailors as black soldiers died in the war, about 20.6 percent). Because an age distribution for black men is not available in the 1870 census, the age distribution used comes from the nearest census with complete information, 1860. In 1860, 44.7 percent of black men were aged twenty years or older. Assuming that this age distribution did not change significantly between 1860 and 1870, there were about 945,575 black men twenty or older in 1870 (2,115,380 black males total multiplied by 44.7 percent). Hence, approximately 16.5 percent (156,420 divided by 945,575) of the adult black male population in 1870 was Civil War veterans. See Ira Berlin, Joseph P. Reidy, and Leslie S. Rowland, eds., *Freedom: A Documentary History of Emancipation, 1861–1867,* Series II,

# After the Glory

*The Black Military Experience* (Cambridge: Cambridge University Press, 1982), 12; Joseph P. Reidy, "Black Men in Navy Blue during the Civil War," *Prologue* 33 (Fall 2001): 156; Frederick H. Dyer, *A Compendium of the War of the Rebellion*, vol. 1 (New York: Thomas Yoseloff, 1908), 12; U.S. Census Bureau, *Population of the United States in 1860; Compiled from the Original Returns of the Eighth Census* (Washington, D.C.: GPO, 1864), 594–95; U.S. Census Bureau, *A Compendium of the Ninth Census (June 1, 1870)* (Washington, D.C.: GPO, 1872), 548–49.

17. Unlike their Southern comrades, who managed to gain office in significant numbers in some states in the South by the late 1860s, black veterans in the North—like other African Americans in that region—remained largely excluded from any meaningful role in Northern politics. Indeed, only three black Civil War veterans served in statewide political office in the North, and only one during the Reconstruction era. Charles L. Mitchell gained a seat in the lower house of the Massachusetts legislature in 1866. George W. Williams, with the support of Cincinnati's Republican party, won election to the Ohio legislature in 1879. James M. Townsend was elected to the Indiana legislature in 1884. Both Mitchell and Williams, however, served only one term. It is not known how many terms Townsend served. See John Hope Franklin, *George Washington Williams: A Biography* (Chicago: University of Chicago Press, 1985), 48–99; Rayford W. Logan and Michael R. Winston, eds., *Dictionary of American Negro Biography* (New York: W. W. Norton, 1982), 188, 603; William J. Simmons, *Men of Mark: Eminent, Progressive, Rising* (Cleveland, Ohio: Geo. M. Rewell Co., 1887), 1138.

18. Of the twenty-nine black veterans who held office in South Carolina during Reconstruction, eleven lived in the North before the war.

19. Charles E. Nash and Josiah Walls served as soldiers in the Union army. Robert Smalls commanded the *Planter*, guiding Union vessels in the waters around Charleston, South Carolina. John R. Lynch labored as a cook for the Union army and as a waiter in the Union navy. Hiram Revels recruited soldiers for the Union army. Robert C. DeLarge worked as a civilian employee of the Confederate navy during the Civil War. Foner, *Freedom's Lawmakers*, 61, 138–39, 158, 180, 197–98, 222–23.

20. Ibid., 216. Turner was technically not a Union soldier during the war but a body servant of a Union officer. For a full-length biography of Turner, including a discussion of his diplomatic career, see Gary L. Kremer, *James Milton Turner and the Promise of America: The Public Life of a Post–Civil War Black Leader* (Columbia: University of Missouri Press, 1991).

21. Foner, *Freedom's Lawmakers*, xxii, xviii.

22. Eric Foner, *Reconstruction: America's Unfinished Revolution, 1863–1877* (New York: Harper and Row, 1988), 105.

23. Foner, *Freedom's Lawmakers*, 234.

24. Ibid., 103, 106, 114, 172, 213.

25. Ibid., xxvii.

26. John W. Blassingame, *Black New Orleans: 1860–1880* (Chicago: University of Chicago Press, 1973), 213; Charles Vincent, *Black Legislators in Louisiana during Reconstruc-*

*tion* (Baton Rouge: Louisiana State University Press, 1976), xiii–xiv, 1–15; see also David C. Rankin, "The Origins of Black Leadership in New Orleans during Reconstruction," *Journal of Southern History* 40 (August 1974): 434.

27. Foner, *Freedom's Lawmakers*, xvi, 8–9, 67–68, 171–72. It is probable that Oscar J. Dunn was not really a Civil War veteran. His name does not appear in the "Index to Compiled Military Service Records of Volunteer Union Soldiers Who Served with the United States Colored Troops" (Microfilm No. M589) at the National Archives in Washington, D.C. The source that indicates that Dunn served in the Civil War is James Grant Wilson and John Fiske, eds., *Appleton's Cyclopedia of American Biography*, vol. 2 (New York: D. Appleton and Company, 1888), 260. Wilson and Fiske state that Dunn attained the rank of captain and resigned from the Union army after he was passed over for promotion to major. However, given that he claimed to be an officer, he should appear in the National Archives index, unless he served under a different name. Considering the strong presence of veterans in Louisiana politics after the war, it is possible that Dunn felt compelled to claim military service in order to compete with them, or the *Appleton* editors may have received erroneous biographical information.

28. There is speculation that his political opponents, such as Warmoth and Pinchback, poisoned Dunn. See Marcus B. Christian, "The Theory of the Poisoning of Oscar J. Dunn," *Phylon* 6 (1945): 264.

29. Pinchback himself confirmed his corrupt behavior. He admitted using inside information, to which he was privy as a state legislator, to guide his investment decisions (what George W. Plunkitt would later call "honest graft"). Congressional investigations also found evidence that Pinchback took bribes, suggesting that whereas the going rate for the vote of a Louisiana legislator was $800 during Reconstruction, Pinchback's key committee chairmanships raised his price to $2,000. See Foner, *Freedom's Lawmakers*, 171; Joe Gray Taylor, *Louisiana Reconstructed: 1863–1877* (Baton Rouge: Louisiana State University Press, 1974), 199; Alice Smith Grosz, "The Political Career of Pinckney Benton Stewart Pinchback," *Louisiana Historical Quarterly* 27 (1944): 543.

30. Grosz, "Political Career of Pinchback," 538–47; James Haskins, *Pinckney Benton Stewart Pinchback* (New York: Macmillan, 1973), 50–56, 74–86.

31. Foner, *Freedom's Lawmakers*, 1, 61, 104–5, 111–12, 233.

32. Ibid., 9, 13, 15–16, 21, 59, 90, 105–6, 130, 132, 175–76, 207–8, 219, 228–29; Dyer, *Compendium*, 3:1266–67, 1597–98, 1723, 1727–28, 1735, 1738.

33. Edward A. Miller Jr., *Gullah Statesman: Robert Smalls from Slavery to Congress, 1839–1915* (Columbia: University of South Carolina Press, 1995), 1–34; Okon Edet Uya, *From Slavery to Public Service: Robert Smalls, 1839–1915* (New York: Oxford University Press, 1971), 1–31.

34. Miller, *Gullah Statesman*, 35–250; Uya, *From Slavery to Public Service*, 32–151. Military heroism was not the only way black veterans broke into postwar politics. The suffrage and equal rights movement in the black community after the Civil War provided some veterans with their first favorable public exposure. Other former soldiers became public figures through service with the Freedmen's Bureau or as organizers for the Republican

party and the Union League. Veterans also gained attention as ministers, as teachers, or in other professions. Often ex-soldiers got into politics through a combination of the aforementioned means. See Foner, *Freedom's Lawmakers*, 7–10, 13, 15, 54, 60, 62, 67–68, 72–73, 78, 81–83, 96, 100, 105–6, 113–16, 127–28, 132, 143, 155, 168, 171, 173, 176, 180, 189–90, 207–8, 215–16, 221, 226, 233.

35. Franklin Lincoln Mather, ed., *Who's Who of the Colored Race: A General Biographical Dictionary of Men and Women of Negro Descent*, vol. 1 (Chicago: Memento Edition, Half-Century of Negro Freedom in the U.S., 1915), 8.

36. Franklin, *George Washington Williams*, 84–85.

37. Simmons, *Men of Mark*, 1138.

38. Logan and Winston, *Dictionary of American Negro Biography*, 16; Foner, *Freedom's Lawmakers*, 133; Charles A. Lofgren, *The Plessy Case: A Legal Historical Interpretation* (New York: Oxford University Press, 1987), 28–32; Willard B. Gatewood, *Aristocrats of Color: The Black Elite, 1880–1920* (Bloomington: Indiana University Press, 1990), 85–86.

39. "In the Aftermath of 'Glory': Black Soldiers and Sailors from Annapolis, Maryland, 1863–1918," Maryland State Archives, Annapolis, Md. I am grateful to Maryland state archivist Edward C. Papenfuse for bringing the John B. Anderson case to my attention.

40. Ibid. *Charles E. Meyers and A. Claude Kalmey, Plaintiffs in Error v. John B. Anderson*, 730 U.S. 22, 806 (1911), 4, 26; *Charles E. Meyers and A. Claude Kalmey, Plaintiffs in Error v. John B. Anderson*, 238 U.S. 368 (1913), 3, 6.

41. Stephen Kantrowitz, *Ben Tillman and the Reconstruction of White Supremacy* (Chapel Hill: University of North Carolina Press, 2000), 235; *State* (Columbia, S.C.), 26 October 1895.

42. Foner, *Freedom's Lawmakers*, 73, 216, 221.

43. Quoted in Nell Irvin Painter, *Exodusters: Black Migration to Kansas after Reconstruction* (New York: Alfred A. Knopf, 1977), 3–4.

44. John Dittmer, "The Education of Henry McNeal Turner," in *Black Leaders of the Nineteenth Century*, ed. Leon F. Litwack and August Meier (Urbana: University of Illinois Press, 1988), 258–61.

45. Victor Ullman, *Martin R. Delany: The Beginning of Black Nationalism* (Boston: Beacon Press, 1971), 500–6.

46. Franklin, *George Washington Williams*, 180–241.

47. Janet Sharp Herman, *The Pursuit of a Dream* (New York: Oxford University Press, 1981), 20, 41–42; David Mark Silver, "In the Eye of the Storm: Isaiah T. Montgomery and the Plight of Black Mississippians, 1847–1924" (honor's thesis, Amherst College, 1993), 29–32.

48. Joel Williamson, *A Rage for Order: Black-White Relations in the American South since Emancipation* (New York: Oxford University Press, 1986), 78–79.

49. August Meier, *Negro Thought in America, 1880–1915: Racial Ideologies in the Age of Booker T. Washington* (Ann Arbor: University of Michigan Press, 1963), 38; Kenneth Marvin Hamilton, *Black Towns and Profit: Promotion and Development in the Trans-*

*Appalachian West, 1877–1915* (Urbana: University of Illinois Press, 1991), 43–55; Herman, *Pursuit of a Dream,* 228–33; Silver, "Eye of the Storm," 43–97.

50. Richard Griggs, *The Life of Richard Griggs of Issaquena County, Mississippi* (Jackson, Miss.: Pilot Steam Book and Job Printing Establishment, 1872), 12, in Civil War Pension File of Richard Griggs, 48th USCI, RG 15.

51. William E. Montgomery, *Under Their Own Vine and Fig Tree: The African-American Church in the South, 1865–1990* (Baton Rouge: Louisiana State University Press, 1993), 156–57.

52. Simmons, *Men of Mark,* 727.

53. Elijah P. Marrs, *Life and History of the Rev. Elijah P. Marrs* (Louisville, Ky.: Bradley and Gilbert Company, 1885), 99–100.

54. Simmons, *Men of Mark,* 92; James T. Moore, "Black Militancy in Readjuster Virginia, 1879–1883," *Journal of Southern History* 41 (May 1975): 167–86.

55. Alexander H. Newton, *Out of the Briars: An Autobiography and Sketch of the Twenty-ninth Regiment Connecticut Volunteers* (Philadelphia: A.M.E. Book Concern, 1910), 99–117.

56. Deposition of Thomas Wilbourn, 14 April 1909, Pension File of Thomas Wilbert (alias Wilbourn), 122d USCI, RG 15.

57. Newton, *Out of the Briars,* 100.

58. Ibid., 88–101.

59. U.S. Census Bureau, *Report on Population of the United States at the Eleventh Census: 1890, Part II* (Washington, D.C.: GPO, 1897), 807.

60. Newton, *Out of the Briars,* 109.

61. Kenneth Ng and Nancy Virts, "The Value of Freedom," *Journal of Economic History* 49 (December 1989): 960–61.

62. Logan and Winston, *Dictionary of American Negro Biography,* 556–58; Simmons, *Men of Mark,* 39–63; George C. Wright, *Life behind a Veil: Blacks in Louisville, Kentucky, 1865–1930* (Baton Rouge: Louisiana State University Press, 1985), 159–61.

63. Logan and Winston, *Dictionary of American Negro Biography,* 463; Meier, *Negro Thought in America,* 230.

64. Logan and Winston, *Dictionary of American Negro Biography,* 19–20, 507–8.

65. Simmons, *Men of Mark,* 278–80.

66. John Phillip Langellier, "Chaplain Allen Allensworth and the 24th Infantry, 1886–1906," *Smoke Signal* (Fall 1990): 192–96.

67. Frank N. Schubert, *Buffalo Soldiers, Braves, and the Brass: The Story of Fort Robinson, Nebraska* (Shippensburg, Pa.: White Mane Publishing Company, 1993), 130–34.

68. Charles Alexander, *Battles and Victories of Allen Allensworth* (Boston: Sherman, French, and Company, 1914), 313–30.

69. *Sentiment Maker,* 15 May 1912, in "Allensworth Collection," California State Department of Parks and Recreation, Sacramento, Calif.

70. Christian A. Fleetwood to John R. Lynch, 7 June 1898, in Christian A. Fleetwood Papers, Library of Congress Manuscript Division, Washington, D.C.

## Chapter 4. Family and Marriage

1. Ira Berlin, Joseph P. Reidy, and Leslie S. Rowland, eds., *Freedom: A Documentary History of Emancipation, 1861–1867*, Series II, *The Black Military Experience* (Cambridge: Cambridge University Press, 1982), 691–92.

2. Ibid., 694–95.

3. Civil War Pension File of Spotswood Rice, 67th USCI, RG 15.

4. Spotswood Rice to Kitty Diggs, [3 September 1864], enclosed in F. W. Diggs to Gen. Rosecrans, 10 September 1864, in Berlin et al., *Black Military Experience, 690*.

5. Ibid.

6. Pvt. Spotswood Rice to his children, 3 September 1864, enclosed in F. W. Diggs to Gen. Rosecrans, 10 September 1864, in ibid., 689.

7. Endorsement of Gen. John M. Palmer, Louisville, Ky., 30 November 1865, in letter of Capt. F. B. Clark, Battery Rodgers, Va., to Lieut. E. T. Lamberton, 15 November 1865, in ibid., 751. Palmer was no doubt referring to the Militia Act of 3 March 1862, which freed the wives and children of black soldiers who belonged to disloyal owners.

8. Laura Edwards also cites former slaveholders' defense of their patriarchy after the war as the basis of their political power. See Laura F. Edwards, *Gendered Strife and Confusion: The Political Culture of Reconstruction* (Urbana: University of Illinois Press, 1997), 25–54.

9. Pension Files of Smith Buchanan (alias Jackson), 136th USCI; Alfred Carruthers (alias Butler), 14th USCI; Pickney Ellsworth (alias Leonard), 51st USCI; Alexander Everly (alias Evans), 12th USCI; Frank Finley (alias Brown), 119th USCI; Mathew McCann (alias Mathias Garner), 116th USCI; George Nicholson (alias Nickerson, alias Brown), 15th and 101st USCI; Luke Riddick (alias White), 38th USCI; Phillip Russell (alias Fry), 114th USCI; Lewis Smith (alias Dick L. Barnett), 77th USCI and 10th USCHA; Toney Smith (alias James T. Keele), 118th USCI; James Watkins (alias Davis), 54th USCI; Edmund Wescott (alias Bayly), 10th USCI; Alfred Williams (alias Allen), 107th USCI; Allen James Walker (alias Allen James), 11th USCI and 7th USCHA, RG 15.

10. Herbert G. Gutman, *The Black Family in Slavery and Freedom, 1750–1925* (New York: Vintage Books, 1976), 230–56.

11. Deposition of Smith Jackson, 7 April 1906, Pension File of Smith Buchanan (alias Jackson), 136th USCI, RG 15.

12. Deposition of Dick Lewis Barnett, 17 May 1911, Pension File of Lewis Smith (alias Dick Lewis Barnett), 77th USCI and 10th USCHA, RG 15.

13. Chaplain James Peet, Vicksburg, Miss., to Brig. Gen. L. Thomas, 30 September 1864, in Berlin et al., *Black Military Experience, 604*.

14. Deposition of John Means Thompson, 19 March 1888, Pension File of Green Colyar, 15th USCI, RG 15.

15. A. W. Greely, *Reminiscences of Adventure and Service: A Record of Sixty-five Years* (New York: Charles Scribner's Sons, 1927), 98–99.

16. Leslie Ann Schwalm, *A Hard Fight for We: Women's Transition from Slavery in South Carolina* (Urbana: University of Illinois Press, 1997), 239.

17. Deposition of Judy Gibson, 23 December 1909, Pension File of Renty Gibson, 21st USCI, RG 15.

18. Gutman, *Black Family in Slavery and Freedom,* 412–18.

19. Deposition of Mary Jane Taylor, 13 May 1919, Pension File of Samuel Taylor, 45th USCI, RG 15.

20. For the purposes of this study, a formal marriage is a union given sanction by the state or a religious institution and solemnized by a ceremony or a legal declaration. An informal union exists when the couple believes that they are married but their union has no legal or religious basis and starts with the commencement of cohabitation.

21. Allen Parker, *Recollections of Slavery Times* (Worcester, Mass.: Charles W. Burbank and Company, 1895), 22–27; Pension Files of Charles Barnett (alias Allen), 92d USCI; Lewis Booth, 50th USCI; Stephen Carson, 42d USCI; Andrew Cassaman (alias Jackson), 2d USCLA; Marshall Hamilton (alias Osborn), 123d USCI; Reuben Martindale, 110th USCI; Kitt Mitchell, 128th USCI; Edward Price (alias Ned Waiters), 135th USCI; Solomon Silbey, 63d USCI, RG 15.

22. Berlin et al., *Black Military Experience,* 672.

23. Laura F. Edwards, "'The Marriage Covenant Is at the Foundation of All Our Rights': The Politics of Slave Marriage in North Carolina after Emancipation," *Law and History Review* 14 (Spring 1996): 99–101.

24. Pension File of Kitt Mitchell, 128th USCI, RG 15.

25. Pension File of Garret Beckley, 114th USCI, RG 15.

26. Pension Files of Alfred Williams, 107th USCI; Samuel Taylor, 45th USCI, RG 15.

27. Noralee Frankel also notes the phenomenon of "taking up" among Civil War veterans in Mississippi. See Noralee Frankel, *Freedom's Women: Black Women and Families in Civil War Era Mississippi* (Bloomington: Indiana University Press, 1999), 90–92.

28. Pension Files of Joseph Bell, 12th USCI; Frederick Clement, 70th and 71st USCI; Edward Gants, 7th USCI; Adam Hayes, 81st USCI (New), 84th USCI, 87th USCI (New), and 95th USCI; George Hibbitt, 14th USCI; Daniel (alias David) Hughes, 27th USCI; Horace Ringgold, 38th USCI; Mack Thompson, 53d USCI; Henry Vass, 2d USCC, RG 15.

29. Affidavit of Morgan Black and Glen Willis, 15 May 1891, Pension File of Phillip Bellfield, 63d USCI, RG 15.

30. Deposition of Rose Baptiste, 19 September 1893, Pension File of Octave Colar (alias Jessie), 96th USCI, RG 15.

31. Pension Files of Walker Bettlesworth (alias Wade), 116th USCI; Jason Brathough (alias Posey), 4th USCC; James Flenoy (alias Robinson), 88th USCI (New) and 3d USCHA; Hector Friar (alias Jones), 78th and 98th USCI; James Henry Gordon (alias Mabin), 60th USCI; Jacob Overall (alias Hutchinson, alias Abraham I. J. Wright), 4th USCHA, RG 15. See also James Smallwood, "Emancipation and the Black Family: A Case Study," *Social Science Quarterly* 57 (March 1977): 850.

32. Pension File of Tony Austin (alias Alston), 21st USCI, RG 15.

33. Pension Files of Walker Bettlesworth (alias Wade), 116th USCI; Peter Bishop, 38th USCI; Jason Brathough (alias Posey), 4th USCC; Henry F. Downing, U.S. Navy; James Flenoy (alias Robinson), 88th USCI (New) and 3d USCHA; Hector Friar (alias Jones),

78th and 98th USCI; James Henry Gordon (alias Mabin), 60th USCI; Daniel (alias David) Hughes, 27th USCI; Jacob Overall (alias Hutchinson, alias Abraham I. J. Wright), 4th USCHA, RG 15.

34. Deposition of Mary Conti, 12 July 1893, Pension File of Wallace Willikey (alias Levi Johnson), 6th USCHA, RG 15.

35. Charles G. Townsend, Louisville, Ky., to the Commissioner of Pensions, Washington, D.C., 29 May 1919, Pension File of Samuel Taylor, 45th USCI, RG 15.

36. U.S. Census Bureau, *Special Reports: Marriage and Divorce, 1867–1906. Part I: Summary, Laws, Foreign Statistics* (Washington, D.C.: GPO, 1909), 22.

37. Edwards, *Gendered Strife and Confusion*, 31–45.

38. Florida and Missouri demanded a new wedding ceremony for freed couples, and Kentucky, Louisiana, and Maryland required them to register their intent to stay together with a justice of the peace. Alabama, Arkansas, the District of Columbia, Georgia, Mississippi, North Carolina, South Carolina, Tennessee, Texas, and Virginia automatically legalized existing slave unions after the war. North Carolina eventually required registration, and Kentucky dropped its registration law in 1910. Delaware, which had a large free population in the antebellum period, merely applied its prewar statutes regarding free black marriages to its entire African-American population after the Civil War. See U.S. Congress, Senate, *Letter of the Secretary of War, Communicating . . . Reports of the Assistant Commissioner of Freedmen and a Synopsis of Laws Respecting Persons of Color in the Slave States*, 39th Congress, 2d sess., 1866–1867, 170–230; Charles Edward Wright, *Marriage and Divorce: A Collation of the Published Decisions of the Department of the Interior, Rendered on Appeal, Appertaining to the Law of Marriage and Divorce in the United States in Its Relation to Pensionable Status* (Washington, D.C.: GPO, 1914), 1–48. Laura Edwards also notes the punitive nature of North Carolina's marriage legalization laws written by white Southerners immediately after the Civil War. See Edwards, *Gendered Strife and Confusion*, 31–45.

Common-law marriage was legal during the postwar period in Alabama, Arkansas, the District of Columbia, Florida, Georgia, Mississippi, Missouri, South Carolina, and Texas. It was illegal in Delaware, Kentucky, Louisiana, Maryland, Tennessee, and Virginia. Informal unions were legal in Oklahoma prior to 1903. See Wright, *Marriage and Divorce*, 1–48.

39. Leslie Schwalm also notes this phenomenon. See Schwalm, *A Hard Fight for We*, 244.

40. Deposition of Cornelius McCray, 7 December 1887, Pension File of Lewis Booth, 50th USCI, RG 15.

41. Deposition of Mollie Fry, 18 April 1911, Pension File of Philip Russell (alias Fry), 114th USCI, RG 15.

42. Deposition of Rosa Farrow, 14 January 1922, Pension File of Volsin Brown (alias Farrow), 80th USCI, RG 15.

43. Pension File of William B. Barrett, 74th USCI, RG 15.

44. In the nineteenth century, common-law marriage was prevalent enough among white Americans for its legitimacy to become a topic of debate in legal circles. See Otto E. Koegel, *Common Law Marriage and Its Development in the United States* (Washing-

ton, D.C.: John Byrne and Company, 1922), 54–172; John E. Semonche, "Common-Law Marriage in North Carolina: A Study in Legal History," *American Journal of Legal History* 9 (October 1965): 320–49; Michael Grossberg, *Governing the Hearth: Law and Family in Nineteenth-Century America* (Chapel Hill: University of North Carolina Press, 1985), 69–90. However, little if any research has been done on the nature of common-law marriage practices in the United States. Hence, it is difficult to compare the origins and practice of informal marriage between former slaves and their nineteenth-century white contemporaries. This topic and the extent of common-law marriage among free persons of color in the antebellum period deserve more research.

There is, however, an extensive literature on the practice of common-law marriage in Europe during the nineteenth century. These studies suggest that although the economic forces encouraging the perpetuation of informal marriage in Western countries were similar, particularly the cost of legal marriage and divorce (which was beyond the means of many working-class people), the context in which informal marriage institutions developed was quite different from country to country. For instance, common-law marriages in nineteenth-century Germany were often the product of means-dependent marriage laws that prevented poor couples from legally marrying (for fear they and their children would become dependent on public relief). See William G. Burgin, "Concubinage: Revolutionary Response or Last Resort? The Attitudes of Town Authorities and of Couples Rejected in Their Marriage Suits in Nineteenth Century Germany," in *Consortium on Revolutionary Europe, 1750–1850: Proceedings* (Tallahassee, Fla.: Institute on Napoleon and the French Revolution, 1983), 271–87; Lynn Abrams, "Concubinage, Cohabitation and the Law: Class and Gender Relations in Nineteenth Century Germany," *Gender and History* 5 (Spring 1993): 81–100. In France and Great Britain, common-law marriage was intimately connected to industrialization and urbanization, phenomena outside the experience of most African Americans in the post–Civil War South. See Jeffrey Kaplow, "Concubinage and the Working Class in Early Nineteenth Century Paris," in *Vom Ancien Regime Zur Franzosischen Revolution*, ed. Ernst Hinrichs, Eberhard Schmitt, and Rudolf Vierhaus (Gottingen: Vandenhoeck and Rurprecht, 1978), 366–67; Lenard R. Berlanstein, "Illegitimacy, Concubinage, and Proletarianization in a French Town, 1760–1914," *Journal of Family History* 5 (Winter 1980): 369–73; John R. Gillis, *For Better, for Worse: British Marriages, 1600 to the Present* (New York: Oxford University Press, 1985), 190–228.

45. Census Bureau, *Marriage and Divorce*, 200–58.

46. Grossberg, *Governing the Hearth*, 251.

47. In his study of antebellum divorce in Maryland, Richard Chused found that attorneys' fees in some divorces amounted to hundreds of dollars and that they constituted the primary costs of divorce. See Richard H. Chused, *Private Acts in Public Places: A Social History of Divorce in the Formative Era of American Family Law* (Philadelphia: University of Pennsylvania Press, 1994), 83 n. 91. Postbellum divorces between black men and women were not as expensive. C. Vance Lewis, a black lawyer in turn-of-the-century Galveston, Texas, charged $25 for a divorce. See Maxwell Bloomfield, "From Deference to Confrontation: The Early Black Lawyers of Galveston, Texas, 1895–1920," in *The New*

*High Priests: Lawyers in Post–Civil War America,* ed. Gerard W. Gawalt (Westport, Conn.: Greenwood Press, 1984), 157. However, even $25 was beyond the means of many African Americans in the late nineteenth and early twentieth centuries.

48. Edwards, "Marriage Covenant," 109.

49. Grossberg, *Governing the Hearth,* 64–102.

50. See note 38.

51. Deposition of Airey Young, 5 August 1892, Pension File of Wilson Fitchett, 10th USCI, RG 15.

52. Deposition of Emma Frederick, 11 April 1903, Pension File of Clement Frederick, 70th and 71st USCI, RG 15.

53. Affidavit of Lucinda Sibley, 18 March 1892, Pension File of Solomon Sibley, 63d USCI, RG 15.

54. Affidavit of Kizzie Sexton, 5 March 1898, Pension File of Henry Sexton, 65th and 67th USCI, RG 15.

55. Affidavits of Thomasine Stephens, 18 January 1909 and 19 May 1913, Pension File of Peter Stephens, 74th and 91st USCI, RG 15.

56. Pension Files of George Bird, 110th USCI; James Henry Gordon (alias Mabin), 60th USCI; James Luckett, 50th USCI; Nimrod Rowley, 20th USCI; George Scott, 54th Massachusetts Infantry; Thomas F. Simons, 26th USCI; Isaac Smith, 117th USCI; John Walker, 31st USCI; Wallace Willikey (alias Levi Johnson), 6th USCHA, RG 15.

57. Frankel, *Freedom's Women,* 135.

58. Pension File of Tony Austin (alias Alston), 21st USCI, RG 15.

59. R. K. Doe, Special Examiner, Charleston, S.C., to the Commissioner of Pensions, Washington, D.C., 25 January 1902, Pension File of Washington Granville, 128th USCI, RG 15.

60. Elizabeth Hafkin Pleck also notes the existence of informal unions among African Americans in postwar Boston; she divides the couples into a series of categories, depending on the level of their commitment to each other. See Elizabeth Hafkin Pleck, *Black Migration and Poverty: Boston, 1865–1900* (New York: Academic Press, 1979), 185–87.

61. Deposition of Lois Jackson, 26 November 1913, Pension File of Lot Lee Barton, 54th Massachusetts Infantry, RG 15; emphasis in original.

62. Deposition of Annie Ross, 4 August 1898, Pension File of William F. Samson, 19th USCI and U.S. Navy, RG 15.

63. Deposition of Elizabeth Vass, 19 May 1903, Pension File of Henry Vass, 2d USCC, RG 15.

64. John Hall Comick to the Commissioner of Pensions, 19 October 1894, Pension File of Jeremiah Bradley, 54th Massachusetts Infantry, RG 15.

65. Deposition of John Craven, 29 December 1909, Pension File of John West, 6th USCI, RG 15.

66. W. E. B. Du Bois to Morris Lewis, c/o Congressman Oscar Depriest, 14 October 1932, Pension File of Henry F. Downing, U.S. Navy, RG 15.

67. Deposition of Diannah Springsteen, 23 September 1915, Pension File of Thomas Simons, 26th USCI, RG 15.

68. Comick to Commissioner, Pension File of Jeremiah Bradley, 54th Massachusetts Infantary, RG 15.

69. Pension File of John H. A. Stephenson, 32d USCI, RG 15.

## Chapter 5. Social Welfare

1. Ira Berlin, Joseph P. Reidy, and Leslie S. Rowland, eds., *Freedom: A Documentary History of Emancipation, 1861–1867*, Series II, *The Black Military Experience* (Cambridge: Cambridge University Press, 1982), 123, 766; Joseph T. Glatthaar, *Forged in Battle: The Civil War Alliance of Black Soldier and White Officers* (New York: Free Press, 1990), 247.

It should be pointed out that not only the federal government paid bounties for black enlistments; some state governments did so as well. For instance, on 6 February 1864, the Maryland legislature authorized the state government to pay a $300 bounty to all volunteers who enlisted for three years, except slaves. When a slave enlisted, his owner received $100, provided the owner manumitted the slave. The slave himself received $50 upon enlistment and the same amount upon being honorably discharged. See *Laws of the State of Maryland, Made and Passed* (Annapolis, Md.: Richard P. Bayly, Printer, 1864), 21.

2. U.S. Congress, House, Committee on Military Affairs, *Bounties to Colored Soldiers: Letter from the Secretary of War in Answer to a Resolution of the House, of the 7th Ultimo, Relative to Collection and Payment of Bounties to Colored Soldiers*, 41st Cong., 2d sess., 1870, 5.

3. Ibid., 57.

4. Theda Skocpol, "America's First Social Security System: The Expansion of Benefits for Civil War Veterans," *Political Science Quarterly* 108 (Spring 1993): 85–86.

5. This sample is different from the main random sample informing this book. A separate sample was necessary because whites were not included in the main sample group, making comparison problematic. The biracial sample to analyze the relative success of whites and blacks in obtaining pensions was drawn from "General Index to Pension Files, 1861–1934" (Microfilm No. T288) at the National Archives in Washington, D.C. The T288 microfilm set contains copies of index cards for all Civil War pension applications made between 1861 and 1934 (as well as index cards of pension applications made during this period for those serving in the Mexican War, Indian Wars, Spanish-American War, Philippine Insurrection, and in peacetime armed forces). The cards are organized alphabetically by the soldier's name and then by unit (for men with the same name). The selection strategy was to choose the first white and black Civil War subject on each of the 545 reels of the T288 index to arrive at a sample of 545 subjects for each race. The index cards contain the name of the soldier; the unit he served in; the application numbers for the veteran, his widow, children, and parent; and, if any of these claims were successful, a certificate number. By comparing the number of index cards for white and black applicants in each class with those containing certificate numbers, it is possible to compile relative statistics on the success of getting on the pension rolls. Black applications are identifiable in the index because of the practice of segregating African Americans into distinct units during the Civil War.

6. U.S. Pension Bureau, *A Treatise on the Practice of the Pension Bureau Governing the Adjudication of Army and Navy Pensions* (Washington, D.C.: GPO, 1898), 55, 75. The booklet stated: "Special provision is made concerning proof of marriage of colored and Indian soldiers by section 4705 of the Revised Statutes, under which marriage is proven by showing the parties 'were joined in marriage by some ceremony deemed by them obligatory, or habitually recognized each other as husband and wife, and were so recognized by their neighbors, and lived together as such up to the date of enlistment, when soldier or sailor died in service, or if otherwise, to the date of death'" (55).

7. The exact eligibility standards changed, generally becoming increasingly relaxed over time. Veterans' pensions were called "invalid" pensions, the theory being that the former soldier was receiving money for some disability that prevented him from earning a living. The general requirements for receiving an invalid pension included some disability verified by a surgical board appointed by the federal government, at least ninety days of wartime service, and an honorable discharge. Until 1890, proof had to be presented that the veteran's disability was in some way related to his military service. After 1890, the disability no longer had to be service related. In 1907, federal law made age a basis for granting a pension, and the invalid pension system formally became an old-age pension system. See *United States Statutes at Large,* 46 vols. (Washington, D.C.: GPO, 1863–1931), 12:566–69, 26:182, 34:879.

For survivors to collect pensions, the men on whom they based their claims had to have had ninety days' service and been honorably discharged. In addition, different types of survivors had to prove other facts. Widows had to show that they were legally married to veterans and had not remarried. After 1882, new legislation disqualified a widow from collecting a pension if she had cohabited or had illicit sexual relations with another man since her husband's death. See *Statutes at Large,* 22:345, and Michelle A. Krowl, "'Her Just Dues': Civil War Pensions of African American Women in Virginia," in *Negotiating Boundaries of Southern Womanhood: Dealing with the Powers that Be,* ed. Janet L Coryell et al. (Columbia: University of Missouri Press, 2000), 58–62. Children had to demonstrate that they were the offspring of a legally married couple and less than sixteen years of age at the time of their father's death. (They lost their pensions on their sixteenth birthdays.) Parents applying for a pension based on the death of their son had to prove that he had helped support them at the time of his death. This requirement was eased in 1873 by legislation authorizing a pension if it could be proved that the son *wished* to help out his parents at the time of his death. The 1890 pension law dropped even this requirement if the son had died while in service during the war. See Megan J. McClintock, "Civil War Pensions and the Reconstruction of Union Families," *Journal of American History* 83 (September 1996): 466–71.

8. About 70 percent of black Civil War veterans applying for pensions could not sign their applications. This rate of illiteracy mirrors the overall rate for African-American men of the Civil War generation: 70.7 percent of black men age sixty-five and older in 1910. The corresponding figure for native-born whites was 15.5 percent, and for foreign-born whites, 14.7 percent. See U.S. Census Bureau, *Negro Population: 1790–1915* (Washington, D.C.: GPO, 1918), 406, 414. In terms of poverty, even the most optimistic estimates

of African-American income in the postwar era acknowledge the wide disparity between per capita white and black incomes. Robert Higgs estimated that the per capita income of African Americans was only 24 percent of white per capita income in the late 1860s, and 35 percent in 1900. See Robert Higgs, *Competition and Coercion: Blacks in the American Economy, 1865–1914* (Cambridge: Cambridge University Press, 1977), 146.

9. The government would not accept affidavits of doctors as sufficient proof of disability. On occasion, a veteran would complain that the bureau had assigned him to a board so far from his home that it was impossible for him to have his disability evaluated. See Deposition of Smith Jackson, 26 March 1895, Civil War Pension File of Smith Buchanan (alias Jackson), 136th USCI; William L. Dickinson, Hardy Station, Miss., to L. C. Woodson, U.S. Pension Bureau, Washington, D.C., 17 January 1903, Pension File of William L. Dixon, 14th USCI; James H. Southard, U.S. Representative, to H. Clay Evans, Commissioner of Pensions, 1 May 1901, Pension File of Reuben Harris, 88th USCI (New) and 9th USCHA; Edward Luntworth, Hampton, Va., to Joshua R. Potts, U.S. Pension Bureau, Washington, D.C., 16 October 1905, Pension File of Edward Luntworth, 36th USCI; Gray Smith, Knoxville, Ark., to Joseph H. Hunter, Washington, D.C., 28 September 1890, Pension File of Gray Smith, 48th USCI; Affidavit of Toliver Thompson, 21 July 1891, Pension File of Toliver Thompson, 83d USCI (New), RG 15.

10. Kenneth Ng and Nancy Virts, "The Value of Freedom," *Journal of Economic History* 49 (December 1989): 960–61.

11. Edward A. Miller Jr. also noted this problem of name inconsistency in his study of a black Illinois regiment. See Edward A. Miller Jr., *The Black Civil War Soldiers of Illinois: The Story of the Twenty-ninth U.S. Colored Infantry* (Columbia: University of South Carolina Press, 1998), 181–86.

12. Pension Files of Smith Buchanan (alias Jackson), 136th USCI; Alfred Carruthers (alias Butler), 14th USCI; Pickney Ellsworth (alias Leonard), 51st USCI; Alexander Everly (alias Evans), 12th USCI; Frank Finley (alias Brown), 119th USCI; Mathew McCann (alias Mathias Garner), 116th USCI; George Nicholson (alias Nickerson, alias Brown), 15th and 101st USCI; Luke Riddick (alias White), 38th USCI; Phillip Russell (alias Fry), 114th USCI; Lewis Smith (alias Dick L. Barnett), 77th USCI and 10th USCHA; Toney Smith (alias James T. Keele), 118th USCI; James Watkins (alias Davis), 54th USCI; Edmund Wescott (alias Bayly), 10th USCI; Alfred Williams (alias Allen), 107th USCI; Allen James Walker (alias Allen James), 11th USCI and 7th USCHA, RG 15. Also see Elizabeth Regosin, *Freedom's Promise: Ex-Slave Families and Citizenship in the Age of Emancipation* (Charlottesville: University of Virginia Press, 2002), 54–78.

13. Pension Files of Samuel Anden (alias Anderson), 5th and 6th USCHA; Joseph E. Armant, 74th and 91st USCI; Alfred Benson, 46th USCI; John Black, 75th USCI; Solomon Bulah, 39th USCI; William L. Dickinson, 14th USCI; Henry Eber, 79th and 81st USCI; Romeo Fee, 10th USCHA; James Flenoy (alias Robinson), 88th USCI (New) and 3d USCHA; Louis Jourdan, 77th USCI and 10th USCHA; Charles Carroll Joyner, 37th USCI; Edward Lunford, 36th USCI; Abraham Northington (alias Norrington), 13th USCI; Charles Crosby (alias Frank Nunn), 86th USCI; Cyrus Ouley (alias Mathias Stephens), 9th USCI; Simon Rappleyea, 26th USCI; Jesse Smith, 52d USCI; Peter Stephens, 74th and 91st USCI, RG 15.

236

## After the Glory

14. Pension Files of William Cullens, 53d USCI; Joseph Ellis, 52d USCI; Charles Morgan, 74th USCI, RG 15.

15. *Statutes at Large,* 34:879.

16. Pension Files of Glen Booker, 2d USCLA; Jackson Bowers, 84th and 87th USCI; Green Colyar, 15th USCI; Nelson Ellis (alias Joseph Ellis), 52d USCI; Renty Gibson, 21st USCI; Washington Granville, 128th USCI; Nelson Jeffries, 125th USCI; Cruel McCray, 33d USCI; John Ransom, 4th USCC; Luke Riddick, 38th USCI; Robert L. Schofield, 26th USCI; Lee Scott, 23d USCI; Isaac Shorter, 14th USCI; Joe Smith, 78th and 83d USCI; Goram Williams, 108th USCI and 5th USCC, RG 15.

17. For a more detailed explanation of the role of pension claims agents, see John William Oliver, *History of the Civil War Military Pensions, 1861–1885,* Bulletin of the University of Wisconsin, No. 844, History Series (Madison: University of Wisconsin, 1917), 53–54.

18. See note 8.

19. Pension Files of Joseph Armant, 74th and 91st USCI; Joseph Arnold, 12th USCI; William Ballinger, 58th USCI; Jeremiah Bradley, 54th Massachusetts Infantry; John H. Clay, 47th USCI; Benjamin Courtney, 51st USCI; John P. Crabb, 24th USCI; George Crawford, 28th USCI; Henry Eber, 79th and 81st USCI; Clement Frederick, 70th and 71st USCI; Phillip Fry (alias Russell), 114th USCI; Washington Granville, 128th USCI; Smith Gray, 48th USCI; Frank Handy, 37th USCI; Thomas Hampton, 115th USCI; William Harmon, 54th Massachusetts Infantry; Samuel Hawkins, 11th USCI (New), 6th and 7th USCHA; George Hinton (alias Beverly Stewart), 102d USCI; Joseph Johnson, 56th USCI; Oscar Johnson, 1st USCHA; William Lucas, 109th USCI; Jacob Luckett, 50th USCI; Amos Matthews, 32d USCI; Jack Matthews, 68th USCI; Charles Morgan, 74th USCI; Abraham Northington (alias Norrington), 13th USCI; Jordan Norton, 70th and 71st USCI; Cornelius Perry (alias Timber), 11th and 113th USCI (New); Isaac Petteway, 37th USCI; Ned Richardson (alias West), 104th USCI; Samuel Sloss, 111th USCI; James A. Smith, 27th USCI; Lloyd Thurston, 9th USCI; General Walker, 88th and 97th USCI; Josiah White, 78th and 83d USCI; Alfred Williams (alias Allen), 107th USCI; Willis Wood, 83d USCI (New), RG 15.

20. Jesse Jeffrey, Special Examiner, Stubenville, Ohio, to the Commissioner of Pensions, Washington, D.C., 17 December 1889, Pension File of James R. Smith, 27th USCI, RG 15.

21. *Statutes at Large,* 20:265.

22. The maximum legal fee in pension cases was $10 in claims made under the 1890 law and $25 in war-related disability claims made under the earlier 1862 or "general law." This money was payable directly to the attorney of record by the Pension Bureau. The law firm then shared a portion of the fee with the claims agent. However, it was apparently common for some agents to appear when the applicant got the initial payment and illegally demand a portion of it, especially if the case involved arrears. For examples of this phenomenon, see Pension Files of George Burton, 41st USCI; Benjamin Courtney, 51st USCI; Nat Jackson, 51st USCI; Jacob Luckett, 50th USCI; Ned Richardson (alias West), 104th USCI; George Scott, 54th Massachusetts Infantry; Cuffie Simmons, 128th USCI; John Smith, 49th USCI; General Walker, 88th and 97th USCI, RG 15.

23. Regosin, *Freedom's Promise*, 35–36.

24. John J. Hibbett, Gallatin, Tenn., to Benton McMillan, U.S. Representative, Washington, D.C., 5 June 1886, Pension File of George Hibbett, 14th USCI, RG 15.

25. I chose white Southerners for comparison because most black soldiers came from the South, thus eliminating regional bias that might have resulted had the white soldiers chosen come from Northern Union regiments. It was also the goal to select white veterans from Southern states in proportions roughly reflective of their contribution to the Union army. The number of subjects chosen from particular Southern states were as follows: Delaware, two; Kentucky, thirteen; Louisiana, one; Maryland, four; Mississippi, one; Missouri, nineteen; North Carolina, one; and Tennessee, nine. Hence, although the sample of white Southerners is not as deep as the group of black veterans to which it is compared, it is fairly geographically representative of the white Southerners in the Union army.

26. Of the 533 pension files examined for the random sample group, 260 (or about 49 percent) contained at least one special examiner's report.

27. The problem of getting specific dates from some black applicants was sufficiently common that the Pension Bureau created a special procedure. "In claims by colored persons," read a bureau manual on special examinations, "it will generally be necessary to call attention to the witnesses to some important event, holiday, &c., to enable them to testify with any approach to accuracy in regard to dates." See U.S. Pension Bureau, *General Instructions to Special Examiners of the U.S. Pension Bureau* (Washington, D.C.: GPO, 1882), 24.

28. Eugene B. Payne, Special Examiner, to the Commissioner of Pensions, Washington, D.C., 23 December 1893, Pension File of Evans Osborne, 18th and 72d USCI, RG 15; emphasis in original.

29. Charles Whitehead, Special Examiner, Memphis, Tenn., to the Commissioner of Pensions, Washington, D.C., 14 July 1905, Pension File of Joseph Smith, 78th and 83d USCI, RG 15.

30. J. B. Steed, Special Examiner, Vicksburg, Miss., to the Commissioner of Pensions, Washington, D.C., 24 May 1918, Pension File of Samuel Anden (alias Anderson), 5th and 6th USCI; A. H. Sweetser, Special Examiner, Richmond, Ky., to the Commissioner of Pensions, Washington, D.C., 31 March 1890, Pension File of Richard Breck, 121st USCI and 13th USCHA; F. G. Sims, Special Examiner, to the Commissioner of Pensions, Washington, D.C., 20 September 1895, Pension File of John Burgess, 11th USCI and 113th USCI (New); L. C. Walsh, Special Examiner, Philadelphia, Pa., to the Commissioner of Pensions, Washington, D.C., 29 December 1906, Pension File of John Demby, 24th USCI; J. S. Collins, Special Examiner, New Albany, Ind., to the Commissioner of Pensions, Washington, D.C., 14 April 1911, Pension File of Phillip Russell (alias Fry), 114th USCI, RG 15.

31. John Hall Comick, Special Examiner, Springfield, Mass., to the Commissioner of Pensions, Washington, D.C., 19 October 1894, Pension File of Jeremiah L. Bradley, 54th Massachusetts Infantry, RG 15.

32. John Lux, Special Examiner, to the Commissioner of Pensions, Washington, D.C., 16 December 1887, Pension File of Lewis Booth, 50th USCI, RG 15.

33. A. H. Sweetser, Special Examiner, Richmond, Ky., to the Commissioner of Pensions, Washington, D.C., 31 March 1890, Pension File of Richard Breck, 121st USCI and 13th USCHA, RG 15.

34. M. Whitehead, Special Examiner, Norfolk, Va., to the Commissioner of Pensions, Washington, D.C., 17 August 1893, Pension File of Lloyd Thurston, 9th USCI, RG 15.

35. M. Whitehead, Special Examiner, New Orleans, La., to the Commissioner of Pensions, Washington, D.C., 21 October 1907, and Deposition of Clementine Chatham, 4 October 1907, Pension File of Henry Eber (alias Herbert), 79th and 81st USCI, RG 15.

36. George P. Rawick, ed., *The American Slave: A Composite Autobiography*, vol. 8, pt. 1, *Arkansas Narratives* (Westport, Conn.: Greenwood Press, 1972), 99.

37. Ibid., vol. 10, pt. 6, 99.

38. Theda Skocpol, *Protecting Soldiers and Mothers: The Political Origins of Social Policy in the United States* (Cambridge, Mass.: Belknap Press of Harvard University Press, 1992), 139–40.

39. Of the 1,044 subjects in the main random sample, 442 (42.3 percent) had a pension file with at least one successful application. This percentage multiplied by the number of black Civil War soldiers and sailors (196,975) produces an estimate of the number of pension files with at least one successful application (83,320). By scrupulously recording the starting and ending dates of pension payments and the payment rate, it is possible to calculate the total pension payments per file and hence the average paid per file. The figure of $313 million was computed by multiplying the estimated number of black pension files with at least one successful application (83,320) by the average amount paid per file ($3,759).

Note that $313 million is a conservative estimate because of the lack of payment information in some pension files, which usually commences in the 1910s. Therefore, this figure probably understates the actual aggregate payment of benefits to black pensioners. The estimate also ignores changes in the price index between the Civil War, when the earliest payments were made, and when the last known black Civil War pensioner, Daisy Anderson, died in 1998.

40. Pauli Murray, *Proud Shoes: The Story of an American Family* (New York: Harper and Row, 1978), 268.

41. Beatrice G. Mickey to the Veterans Administration, 20 September 1962, Pension File of David M. Mickey, 3d USCC, RG 15.

42. Deposition of Kitt Mitchell, 9 June 1903, Pension File of Kitt Michell, 109th USCI, RG 15.

43. Pension File of George Scott, 54th Massachusetts Infantry, RG 15.

44. George P. Rawick, ed., *The American Slave: A Composite Autobiography, Supplement, Series 2*, vol. 9, pt. 8, *Texas Narratives* (Westport, Conn.: Greewood Press, 1979), 3806–7.

45. George P. Rawick, ed., *The American Slave: A Composite Autobiography, Supplement, Series 1*, vol. 9, pt. 4, *Mississippi Narratives* (Westport, Conn.: Greenwood Press, 1977), 1906–7.

46. U.S. Pension Bureau, *Laws of the United States Governing the Granting of Army and Navy Pensions and Bounty Land, Together with the Regulations Relating Thereto* (Washington, D.C.: GPO, 1905), 38–39.

47. Pension File of Charles W. Goodrich, 1st USCI, RG 15.

48. Loaning money to veterans became a sizable racket for some merchants, particularly in small towns and villages, where the storekeeper was often the local postmaster as well. The merchant-postmaster could siphon money from pensioners in three ways: he could charge for cashing the pension check, collect interest on loans, and make the veteran pay for executing the voucher every quarter. Because the storekeeper could execute vouchers, this obviated the need to return the certificate to the pensioner every quarter so that he could go elsewhere to have the voucher executed. See Pension File of Frank Wilson, 36th USCI, RG 15.

49. R. B. Rosenburg, *Living Monuments: Confederate Soldiers' Homes in the New South* (Chapel Hill: University of North Carolina Press, 1993), 5.

50. For most of the history of the National Home for Disabled Volunteer Soldiers, the institution did not keep statistics on the race of residents. However, after 1876, it published the names of residents in its annual report. Until 1905, black veterans were listed separately from white veterans. Hence, it is possible to reconstruct their numbers in the NHDVS homes from 1876 to 1905. See National Home for Disabled Volunteer Soldiers, *Annual Report of the Board of Managers of the National Home for Disabled Volunteer Soldiers* (Washington, D.C.: GPO, 1877–1906).

51. Hezekiah Butler, St. Louis, Mo., to the Governor, National Home for Disabled Volunteer Soldiers, Danville, Ill., 19 June 1907, Hezekiah Butler, Case File, Sample Case Files of Members, 1867–1934, Danville Branch, Danville, Ill., Records of the National Home for Disabled Volunteer Soldiers and the National Homes of the Veterans Administration, RG 15, Records of the Veterans Administration, National Archives and Records Administration—Great Lakes Region (Chicago).

52. Patrick J. Kelley, *Creating a National Home: Building the Veterans' Welfare State* (Cambridge, Mass.: Harvard University Press, 1997), 98; see also E. L. Cobb, *Optic Views and Impressions of the National Soldiers' Home, Southern Branch, N.H.D.V.S., Near Hampton, Virginia, as Seen and Described by One of Its Members* (Hampton, Va.: Southern Branch, NHDVS, 1910), 71.

53. Stephen Fountain, Norfolk, Va., to Benjamin F. Butler, 20 August 1878, Stephen Fountain, Case File, Sample Case Files of Members, 1871–1933, Southern Branch, Hampton, Va., Records of the National Home for Disabled Volunteer Soldiers and the National Homes of the Veterans Administration, RG 15, Records of the Veterans Administration, National Archives and Records Administration—Mid-Atlantic Region (Philadelphia).

54. Etta Hatcher, South Bend, Ind., to London Swift, Dayton, Ohio, 28 December 1922, London Swift, Case File, Sample Case Files of Members, 1867–1934, Central Branch, Dayton, Ohio, Records of the National Home for Disabled Volunteer Soldiers and the National Homes of the Veterans Administration, RG 15, Records of the Veterans Administration, National Archives and Records Administration—Great Lakes Region (Chicago).

55. Stephen Fountain, Case File, RG 15.

56. *Statutes at Large,* 30:1379–80.

57. Pension File of William Edmund, 46th USCI, RG 15.

**After the Glory**

## Chapter 6. Comradeship

1. Mark C. Carnes, *Secret Ritual and Manhood in Victorian America* (New Haven, Conn.: Yale University Press, 1989), 1.

2. Robert B. Beath, *The Grand Army Blue-Book: Rules and Regulations of the Grand Army of the Republic and Official Decisions and Opinions Thereon with Additional Notes* (Philadelphia: n.p., 1888), 4.

3. Nick Salvatore, *We All Got History: The Memory Books of Amos Webber* (New York: Vintage Books, 1997), 168.

4. Beath, *Grand Army Blue-Book,* 1884 ed., 21; 1904 ed., 33.

5. Franklin D. Tappan, *The Passing of the Grand Army of the Republic* (Worcester, Mass.: Commonwealth Press, 1939), 23–25; emphasis in original.

6. Grand Army of the Republic, *Journal of the Twenty-first Annual Session of the National Encampment* (Milwaukee, Wis.: Burdick and Armitage, Printers, 1887), 250–51, 255.

7. Grand Army of the Republic, *Journal of the Twenty-fourth Annual Session of the National Encampment* (Detroit, Mich.: Richmond and Backus Company, 1890), 56–60; Grand Army of the Republic, Department of Louisiana and Mississippi, *Proceedings of the Eighth Annual Encampment* (New Orleans: Patterson and Gray, 1891), 8–9, 17, 25–28, 41.

8. Grand Army of the Republic, *Journal of the Twenty-fifth National Encampment* (Rutland, Vt.: Tuttle Company, Printers, 1891), 259.

9. Ibid., 261–62.

10. Ibid., 254–55.

11. Ibid., 256–57; see also Civil War Pension File of Edmund Richey (alias Edward A. Richey), 115th USCI, RG 15.

12. GAR, *Twenty-fifth National Encampment,* 51.

13. August Meier, *Negro Thought in America, 1880–1915: Racial Ideologies in the Age of Booker T. Washington* (Ann Arbor: University of Michigan Press, 1963), 161–70.

14. Wallace E. Davies, "The Problem of Race Segregation in the Grand Army of the Republic," *Journal of Southern History* 13 (August 1947): 365; Stuart McConnell, *Glorious Contentment: The Grand Army of the Republic, 1865–1900* (Chapel Hill: University of North Carolina Press, 1992), 217.

15. GAR, Department of Louisiana and Mississippi, *Eighth Annual Encampment,* 20; "Roster of the Department of Louisiana and Mississippi, 1884–1892," in Caesar C. Antoine Scrapbook, Southern University Archives, Baton Rouge, La.

16. GAR, *Twenty-fifth National Encampment,* 250.

17. Grand Army of the Republic, Department of Louisiana and Mississippi, *Proceedings of the Fifteenth Annual Encampment of the Department of Louisiana and Mississippi* (New Orleans: Merchants Printing Co., 1898), 27–28.

18. Mary R. Dearing, *Veterans in Politics: The Story of the G.A.R.* (Baton Rouge: Louisiana State University Press, 1952), 418–19.

19. GAR, *Twenty-first National Encampment,* 255.

20. Deposition of William A. Rhegness, 18 May 1922, Pension File of Samuel Hawkins, 11th USCI (New) and 6th and 7th USCHA, RG 15.

21. GAR, *Twenty-first National Encampment,* 251.

22. W. Fitzhugh Brundage, "Race, Memory, and Masculinity: Black Veterans Recall the Civil War," in *The War Was You and Me: Civilians in the American Civil War,* ed. Joan E. Cashin (Princeton, N.J.: Princeton University Press, 2002), 141.

23. Two notable exceptions to the larger pattern of condescension and neglect in the GAR exist at the state level. In 1898, the Department of Louisiana and Mississippi (by then a black-majority department) voted a resolution asking the state constitutional convention not to take away the right of black men to vote. Likewise, a GAR departmental encampment in Arkansas approved a resolution in 1912 opposing an attempt to amend the state constitution to include a grandfather clause to disfranchise black voters. These two cases demonstrate that on at least some occasions the GAR did take formal stands in favor of its African-American members. See GAR, *Fifteenth Annual Encampment,* 27; Grand Army of the Republic, Department of Arkansas, *Proceedings of the Twenty-third Annual Encampment* (Siloam Springs, Ark.: Press of the Daily Register, [1912]), 18.

According to Mary Dearing, members of the Union Veterans' Union, a more exclusive organization (membership required six months of uninterrupted wartime service or a disability discharge, as opposed to only ninety days of service for the GAR), criticized white Southerners in 1899 "for depriving Negroes of their legal and political equality." See Dearing, *Veterans in Politics,* 495.

24. Soekland went on to suggest that fraud had characterized the relationship between the Arkansas department and its black posts prior to his tenure. "They received money from these deluded creatures, for dues, year after year," he claimed, "and never placed one cent to their credit." See Grand Army of the Republic, Department of Arkansas, *Proceedings of the Sixteenth Annual Encampment* (Fayetteville, Ark.: W. D. Mathews and Son, [1898]), 5.

25. Barbara A. Gannon, "Sites of Memory, Sites of Glory: African-American Grand Army of the Republic Posts in Pennsylvania," in *Making and Remaking Pennsylvania's Civil War,* ed. William Blair and William Pencak (University Park: Pennsylvania State University Press, 2001), 165–87.

26. Records of Miscellaneous Posts, 1861–1940, Grand Army of the Republic, Department of Pennsylvania, Archives of Industrial Society, University of Pittsburgh, Pittsburgh, Pa.

27. Gannon, "Sites of Memory," 174–79.

28. Robert Anderson, *From Slavery to Affluence: Memoirs of Robert Anderson, Ex-Slave* (Hemingford, Nebr.: Hemingford Ledger, 1927), 4; 1890 Special Census of Union Veterans and Their Widows, Box Butte County, Nebr., Microfilm No. M123, National Archives, Washington, D.C. In fairness, the Hemingford GAR post was likely able to draw on men farther out in Box Butte County. Robert Anderson is not listed as having a Hemingford post office address. Nonetheless, the special census found only 133 Union veterans residing in Box Butte County in 1890.

29. Salvatore, *We All Got History,* 169.

30. GAR, *Twenty-fifth National Encampment,* 261–62.

31. *Cleveland Gazette,* 11 June 1887.

32. Grand Army of the Republic, Department of Pennsylvania, *Roster for 1885, General Orders of 1884, and Proceedings of the 36th and 37th Encampments of the Department of Pennsylvania, Grand Army of the Republic* (Philadelphia: n.p., 1885), 260–61.

33. Gannon, "Sites of Memory," 173.

34. *Cleveland Gazette*, 4 December 1886.

35. Carnes, *Secret Ritual and Manhood*, 14.

36. Pension File of Denny Milton (alias Charles Davis), 65th USCI, RG 15.

37. Pension File of Jacob Hutchinson (alias Abraham I. J. Wright), 4th USCHA, RG 15.

38. Pension File of Oscar Johnson, 1st USCHA, RG 15.

39. Pension File of John Spencer, 77th USCI and 10th USCHA, RG 15.

40. Of the 369 veterans in the random sample group who had applied for pensions, 305 (82.7 percent) had at least one successful pension application. Of the 128 members of the O. P. Morton Post in 1888 who applied for pensions, all but 4, or nearly 97 percent, were successful. See Civil War Pension Files, RG 15; James S. Wyekoff, comp., *Roster of the Department of the Potomac, Grand Army of the Republic* (Washington, D.C.: Gibson Brothers, Printers, 1888), 24–26.

41. Grand Army of the Republic, Department of Georgia, *Roster and History of the Department of Georgia, States of Georgia and South Carolina, Grand Army of the Republic* (Atlanta: Syl. Lester and Company, Printers, 1894), 24–33.

42. Pension Files of Lot Lee Barton, 54th Massachusetts Infantry; George Crawford, 28th USCI; Erastus Green, 1st USCI; George Seymour (alias Madison), 83d USCI (New), RG 15; *New York Freeman*, 7 March 1885, 3.

43. Pension Files of Edwin Freeman, 29th Connecticut Infantry; Louis Page, 74th and 91st USCI; Matthew Shavers, 34th USCI, RG 15.

44. Pension File of Lindsay Brown, 13th USCHA, RG 15.

45. GAR, *Twenty-fifth National Encampment*, 256. For information on Johnson's personal background, see Civil War Pension File of Robert Johnson, 43d USCI, RG 15.

46. *Cleveland Gazette*, 30 January 1886.

47. Grand Army of the Republic, Department of Ohio, *Proceedings of the Twenty-second Annual Encampment of the Department of Ohio, Grand Army of the Republic* (Springfield, Ohio: Globe Printing and Publishing Company, 1888), 131–32, 138.

48. *Boston Journal*, 30 December 1894, in the George T. Garrison Clippings, vol. 4, Garrison Family Papers, Sophia Smith Collection, Smith College, Northampton, Mass.

49. GAR, Department of Louisiana and Mississippi, *Eighth Annual Encampment*, 5; Grand Army of the Republic, Department of Louisiana and Mississippi, *Proceedings of the Ninth Annual Encampment* (n.p., [1892]), 4–5; *Proceedings of the Tenth Annual Encampment* (n.p., [1893]), 4; *Proceedings of the Eleventh Annual Encampment* (n.p., [1894]), 4; *Proceedings of the Twelfth Annual Encampment* (New Orleans, La.: Paragon Printing Company, 1895), 4–5; *Proceedings of the Thirteenth Annual Encampment* (New Orleans, La.: Crusader Print, 1896), 4; *Proceedings of the Fourteenth Annual Encampment* (New Orleans, La.: Meine and Weihing, 1897), 3; *Fifteenth Annual Encampment*, 4–5; *Proceedings of the Sixteenth Annual Encampment* (New Orleans, La.: Merchants Printing Company, 1899), 2; *Proceedings of the Seventeenth and Eighteenth Annual En-*

*campments* (New Orleans, La.: Merchants Printing Company, 1901), 5–6, 35–36; *Proceedings of the 19th Annual Encampment* (New Orleans, La.: E. S. Upton Print, 1902), 3, 6; *Proceedings of the Twentieth Annual Encampment* (New Orleans, La.: E. S. Upton Print, 1902), 5–6.

50. Paul Bruce, a former private in the 81st USCI, was the commander for the Department of Louisiana and Mississippi for 1901. Felix C. Antoine, the younger brother of Caesar C. Antoine, is listed as a "Past Department Commander," apparently preceding Bruce. See GAR, *Proceedings of the Twenty-first Annual Encampment* (New Orleans, La.: E. S. Upton Print, 1903), 5.

51. *Cleveland Gazette,* 12 July 1884.

52. Salvatore, *We All Got History,* 280–81.

53. *Cleveland Gazette,* 30 January 1886.

54. Ibid.

55. *Boston Journal,* 2 and 3 August 1887, in Garrison Clippings.

56. Ibid., 3 August 1887.

57. Grand Army of the Republic, Department of the Potomac, *Journal of the Thirty-third Annual Encampment, Department of the Potomac, Grand Army of the Republic* (Washington, D.C.: Gibson Brothers, Printers and Bookbinders, 1901), 22–25, 31–33.

58. GAR, *Tenth Annual Encampment,* 12–13.

59. Stuart McConnell points out that in the 1880s and 1890s, some white GAR posts created "associate" or "honorary" memberships for prominent nonveterans. Many former soldiers and sailors who wished to limit membership to Union veterans exclusively were opposed to this practice. Although a similar custom was apparently common in some African-American posts, there is no evidence that former military laborers or buffalo soldiers had anything but full membership in the GAR. Full membership in turn suggests that black Union veterans saw these men as their equals and that they fit within their conception of veteranhood. See McConnell, *Glorious Contentment,* 120–21.

60. Roland C. McConnell, "Selected African American Musicians and Bands in the United States Military from Colonial Times through the Civil War," *Journal of the Afro-American Historical and Genealogical Society* 12 (Spring and Summer 1991): 11–15. It should be noted that Edward C. Papenfuse, Maryland state archivist and commissioner of land patents; his associates; and summer interns at the Maryland State Archives did most of the groundbreaking research on Brigade Band No. 1. I appreciate their willingness to share information on this unit.

61. Deposition of James Hill, 18 September 1889, Pension File of Joseph Moxley, Brigade Band No. 1, RG 15.

62. Deposition of Thomas Henry, 17 September 1889, in ibid.

63. Deposition of Robert Moxley, 2 March 1896, Pension File of Thomas Henry, Brigade Band No. 1, RG 15.

64. Pension Files of Joseph Moxley, James Hill, Thomas Henry, Perry Moxley, and Robert Moxley, Brigade Band No. 1, RG 15.

65. Deposition of Robert Moxley, 15 September 1897, Pension File of Thomas Henry, Brigade Band No. 1, RG 15.

66. Pension File of Andrew J. Smith, 55th Massachusetts Infantry, RG 15; Civil War Service Record of Andrew J. Smith, 55th Massachusetts Infantry, RG 94; "Biography," in Letters and Memorabilia of Color-Sergeant Andrew J. Smith, Co. B, 55th Massachusetts Infantry Regiment, 1842–1932, Civil War Miscellaneous Collection, U.S. Army Military History Institute, Carlisle, Pa. Smith's Civil War service record indicates that he was free-born in Illinois, but the oral history passed down by his descendants claims that he was the son of a slave and a Kentucky plantation owner. Family lore asserts that when he was sixteen years old his father sent him north to freedom. Smith became a boatman there and in May 1863 joined the 55th Massachusetts Infantry. Smith rose to the rank of sergeant in the 55th, winning promotions for bravery.

67. William H. Dupree to Andrew J. Smith, 17 July 1890, in ibid.

68. David Lee to Andrew J. Smith, 18 April 1914, in ibid.

69. George S. Walker to Andrew J. Smith, 5 August 1915, in ibid.

70. George S. Walker to Andrew J. Smith, 20 October 1915, in ibid.

71. Ibid.

72. Wilder's efforts failed because the War Department could find no account of Smith's bravery in its official records, and the act of Congress authorizing the medal permitted it to be awarded only on the basis of official military records. See Burt G. Wilder to Commissioner of Pensions, 21 December 1916, and Adjutant General to Burt G. Wilder, 3 January 1917, in ibid.

73. Burt G. Wilder to Andrew J. Smith, 15 February 1913, in ibid.

74. Burt G. Wilder to Andrew J. Smith, 17 August 1913, in ibid.

75. Avis Thomas-Lester, "North Brentwood Savors, Sustains Proud Heritage," *Washington Post*, 30 March 1995, E1.

76. Thomas W. Higginson, "Some War Scenes Revisited," *Atlantic Monthly* 42 (July 1878): 1–9.

77. Garrison Clippings.

78. Philip S. Foner and George E. Walker, eds., *Proceedings of the Black National and State Conventions, 1865–1900*, vol. 1 (Philadelphia: Temple University Press, 1986), 294–95; Salvatore, *We All Got History*, 280–85; *Boston Journal*, 2 and 3 August 1887, in Garrison Clippings.

79. Edward Cahill to Henry Taylor, 20 May 1892, Pension File of Henry Taylor, 102d USCI, RG 15.

## Chapter 7. Memory

1. Stuart McConnell, *Glorious Contentment: The Grand Army of the Republic, 1865–1900* (Chapel Hill: University of North Carolina Press, 1992), 219.

2. *New York Freeman*, 20 August 1887.

3. Ibid.

4. Barbara Gannon, "Colored Comrades: African Americans in the Grand Army of the Republic and the Construction of Interracial Veteranhood" (paper presented at the annual meeting of the Southern Historical Association, November 1999), 5–6.

5. *New York Globe,* 24 February 1883; *New York Freeman,* 30 May 1855 and 29 May 1886.

6. Ibid; *Washington Bee,* 4 June 1887; *New York Age,* 9 June 1888.

7. *New York Globe,* 2 June 1883; *New York Freeman,* 30 May 1885 and 29 May 1886; *New York Age,* 25 May 1889 and 9 January 1890.

8. Grand Army of the Republic, *Roster of the Department of Louisiana and Mississippi, 1884–1897* (n.p., [1897]); Grand Army of the Republic, Department of the Potomac, *Journal of the Thirty-third Annual Encampment* (Washington, D.C.: Gibson Brothers, Printers and Bookbinders, 1901), 11.

9. James G. Hollandsworth Jr., *The Louisiana Native Guards: The Black Military Experience during the Civil War* (Baton Rouge: Louisiana State University Press, 1995), 112; Stephen J. Ochs, *A Black Patriot and a White Priest: André Cailloux and Claude Paschal Maistre in Civil War New Orleans* (Baton Rouge: Louisiana State University Press, 2000).

10. *New York Globe,* 2 June 1883.

11. *New York Freeman,* 30 May 1885.

12. Ibid., 5 June 1886.

13. W. Fitzhugh Brundage, "Race, Memory, and Masculinity: Black Veterans Recall the Civil War," in *The War Was You and Me: Civilians in the American Civil War,* ed. Joan E. Cashin (Princeton, N.J.: Princeton University Press, 2002), 143.

14. Ibid., 144–46.

15. Minute Book, August 7, 1885–December 8, 1887, Robert G. Shaw Post No. 206, Records of Miscellaneous Posts, 1861–1940, Grand Army of the Republic, Department of Pennsylvania, Archives of Industrial Society, University of Pittsburgh, Pittsburgh, Pa.

16. Minute Book, June 5, 1897–September 17, 1894, in ibid.

17. *New York Freeman,* 19 February 1887.

18. Laurie F. Maffly-Kipp, "Redeeming Southern Memory: The Negro Race History, 1874–1915," in *Where These Memories Grow: History, Memory, and Southern Identity,* ed. W. Fitzhugh Brundage (Chapel Hill: University of North Carolina Press, 2000), 169–70.

19. William Wells Brown, *The Negro in the American Rebellion: His Heroism and His Fidelity* (Boston: Lee and Shepard, 1867), 309; William T. Alexander, *History of the Colored Race in America* (Kansas City, Mo.: Palmetto Publishing Company, 1887), 346–47; P. Thomas Stanford, *The Tragedy of the Negro in America* (Boston: n.p., 1898), 98; T. G. Steward, *The Colored Regulars in the United States Army* (Philadelphia: A.M.E. Book Concern, 1904), 69; H. M. Tarver, *The Negro in the History of the United States* (Austin, Tex.: State Printing Company, 1905), 104–5; Edward A. Johnson, *A School History of the Negro Race in America from 1619 to 1890* (New York: Isaac Goldmann, 1911), 106–30.

20. E[dward] A. Pollard, *Southern History of the War,* vol. 2 (New York: Charles B. Richardson, 1866), 197.

21. Theo F. Brewer, "Storming of Fort Pillow," *Confederate Veteran* 33 (December 1925): 459, 478; James Dinkins, "The Capture of Fort Pillow," *Confederate Veteran* 33 (December 1925): 460–62.

22. Vance Robert Skarstedt, "The Confederate Veteran Movement and National Reunification" (Ph.D. diss., Florida State University, 1993), 230–31.

23. Ervin L. Jordan Jr., *Black Confederates and Afro-Yankees in Civil War Virginia* (Charlottesville: University of Virginia Press, 1995), 185–200.

24. *Confederate Veteran* 2 (July 1884): 233; 23 (September 1915): 425; Skarstedt, "Confederate Veteran Movement," 250–51.

25. R. B. Rosenburg, *Living Monuments: Confederate Soldiers' Homes in the New South* (Chapel Hill: University of North Carolina Press, 1993), xi–xiii, 151–52.

26. *Confederate Veteran* 29 (July 1921): 284; 30 (February 1922): 77. Pensions were eventually awarded to "faithful Negroes" in the following states (according to mail inquiries to state archives in the South): Arkansas, Georgia, Mississippi, North Carolina, South Carolina, Tennessee, and Virginia. Alabama, Florida, Maryland, and Texas did not pay pensions to African Americans who served the Confederacy. Inquiries did not settle whether Kentucky, Louisiana, or Missouri paid such state pensions to African Americans for Confederate service. See also Jordan, *Black Confederates and Afro-Yankees,* 196–99.

27. George P. Rawick, ed., *The American Slave: A Composite Autobiography, Supplement, Series 1,* vol. 10, pt. 5, *Mississippi Narratives* (Westport, Conn.: Greenwood Press, 1977), 2017–18.

28. Ibid., vol. 8, pt. 3, 1107.

29. Ibid.

30. R. B. Rosenburg also notes the presence of former African-American body servants as residents in Southern old soldiers' homes. See Rosenburg, *Living Monuments,* 136.

31. Joseph T. Glatthaar, *Forged in Battle: The Civil War Alliance of Black Soldiers and White Officers* (New York: Free Press, 1990), 238–42.

32. Garth W. James, "The Assault on Fort Wagner," in *War Papers Read before the Commandery of the State of Wisconsin, Military Order of the Loyal Legion of the United States* (Milwaukee, Wis.: Burdick, Armitage, and Allen, 1891), 30.

33. William Eliot Furness, "The Negro as a Soldier," in *Military Essays and Recollections: Papers Read before the Commandery of the State of Illinois, Military Order of the Loyal Legion of the United States,* vol. 2 (Chicago: A. C. McClurg and Company, 1894), 459.

34. James H. Rickard, *Service with Colored Troops in Burnside's Corps* (Providence, R.I.: Providence Press for Rhode Island Soldiers and Sailors Historical Society, 1894), 38.

35. Thomas J. Morgan, "Reminiscences of Service with Colored Troops," in *Personal Narratives of Events in the War of the Rebellion Being Papers Read before the Rhode Island Soldiers and Sailors Historical Society* (Providence, R.I.: Rhode Island Soldiers and Sailors Historical Society, 1885), 8–9; Furness, "The Negro as a Soldier," 468–69; Norwood P. Hallowell, *The Negro as a Soldier in the War of the Rebellion* (Boston: Little, Brown, 1897), 9–11; William H. Armstrong, "The Negro as a Soldier," in *War Papers Read before the Indiana Commandery, Military Order of the Loyal Legion of the United States* (Indianapolis: Indiana Commandery, Military Order of the Loyal Legion of the United States, 1898), 316; Henry Allyn Norton, "Colored Troops in the War of the Rebellion," in *Glimpses of the Nations Struggle* (St. Paul, Minn.: Review Publishing Company, 1908), 68, 72; A. W. Greely, *Reminiscences of Adventure and Service: A Record of Sixty-five Years* (New York: Charles Scribner's Sons, 1927), 98–99.

36. William A. Crafts, *The Southern Rebellion* (Boston: Samuel Walker and Company, 1870), 385.

37. Henry Stacke, *The Story of the American War, 1861–1865* (London: Frederick Warne and Company, 1866), 128–129, 178, 180, 184–86, 203, 221; Rossiter Johnson, *A Short History of the War of Secession, 1861–1865* (Boston: Houghton, Mifflin, 1889), 313–14, 340–41, 449; John A. Logan, *The Great Conspiracy: Its Origins and History* (New York: A. R. Hart and Company, Publishers, 1886), 501–12.

38. Logan, *The Great Conspiracy*, 502–3.

39. Thomas P. Kettell, *History of the Great Rebellion* (Hartford, Conn.: L. Stebbins, 1865), 506, 662.

40. John William Draper, *History of the American Civil War* (New York: Harper and Brothers, 1870), 207–8.

41. George B. Herbert, *The Popular History of the Civil War in America* (New York: F. M. Lupton, 1884), 329–30.

42. Theodore Ayrault Dodge, *A Bird's-Eye View of Our Civil War* (Cambridge, Mass.: Riverside Press, 1883), 162–66, 248–51.

43. John Hope Franklin, *George Washington Williams: A Biography* (Chicago: University of Chicago Press, 1985), 1–133.

44. George W. Williams, *A History of the Negro Troops in the War of the Rebellion, 1861–1865* (New York: Harper and Brothers, 1888), xiii.

45. Ibid., 145.

46. Ibid., 167–69.

47. Ibid., 320, 324; emphasis in original.

48. Eric Foner, *Freedom's Lawmakers: A Directory of Black Officeholders during Reconstruction* (New York: Oxford University Press, 1993), 233–34; Civil War Service Record of Joseph T. Wilson, 74th USCI (2d Louisiana Native Guards) and 54th Massachusetts Infantry, RG 94.

49. Joseph T. Wilson, *The Black Phalanx: A History of the Negro Soldiers in the Wars of 1775–1812, 1861–'65* (Hartford, Conn.: American Publishing Company, 1887), 13; emphasis in original.

50. Ibid., 377.

51. Brown, *The Negro in the American Rebellion*, 309–22.

52. Alexander, *History of the Colored Race*, 346–47; Stanford, *Tragedy of the Negro*, 98; Steward, *Colored Regulars*, 69; Tarver, *The Negro in the History of the United States*, 104–5; Johnson, *A School History of the Negro Race*, 106–30.

53. Williams, *History of Negro Troops*, 320.

54. Larry M. Logue, *To Appomattox and Beyond: The Civil War Soldier in War and Peace* (Chicago: Ivan R. Dee, 1996), 84.

55. Glatthaar, *Forged in Battle*, 253–56.

56. Christian A. Fleetwood, *The Negro as a Soldier* (Washington, D.C.: Howard University Print, 1895), 18.

57. Williams, *History of Negro Troops*, 328.

58. Brundage, "Race, Memory, and Masculinity," 152.

59. Williams, *History of the Negro Troops,* 328–32.

60. *Cleveland Gazette,* 13 December 1884.

61. For more about Saint-Gaudens's monument, see David W. Blight, "The Shaw Memorial in the Landscape of Civil War Memory," 79–93; Kathryn Greenthal, "Augustus Saint-Gaudens and the Shaw Memorial," 116–29; and Kirk Savage, "Uncommon Soldiers: Race, Art, and the Shaw Memorial," all in *Hope and Glory: Essays on the Legacy of the Fifty-fourth Massachusetts Regiment,* ed. Martin H. Blatt, Thomas J. Brown, and Donald Yacovone (Amherst: University of Massachusetts Press, 2001), 156–67.

62. McConnell, *Glorious Contentment,* 232.

63. Grand Army of the Republic, *Journal of the Twenty-fifth National Encampment* (Rutland, Vt.: Tuttle Company, Printers, 1891), 260.

64. Brundage, "Race, Memory, and Masculinity," 141.

65. David W. Blight, *Race and Reunion: The Civil War in American Memory* (Cambridge, Mass.: Belknap Press of Harvard University Press, 2001), 2.

66. Ibid., 256.

67. Grand Army of the Republic, *Journal of the Twenty-fourth Annual Session of the National Encampment* (Detroit, Mich.: Richmond and Backus Company, 1890), 258.

68. GAR, *Twenty-fifth National Encampment,* 257.

69. Williams, *History of the Negro Troops,* 330–31.

70. GAR, *Twenty-fifth National Encampment,* 256.

**Epilogue**

1. *New Orleans Item,* 13 July 1951.

2. Civil War Pension File and Civil War Service Record of Joseph Clovese, 63d USCI, RG 15.

3. Ibid.

4. Lenwood G. Davis and George Hill, comp., *Blacks in the Armed Forces, 1776–1983: A Bibliography* (Westport, Conn.: Greenwood Press, 1985), xiv.

5. Dudley Taylor Cornish, *The Sable Arm: Negro Troops in the Union Army, 1861–1865* (New York: Longmans, Green, 1956), xi.

6. Cathy Stanton and Stephen Belyea, "'Their Time Will Yet Come': The African American Presence in Civil War Reenactment," in *Hope and Glory: Essays on the Legacy of the Fifty-fourth Massachusetts Regiment,* ed. Martin H. Blatt, Thomas J. Brown, and Donald Yacovone (Amherst: University of Massachusetts Press, 2001), 260.

7. W. Fitzhugh Brundage, "Race, Memory, and Masculinity: Black Veterans Recall the Civil War," in *The War Was You and Me: Civilians in the American Civil War,* ed. Joan E. Cashin (Princeton, N.J.: Princeton University Press, 2002), 142, 154 n. 17.

# Bibliography

**Primary Sources**

*Manuscript Sources at the National Archives, Washington, D.C.*
"General Index to Pension Files, 1861–1934" (Microfilm No. T288).
"Index to Compiled Service Records of Volunteer Union Soldiers Who Served with the United States Colored Troops" (Microfilm No. M589).
"Organization Index to Pension Files of Veterans Who Served between 1861 and 1900" (Microfilm No. T289).
RG 15, Records of the Veterans Administration.
RG 94, Records of the Adjutant General's Office, 1780s–1917.
RG 105, Records of the Bureau of Refugees, Freedmen, and Abandoned Lands.
RG 153, Records of the Office of the Judge Advocate General, Army.
RG 217, Records of the United States General Accounting Office.
RG 233, Records of the U.S. House of Representatives.
RG 393, Records of the United States Army Continental Commands, 1821–1920.

*Other Manuscript Collections*
Allensworth, Allen. Allensworth Collection. California State Department of Parks and Recreation, Sacramento, Calif.
Antoine, Caesar C. Scrapbook. Southern University Archives, Baton Rouge, La.
Dun, R. G., and Company. Credit Ledgers. Business School Archives, Baker Library, Harvard University, Cambridge, Mass.
Fleetwood, Christian A. Papers. Library of Congress Manuscript Division, Washington, D.C.
Freedmen and Southern Society Project Files. University of Maryland, College Park.
Garrison, George T. Clippings. Garrison Family Papers, Smith College, Northampton, Mass.
Harris, Middleton "Spike" A. Papers. Schomburg Center for Research of Black Culture, New York, N.Y.
"In the Aftermath of 'Glory': Black Soldiers and Sailors from Annapolis, Maryland, 1863–1918." Maryland State Archives, Documents for the Classroom. MSA SC 2221–8. Maryland State Archives, Annapolis.
Kinsley, Edward W. Papers. Special Collections Library, Duke University, Durham, N.C.
Latimer, Lewis H. Papers. Schomburg Center for Research of Black Culture, New York, N.Y.
Pinchback, P. B. S. Papers. Moorland-Spingarn Research Center, Howard University, Washington, D.C.

Purvis, Charles Burleigh. Grimke Papers. Moorland-Spingarn Research Center, Howard University, Washington, D.C.

Smith, Andrew J. Letters and Memorabilia of Color-Sergeant Andrew J. Smith, Co. B. 55th Massachusetts Infantry Regiment, 1842–1932. Civil War Miscellaneous Collection, U.S. Army Military History Institute, Carlisle, Pa.

Trotter, James Monroe. "Biographical Sketch of James Monroe Trotter," by George W. Forbes. Rare Books Room, Boston Public Library, Boston, Mass.

Turner, Henry M. Turner Papers. Moorland-Spingarn Research Center, Howard University, Washington, D.C.

*Published Sources*

Abbott, Abial R. "The Negro in the War of the Rebellion." In *Military Essays and Recollections: Papers Read before the Commandery of the State of Illinois, Military Order of the Loyal Legion of the United States.* Vol. 3. Chicago: Dial Press, 1899.

Addeman, Joshua McLancthon. *Reminiscences of Two Years with the Colored Troops.* Providence, R.I.: N. Bang Williams, 1880.

Alexander, Charles. *Battles and Victories of Allen Allensworth.* Boston: Sherman, French, and Company, 1914.

———. *One Hundred Distinguished Leaders.* Atlanta: Franklin Printing and Publishing Co., 1899.

Alexander, William T. *History of the Colored Race in America.* Kansas City, Mo.: Palmetto Publishing Company, 1887.

Anderson, Robert. *From Slavery to Affluence: Memoirs of Robert Anderson, Ex-Slave.* Hemingford, Nebr.: Hemingford Ledger, 1927.

Armstrong, William H. "The Negro as a Soldier." In *War Papers Read before the Indiana Commandery, Military Order of the Loyal Legion of the United States.* Indianapolis: Indiana Commandery, Military Order of the Loyal Legion of the United States, 1898.

Baird, George W. *The 32d Regiment, U.S.C.T. at the Battle of Honey Hill.* N.p., [1889].

Beath, Robert B. *The Grand Army Blue-Book: Rules and Regulations of the Grand Army of the Republic and Official Decisions and Opinions Thereon with Additional Notes.* Philadelphia: n.p., 1888.

Berlin, Ira, Joseph P. Reidy, and Leslie S. Rowland, eds. *Freedom: A Documentary History of Emancipation, 1861–1867. Series II: The Black Military Experience.* Cambridge: Cambridge University Press, 1982.

Brown, Frederick W. *My Service in the U.S. Colored Cavalry.* Cincinnati, Ohio: n.p., 1908.

Brown, William Wells. *The Negro in the American Rebellion: His Heroism and His Fidelity.* Boston: Lee and Shepard, 1867.

Bruce, John Edward. *Defence of the Colored Soldiers Who Fought in the War of the Rebellion.* Yonkers, N.Y.: n.p., n.d.

Bruner, Peter. *A Slave's Adventures toward Freedom: Not Fiction, but the True Story of a Struggle.* Oxford, Ohio: Author, 1925.

Carter, Solon A. *Fourteen Months' Service with Colored Troops.* Boston: Massachusetts Commandery, Military Order of the Loyal Legion of the United States, 1900.

Cobb, E. L. *Optic Views and Impressions of the National Soldiers' Home, Southern Branch, N.H.D.V.S., Near Hampton, Virginia, as Seen and Described by One of Its Members.* Hampton, Va.: Southern Branch NHDVS, 1910.

Cooney, Charles F., ed. "I Was . . . Eager to Become a Soldier." *Manuscripts* 26 (Fall 1974): 280–82.

Crafts, William A. *The Southern Rebellion.* Boston: Samuel Walker and Company, 1870.

Dodge, Theodore Ayrault. *A Bird's-Eye View of Our Civil War.* Cambridge, Mass.: Riverside Press, 1883.

Douglass, Frederick, *Narrative of the Life of Frederick Douglass.* Boston: Anti-Slavery Office, 1845.

Draper, John William. *History of the American Civil War.* New York: Harper and Brothers, 1870.

Eldridge, Hope T., and Dorothy Swaine Thomas. *Population Redistribution and Economic Growth: United States, 1870–1950. Part III: Demographic Analyses and Interrelations.* Philadelphia: American Philosophical Society, 1964.

Fleetwood, Christian A. *The Negro as a Soldier.* Washington, D.C.: Howard University Print, 1895.

Foner, Philip S., and George E. Walker, eds. *Proceedings of the Black National and State Conventions, 1865–1900.* Vol. 1. Philadelphia: Temple University Press, 1986.

Furness, William Eliot. "The Negro as a Soldier." In *Military Essays and Recollections: Papers Read before the Commandery of the State of Illinois, Military Order of the Loyal Legion of the United States.* Vol. 2. Chicago: A. C. McClurg and Company, 1894.

Gibson, J. W., and W. H. Crogman. *The Colored American: From Slavery to Honorable Citizenship.* Atlanta: J. L. Nichols and Co., 1902.

Glasson, William H. *Federal Military Pensions in the United States.* New York: Oxford University Press, 1918.

Grand Army of the Republic. *Journal of the National Encampment.* Publisher and place of publication varies, 1887–1891.

———. Department of Arkansas. *Proceedings of the Annual Encampment.* Publisher and place of publication varies, 1894–1912.

———. Department of Delaware. *Journal of the Twenty-fourth Annual Encampment.* Wilmington, Del.: Hubert A. Roop, Printer, 1905.

———. Department of Georgia. *Roster and History of the Department of Georgia, States of Georgia and South Carolina, Grand Army of the Republic.* Atlanta: Syl. Lester and Company, Printers, 1894.

———. Department of Louisiana and Mississippi. *Proceedings of the Annual Encampment.* Publisher and place of publication varies, 1891–1903.

———. Department of Louisiana and Mississippi. *Roster of the Department of Louisiana and Mississippi, 1884–1897.* N.p., [1897].

————. Department of Pennsylvania. *Roster for 1885, General Orders of 1884, and Proceedings of the 36th and 37th Encampments of the Department of Pennsylvania, Grand Army of the Republic.* Philadelphia: n.p., 1885.

————. Department of the Potomac. *Proceedings* [later *Journals*] *of the Annual Encampment.* Publisher and place of publication varies, 1896–1901.

————. Department of Ohio. *Proceedings of the Twenty-second Annual Encampment of the Department of Ohio, Grand Army of the Republic.* Springfield, Ohio: Globe Printing and Publishing Company, 1888.

Greely, A. W. *Reminiscences of Adventure and Service: A Record of Sixty-five Years.* New York: Charles Scribner's Sons, 1927.

Griggs, Richard. *The Life of Richard Griggs of Issaquena County, Mississippi.* Jackson, Miss.: Pilot Steam Book and Job Printing Establishment, 1872.

Grimes, William W. *Thirty-three Years Experience of an Itinerant Minister of the A.M.E. Church.* Lancaster, Pa.: Eml. S. Speaker, 1887.

Hallowell, Norwood P. *The Negro as a Soldier in the War of the Rebellion.* Boston: Little, Brown, 1897.

Harrison, Samuel. *Rev. Samuel Harrison: His Life Story as Told by Himself.* Pittsfield, Mass.: Press of the Eagle Publishing Company, 1899.

Herbert, George B. *The Popular History of the Civil War in America.* New York: F. M. Lupton, 1884.

Higginson, T[homas] W[entworth]. "Some War Scenes Revisited." *Atlantic Monthly* 42 (July 1878): 3.

Hobart, Edwin L. *Semi-History of a Boy-Veteran of the Twenty-eighth Regiment Illinois Infantry Volunteers in a Black Regiment.* n.p., 1909.

James, Garth W. "The Assault on Fort Wagner." In *War Papers Read before the Commandery of the State of Wisconsin, Military Order of the Loyal Legion of the United States.* Milwaukee, Wis.: Burdick, Armitage, and Allen, 1891.

Johnson, Edward A. *A School History of the Negro Race in America from 1619 to 1890.* New York: Isaac Goldmann, 1911.

Johnson, Rossiter. *A Short History of the War of Secession, 1861–1865.* Boston: Houghton, Mifflin, 1889.

Johnson, William Henry. *Autobiography of William Henry Johnson.* Albany, N.Y.: Argis Company, Printers, 1900.

Kettell, Thomas P. *History of the Great Rebellion.* Hartford, Conn.: L. Stebbins, 1865.

Kletzing, H. F., and W. H. Crogman. *Progress of a Race: The Remarkable Advancement of the American Negro from the Bondage of Slavery, Ignorance and Poverty to the Freedom of Citizenship, Intelligence, Affluence, Honor and Trust.* Atlanta: J. L. Nichols and Co., 1897.

*Laws of the State of Maryland, Made and Passed.* Annapolis, Md.: Richard P. Bayly, Printer, 1864.

Logan, John A. *The Great Conspiracy: Its Origins and History.* New York: A. R. Hart and Company, 1886.

Long, Richard A., ed. *Black Writers and the Civil War.* Secaucus, N.J.: Blue and Grey Press, 1988.

# Bibliography

Lynch, John Roy. *Reminiscences of an Active Life: The Autobiography of John Roy Lynch.* Edited by John Hope Franklin. Chicago: University of Chicago Press, 1970.

Main, Edwin M. *The Story of the Marches, Battles and Incidents of the Third United States Colored Cavalry.* Louisville, Ky.: Globe Printing Company, 1908.

Mallory, William. *Old Plantation Days.* Hamilton, Ontario, Canada: n.p., [1902].

Marrs, Elijah P. *Life and History of the Rev. Elijah P. Marrs.* Louisville, Ky.: Bradley and Gilbert Company, 1885.

Mather, Frank Lincoln, ed. *Who's Who of the Colored Race: A General Biographical Dictionary of Men and Women of Negro Descent.* Vol. 1. Chicago: Memento Edition, Half-Century Anniversary of Negro Freedom in U.S., 1915.

Montgomery, Isaiah T. "The Negro in Business." *Outlook* 16 (November 1901): 733–34.

Moore, John. *What the Negro Has Done for Liberty in America.* Boston: B. Wilkins and Co., 1895.

Morgan, Thomas J. "Reminiscences of Service with Colored Troops." In *Personal Narratives of Events in the War of the Rebellion Being Papers Read before the Rhode Island Soldiers and Sailors Historical Society.* Providence, R.I.: Rhode Island Soldiers and Sailors Historical Society, 1885.

Murray, Pauli. *Proud Shoes: The Story of an American Family.* New York: Harper and Row, 1978.

National Home for Disabled Volunteer Soldiers. *Annual Report of the Board of Managers of the National Home for Disabled Volunteer Soldiers.* Washington, D.C.: GPO, 1877–1906.

Newton, Alexander H. *Out of the Briars: An Autobiography and Sketch of the Twenty-ninth Regiment Connecticut Volunteers.* Philadelphia: A.M.E. Book Concern, 1910.

Nichols, J. L., and William H. Crogman. *Progress of a Race: The Remarkable Advancement of the American Negro from the Bondage of Slavery, Ignorance and Poverty to the Freedom of Citizenship, Intelligence, Affluence, Honor and Trust,* revised and enlarged. Naperville, Ill.: J. L. Nichols and Co., 1920.

Norton, Henry Allyn. "Colored Troops in the War of the Rebellion." In *Glimpses of the Nation's Struggle.* St. Paul, Minn.: Review Publishing Company, 1908.

Oliver, John William. *History of the Civil War Military Pensions, 1861–1885.* Bulletin of the University of Wisconsin, No. 844, History Series. Madison: University of Wisconsin, 1917.

Parker, Allen. *Recollections of Slavery Times.* Worcester, Mass.: Charles W. Burbank and Company, 1895.

Penn, I. Garland. *The Afro-American Press and Its Editors.* Springfield, Mass.: Willey and Company, 1891.

Pollard, E[dward] A. *Southern History of the War.* Vol. 2. New York: Charles B. Richardson, 1866.

Ponton, M. M. *Life and Times of Henry M. Turner.* Atlanta: A. B. Caldwell Publishing Company, 1917.

Rawick, George P., ed. *The American Slave: A Composite Autobiography.* Westport, Conn.: Greenwood Press, 1972.

———. *The American Slave: A Composite Autobiography, Supplement, Series 1.* Westport, Conn.: Greenwood Press, 1977.

————. *The American Slave: A Composite Autobiography, Supplement, Series 2.* Westport, Conn.: Greenwood Press, 1979.

Redkey, Edwin S., ed. *A Grand Army of Black Men: Letters from African American Soldiers in the Union Army, 1861–1865.* Cambridge: Cambridge University Press, 1982.

————. *Respect Black: The Writings and Speeches of Henry McNeal Turner.* New York: Arno Press, 1971.

Richardson, Clement, et al., eds. *The National Cyclopedia of the Colored Race.* Montgomery, Ala.: National Publishing Company, 1919.

Rickard, James H. *Service with Colored Troops in Burnside's Corps.* Providence, R.I.: Providence Press for Rhode Island Soldiers and Sailors Historical Society, 1894.

Robinson, William H. *From Log Cabin to Pulpit: Reminiscences of My Early Life While in Slavery.* Eau Claire, Wis.: James H. Tifft, Publishing Printer, 1913.

Sherman, George R. *The Negro as a Soldier.* Providence, R.I.: Rhode Island Soldiers and Sailors Historical Society, 1913.

Simmons, William J. *Men of Mark: Eminent, Progressive, Rising.* Cleveland, Ohio: Geo. M. Rewell Co., 1887.

Singleton, Henry William. *Recollections of My Slavery Days.* Edited by Katherine Mellon Charron and David S. Cecelski. Raleigh: Division of Archives and History, North Carolina Department of Cultural Resources, 1999.

Sluby, Paul E., Sr., and Stanton L. Wormley, eds. *Diary of Charles B. Fisher.* Washington, D.C.: Columbian Harmony Society, 1983.

Stacke, Henry. *The Story of the American War, 1861–1865.* London: Frederick Warne and Company, 1866.

Stanford, Thomas. *The Tragedy of the Negro in America.* Boston: n.p., 1898.

Steward, T. G. *The Colored Regulars in the United States Army.* Philadelphia: A.M.E. Book Concern, 1904.

Tappan, Franklin D. *The Passing of the Grand Army of the Republic.* Worcester, Mass.: Commonwealth Press, 1939.

Tarver, H. M. *The Negro in the History of the United States.* Austin, Tex.: State Printing Company, 1905.

Trotter, James M. *Music and Some Highly Musical People.* Boston: Lee and Shepard, 1881.

U.S. Census Bureau. *Census Reports. Twelfth Census of the United States Taken in the Year 1900: Population.* Vol. 1. Washington, D.C.: GPO, 1901.

————. *Compendium of the Eleventh Census: 1890.* Washington, D.C.: GPO, 1897.

————. *A Compendium of the Ninth Census (June 1, 1870).* Washington, D.C.: GPO, 1872.

————. *Negro Population: 1790–1915.* Washington, D.C.: GPO, 1918.

————. *Population of the United States in 1860: Compiled from the Original Returns of the Eighth Census.* Washington, D.C.: GPO, 1864.

————. *Report on the Mortality and Vital Statistics of the United States as Returned at the Tenth Census (June 1, 1880).* Washington D.C.: GPO, 1885.

————. *Report on Population of the United States at the Eleventh Census: 1890.* Washington, D.C.: GPO, 1897.

————. *The Seventh Census of the United States: 1850.* Washington, D.C.: Robert Armstrong, Public Printer, 1853.

————. *Special Reports: Marriage and Divorce, 1867–1906. Part 1: Summary, Laws, Foreign Statistics.* Washington, D.C.: GPO, 1909.

————. *Statistics on Population of the United States at the Tenth Census.* Washington, D.C.: GPO, 1883.

U.S. Congress. House. Committee on Military Affairs. *Bounties to Colored Soldiers: Letter from Secretary of War in Answer to a Resolution of the House, of the 7th Ultimo. Relative to Collection and Payment of Bounties to Colored Soldiers.* 41st Cong., 2d sess., 1870.

U.S. Congress. Senate. *Letter of the Secretary of War, Communicating . . . Reports of the Assistant Commissioner of Freedmen and a Synopsis of Laws Respecting Persons of Color in the Slave States.* 39th Cong., 2d sess., 1866–1867.

U.S. Pension Bureau. *General Instructions to Special Examiners of the U.S. Pension Bureau.* Washington, D.C.: GPO, 1882.

————. *Laws of the United States Governing the Granting of Army and Navy Pensions and Bounty Land, Together with the Regulations Relating Thereto.* Washington, D.C.: GPO, 1905.

————. *A Treatise on the Practice of the Pension Bureau Governing the Adjudication of Army and Navy Pensions.* Washington, D.C.: GPO, 1898.

*U.S. Statutes at Large.* Vols. 1–46. Washington D.C.: GPO, 1863–1931.

Wallace, John. *Carpetbag Rule in Florida.* Jacksonville, Fla.: Da Costa, 1888.

Webb, William. *The History of William Webb, Composed by Himself.* Detroit, Mich.: E. Hoekstra, 1873.

Williams, George W. *A History of the Negro Troops in the War of the Rebellion, 1861–1865.* New York: Harper and Brothers, 1888.

Wilson, James Grant, and John Fiske, eds. *Appleton's Cyclopedia of American Biography.* Vol. 2. New York: D. Appleton and Company, 1888.

Wilson, Joseph T. *The Black Phalanx: A History of the Negro Soldiers of the United States in the Wars of 1775–1812, 1861–'65.* Hartford, Conn.: American Publishing Company, 1887.

Wright, Charles Edward. *Marriage and Divorce: A Collation of the Published Decisions of the Department of the Interior, Rendered on Appeal, Appertaining to the Law of Marriage and Divorce in the United States in Its Relation to Pensionable Status.* Washington, D.C.: GPO, 1914.

Wyekoff, James S., comp. *Roster of the Department of the Potomac. Grand Army of the Republic.* Washington, D.C.: Gibson Brothers, Printers, 1888.

## Secondary Sources

*Books*

Adjaye, Joseph K., ed. *Time in the Black Experience.* Westport, Conn.: Greenwood Press, 1994.

Angell, Stephen Ward. *Bishop Henry McNeal Turner and African American Religion in the South.* Knoxville: University of Tennessee Press, 1992.

Ayers, Edward. *The Promise of the New South.* New York: Oxford University Press, 1992.

Bailey, Fred Arthur. *Class and Tennessee's Confederate Generation.* Chapel Hill: University of North Carolina Press, 1987.

Bailey, N. Louise, et al. *Neither Carpetbaggers nor Scalawags: Black Officeholders during the Reconstruction of Alabama, 1867–1878.* Montgomery, Ala.: R. Bailey Publishers, 1991.

Bederman, Gail. *Manliness and Civilization: A Cultural History of Gender and Race in the United States, 1880–1917.* Chicago: University of Chicago Press, 1995.

Black, Daniel P. *Dismantling Black Manhood: An Historical and Literary Analysis of the Legacy of Slavery.* New York: Garland Publishing, 1997.

Blair, William, and William Pencak, eds. *Making and Remaking Pennsylvania's Civil War.* University Park: Pennsylvania State University Press, 2001.

Blassingame, John W. *Black New Orleans: 1860–1880.* Chicago: University of Chicago Press, 1973.

———. *The Slave Community: Plantation Life in the Antebellum South.* New York: Oxford University Press, 1972.

Blatt, Martin H., Thomas J. Brown, and Donald Yacovone, eds. *Hope and Glory: Essays on the Legacy of the Fifty-fourth Massachusetts Regiment.* Amherst: University of Massachusetts Press, 2001.

Blight, David W. *Frederick Douglass' Civil War: Keeping Faith in Jubilee.* Baton Rouge: Louisiana State University Press, 1989.

———. *Race and Reunion: The Civil War in American Memory.* Cambridge, Mass.: Belknap Press of Harvard University, 2001.

Brundage, W. Fitzhugh, ed. *Where These Memories Grow: History, Memory, and Southern Identity.* Chapel Hill: University of North Carolina Press, 2000.

Burton, Orville, and Robert C. McGrath Jr., eds. *Toward a New South? Studies in Post–Civil War Southern Communities.* Westport, Conn.: Greenwood Press, 1982.

Carnes, Mark C. *Secret Ritual and Manhood in Victorian America.* New Haven, Conn.: Yale University Press, 1989.

Cashin, Joan E., ed. *The War Was You and Me: Civilians in the American Civil War.* Princeton, N.J.: Princeton University Press, 2002.

Chused, Richard H. *Private Acts in Public Places: A Social History of Divorce in the Formative Era of American Family Law.* Philadelphia: University of Pennsylvania Press, 1994.

Clawson, Mary Ann. *Constructing Brotherhood: Class, Gender, and Fraternalism.* Princeton, N.J.: Princeton University Press, 1989.

Clinton, Catherine, and Nina Silber, eds. *Divided Houses: Gender and the Civil War.* New York: Oxford University Press, 1992.

Cohen, William. *At Freedom's Edge: Black Mobility and the Southern White Quest for Racial Control, 1861–1915.* Baton Rouge: Louisiana State University Press, 1991.

Cornish, Dudley Taylor. *The Sable Arm: Negro Troops in the Union Army, 1861–1865.* New York: Longmans, Green, 1956.

Coryell, Janet L., et al., eds. *Negotiating Boundaries of Southern Womanhood: Dealing with the Powers That Be.* Columbia: University of Missouri Press, 2000.

David, Paul A., et al., eds. *Reckoning with Slavery: A Critical Study in the Quantitative History of American Negro Slavery.* New York: Oxford University Press, 1976.

Davis, Lenwood G., and George Hill, comps. *Blacks in the Armed Forces, 1776–1983: A Bibliography.* Westport, Conn.: Greenwood Press, 1985.

Dean, Eric T. *Shook over Hell: Post-Traumatic Stress, Vietnam, and the Civil War.* Cambridge, Mass.: Harvard University Press, 1997.

Dearing, Mary R. *Veterans in Politics: The Story of the G.A.R.* Baton Rouge: Louisiana State University Press, 1952.

Doyle, Don. *New Men, New Cities, New South: Atlanta, Nashville, Charleston, Mobile, 1860–1910.* Chapel Hill: University of North Carolina Press, 1990.

Drago, Edmund L. *Black Politicians and Reconstruction in Georgia: A Splendid Failure.* Athens: University of Georgia Press, 1992.

Du Bois, W. E. Burghardt. *Black Reconstruction in America: An Essay toward a History of the Part Which Black Folk Played in the Attempt to Reconstruct Democracy in America, 1860–1880.* New York: Harcourt, Brace, 1935.

Dyer, Frederick H. *A Compendium of the War of the Rebellion.* Vols. 1–3. New York: Thomas Yoseloff, 1908.

Edwards, Laura F. *Gendered Strife and Confusion: The Political Culture of Reconstruction.* Urbana: University of Illinois Press, 1997.

Elkins, Stanley. *Slavery: A Problem in American Institutional and Intellectual Life.* Chicago: University of Chicago Press, 1959.

Farley, Reynolds. *Growth of the Black Population: A Study of Demographic Trends.* Chicago: Markham Publishing Company, 1971.

Foner, Eric. *Free Soil, Free Labor, Free Men: The Ideology of the Republican Party before the Civil War.* New York: Oxford University Press, 1970.

———. *Freedom's Lawmakers: A Directory of Black Officeholders during Reconstruction.* New York: Oxford University Press, 1993.

———. *Reconstruction: America's Unfinished Revolution, 1863–1877.* New York: Harper and Row, 1988.

Fowler, William M. *Under Two Flags: The American Navy in the Civil War.* New York: W. W. Norton, 1990.

Frankel, Noralee. *Freedom's Women: Black Women and Families in Civil War Era Mississippi.* Bloomington: Indiana University Press, 1999.

Franklin, John Hope. *George Washington Williams: A Biography.* Chicago: University of Chicago Press, 1985.

Fredrickson, George M. *The Black Image in the White Mind: The Debate on Afro-American Character and Destiny, 1817–1914.* New York: Harper and Row, 1971.

Gatewood, Willard B. *Aristocrats of Color: The Black Elite, 1880–1920.* Bloomington: University of Indiana Press, 1990.

Gawalt, Gerard W., ed. *The New High Priests: Lawyers in Post–Civil War America.* Westport, Conn.: Greenwood Press, 1984.

Geary, James W. *We Need Men: The Union Draft in the Civil War.* De Kalb: Northern Illinois University Press, 1991.

Genovese, Eugene D. *Roll, Jordan, Roll: The World the Slaves Made.* New York: Vintage Books, 1974.

Gerber, David A. *Black Ohio and the Color Line: 1860–1915.* Urbana: University of Illinois Press, 1976.

Gillis, John R. *For Better, for Worse: British Marriages, 1600 to the Present.* New York: Oxford University Press, 1985.

Glatthaar, Joseph T. *Forged in Battle: The Civil War Alliance of Black Soldiers and White Officers.* New York: Free Press, 1990.

Grossberg, Michael. *Governing the Hearth: Law and Family in Nineteenth-Century America.* Chapel Hill: University of North Carolina Press, 1985.

Gutman, Herbert G. *The Black Family in Slavery and Freedom, 1750–1925.* New York: Vintage Books, 1976.

Hamilton, Kenneth Marvin. *Black Towns and Profit: Promotion and Development in the Trans-Appalachian West, 1877–1915.* Urbana: University of Illinois Press, 1991.

Harris, William C. *The Day of the Carpetbagger: Republican Reconstruction in Mississippi.* Baton Rouge: Louisiana State University Press, 1979.

Harris, William H. *The Harder We Run: Black Workers since the Civil War.* New York: Oxford University Press, 1982.

Haskins, James. *Pinckney Benton Stewart Pinchback.* New York: Macmillan, 1973.

Herman, Janet Sharp. *The Pursuit of a Dream.* New York: Oxford University Press, 1981.

Higginbotham, Evelyn Brooks. *Righteous Discontent: The Women's Movement in the Black Baptist Church, 1880–1920.* Cambridge, Mass.: Harvard University Press, 1993.

Higgs, Robert. *Competition and Coercion: Blacks in the American Economy, 1865–1914.* Cambridge: Cambridge University Press, 1977.

Hine, Darlene Clark, and Earnestine Jenkins, eds. *A Question of Manhood: A Reader in U.S. Black Men's History and Masculinity.* 2 vols. Bloomington: University of Indiana Press, 1999–2001.

Hinrichs, Ernst, Eberhard Schmitt, and Rudolf Vierhaus, eds. *Vom Ancien Regime Zur Franzosischen Revolution.* Gottingen, Germany: Vandenhoeck and Rurprecht, 1978.

Hollandsworth, James G., Jr. *An Absolute Massacre: The New Orleans Race Riot of July 30, 1866.* Baton Rouge: Louisiana State University Press, 2001.

————. *The Louisiana Native Guards: The Black Military Experience during the Civil War.* Baton Rouge: Louisiana State University Press, 1995.

Holt, Thomas. *Black over White: Negro Political Leadership in South Carolina during Reconstruction.* Urbana: University of Illinois Press, 1977.

Horton, James Oliver, ed. *Free People of Color: Inside the African-American Community.* Washington, D.C.: Smithsonian Institution Press, 1993.

Horton, James Oliver, and Lois E. Horton. *Black Bostonians: Family Life and Community Struggle in the Antebellum North.* New York: Holmes and Meier, 1979.

Innes, Stephen, ed. *Work and Labor in Early America.* Chapel Hill: University of North Carolina Press, 1988.

Jones, Jacqueline. *Labor of Love, Labor of Sorrow: Black Women, Work, and the Family from Slavery to the Present*. New York: Basic Books, 1985.

Jones, Norrece T., Jr. *Born a Child of Freedom, Yet a Slave: Mechanisms of Control and Strategies of Resistance in Antebellum South Carolina*. Hanover, N.H.: University Press of New England, 1990.

Jordan, Ervin L., Jr. *Black Confederates and Afro-Yankees in Civil War Virginia*. Charlottesville: University of Virginia Press, 1995.

Kantrowitz, Stephen. *Ben Tillman and the Reconstruction of White Supremacy*. Chapel Hill: University of North Carolina Press, 2000.

Katzman, David M. *Before the Ghetto: Black Detroit in the Nineteenth Century*. Urbana: University of Illinois Press, 1973.

Kelley, Patrick J. *Creating a National Home: Building the Veterans' Welfare State*. Cambridge, Mass.: Harvard University Press, 1997.

Klingman, Peter. *Josiah Walls: Florida's Black Congressman of Reconstruction*. Gainesville: University Presses of Florida, 1976.

Koegel, Otto E. *Common Law Marriage and Its Development in the United States*. Washington, D.C.: John Byrne and Company, 1922.

Kremer, Gary L. *James Milton Turner and the Promise of America: The Public Life of a Post–Civil War Black Leader*. Columbia: University of Missouri Press, 1991.

Kusmer, Kenneth L. *A Ghetto Takes Shape: Black Cleveland, 1870–1930*. Urbana: University of Illinois Press, 1976.

Levine, Lawrence W. *Black Culture and Black Consciousness: Afro-American Folk Thought from Slavery to Freedom*. New York: Oxford University Press, 1977.

Link, William A. *The Paradox of Southern Progressivism, 1880–1930*. Chapel Hill: University of North Carolina Press, 1992.

Litwack, Leon F. *North of Slavery: The Negro in the Free States, 1790–1860*. Chicago: University of Chicago Press, 1961.

Litwack, Leon F., and August Meier, eds. *Black Leaders of the Nineteenth Century*. Urbana: University of Illinois, 1988.

Lofgren, Charles A. *The Plessy Case: A Legal Historical Interpretation*. New York: Oxford University Press, 1987.

Logan, Rayford W., and Michael R. Winston, eds. *Dictionary of American Negro Biography*. New York: W. W. Norton, 1982.

Logue, Larry M. *To Appomattox and Beyond: The Civil War Soldier in War and Peace*. Chicago: Ivan R. Dee, 1996.

Long, E. B., with Barbara Long. *The Civil War Day by Day: An Almanac, 1861–1865*. New York: Da Capo Press, 1971.

Lonn, Ella. *Desertion during the Civil War*. New York: Century Company, 1928.

McBride, David. *From TB to AIDS: Epidemics among Urban Blacks since 1900*. Albany: State University of New York Press, 1991.

McConnell, Stuart. *Glorious Contentment: The Grand Army of the Republic, 1865–1900*. Chapel Hill: University of North Carolina Press, 1992.

McMillen, Neil. *Dark Journey: Black Mississippians in the Age of Jim Crow.* Urbana: University of Illinois Press, 1989.

McPherson, James M. *Battle Cry of Freedom: The Civil War Era.* New York: Ballantine Books, 1988.

Meier, August. *Negro Thought in America, 1880–1915: Racial Ideologies in the Age of Booker T. Washington.* Ann Arbor: University of Michigan Press, 1963.

Miller, Edward A., Jr. *The Black Civil War Soldiers of Illinois: The Story of the Twenty-ninth U.S. Colored Infantry.* Columbia: University of South Carolina Press, 1998.

———. *Gullah Statesman: Robert Smalls from Slavery to Congress, 1839–1915.* Columbia: University of South Carolina Press, 1995.

Mintz, Steven, and Susan Kellogg. *Domestic Revolutions: A Social History of American Family Life.* New York: Free Press, 1988.

Mitchell, Reid. *The Vacant Chair: The Northern Soldier Leaves Home.* New York: Oxford University Press, 1993.

Montgomery, William E. *Under Their Own Vine and Fig Tree: The African American Church in the South, 1865–1900.* Baton Rouge: Louisiana State University Press, 1993.

Morgan, Lynda J. *Emancipation in Virginia's Tobacco Belt, 1850–1870.* Athens: University of Georgia Press, 1992.

Morris, Robert C. *Reading, 'Riting, and Reconstruction: The Education of Freedmen in the South, 1861–1870.* Chicago: University of Chicago Press, 1981.

Murdock, Eugene C. *One Million Men: The Civil War Draft in the North.* Westport, Conn.: Greenwood Press, 1980.

Ochs, Stephen J. *A Black Patriot and a White Priest: André Cailloux and Claude Paschal Maistre in Civil War New Orleans.* Baton Rouge: Louisiana State University Press, 2000.

Oubre, Claude F. *Forty Acres and a Mule: The Freedmen's Bureau and Black Land Ownership.* Baton Rouge: Louisiana State University Press, 1978.

Painter, Nell Irvin. *Exodusters: Black Migration to Kansas after Reconstruction.* New York: Alfred A. Knopf, 1977.

———. *Standing at Armageddon: The United States, 1877–1919.* New York: W. W. Norton, 1987.

Pleck, Elizabeth Hafkin. *Black Migration and Poverty: Boston, 1865–1900.* New York: Academic Press, 1979.

Rabinowitz, Howard N. *Race Relations in the Urban South, 1865–1890.* New York: Oxford University Press, 1978.

———, ed. *Southern Black Leaders of the Reconstruction Era.* Urbana: University of Illinois Press, 1982.

Rable, George C. *But There Was No Peace: The Role of Violence in the Politics of Reconstruction.* Athens: University of Illinois Press, 1984.

Ramold, Steven J. *Slaves, Sailors, Citizens: African Americans in the Union Navy.* De Kalb: Northern Illinois University Press, 2002.

Regosin, Elizabeth. *Freedom's Promise: Ex-Slave Families and Citizenship in the Age of Emancipation.* Charlottesville: University of Virginia Press, 2002.

Rose, Anne C. *Victorian America and the Civil War*. Cambridge: Cambridge University Press, 1992.

Rosenburg, R. B. *Living Monuments: Confederate Soldiers' Homes in the New South*. Chapel Hill: University of North Carolina Press, 1993.

Rotundo, E. Anthony. *American Manhood: Transformations in Masculinity from the Revolution to the Modern Era*. New York: Basic Books, 1993.

Salvatore, Nick. *We All Got History: The Memory Books of Amos Webber*. New York: Vintage Books, 1997.

Savage, Kirk. *Standing Soldiers, Kneeling Slaves: Race, War, and Monument in Nineteenth-Century America*. Princeton, N.J.: Princeton University Press, 1997.

Saville, Julie. *The Work of Reconstruction: From Slave to Wage Labor in South Carolina, 1860–1870*. Cambridge: Cambridge University Press, 1994.

Schubert, Frank N. *Buffalo Soldiers, Braves, and the Brass: The Story of Fort Robinson, Nebraska*. Shippensburg, Pa.: White Mane Publishing Company, 1993.

———. *On the Trail of the Buffalo Soldier: Biographies of African Americans in the U.S. Army, 1866–1917*. Wilmington, Del.: Scholarly Resources, 1995.

Schwalm, Leslie Ann. *A Hard Fight for We: Women's Transition from Slavery in South Carolina*. Urbana: University of Illinois Press, 1997.

Schweninger, Loren. *Black Property Owners in the South, 1790–1915*. Urbana: University of Illinois Press, 1990.

Severo, Richard, and Lewis Milford. *The Wages of War: When America's Soldiers Came Home from Valley Forge to Vietnam*. New York: Simon and Schuster, 1989.

Silber, Nina. *The Romance of Reunion: Northerners and the South, 1865–1900*. Chapel Hill: University of North Carolina Press, 1993.

Skocpol, Theda. *Protecting Soldiers and Mothers: The Political Origins of Social Policy in the United States*. Cambridge, Mass.: Belknap Press of Harvard University Press, 1992.

Stampp, Kenneth M. *The Peculiar Institution: Slavery in the Ante-bellum South*. New York: Knopf, 1956.

Steiner, Paul E. *Medical History of a Civil War Regiment: Disease in the Sixty-fifth United States Colored Infantry*. Clayton, Mo.: Institute of Civil War Studies, 1977.

Taylor, Joe Gray. *Louisiana Reconstructed: 1863–1877*. Baton Rouge: Louisiana State University Press, 1974.

Thernstrom, Stephan. *The Other Bostonians: Poverty and Progress in the American Metropolis, 1880–1970*. Cambridge, Mass.: Harvard University Press, 1973.

Trudeau, Noah Andre. *Like Men of War: Black Troops in the Civil War, 1862–1865*. Boston: Little, Brown, 1998.

Tunnell, Ted. *Crucible of Reconstruction: War, Radicalism and Race in Louisiana, 1862–1877*. Baton Rouge: Louisiana State University Press, 1984.

Ullman, Victor. *Martin R. Delany: The Beginnings of Black Nationalism*. Boston: Beacon Press, 1971.

Uya, Okon Edet. *From Slavery to Public Service: Robert Smalls, 1839–1915*. New York: Oxford University Press, 1971.

Valuska, David L. *The African American in the Union Navy: 1861–1865.* New York: Garland Publishing, 1993.

Vandal, Gilles. *The New Orleans Riot of 1866: Anatomy of a Tragedy.* Lafayette, La.: Center for Louisiana Studies, University of Southwestern Louisiana, 1983.

Vincent, Charles. *Black Legislators in Louisiana during Reconstruction.* Baton Rouge: Louisiana State University Press, 1976.

Walker, Clarence G. *A Rock in a Weary Land: The African Methodist Episcopal Church during the Civil War and Reconstruction, 1861–1881.* Baton Rouge: Louisiana State University Press, 1982.

Wang, Xi. *The Trial of Democracy: Black Suffrage and Northern Republicans, 1860–1910.* Athens: University of Georgia Press, 1997.

Washington, Versalle F. *Eagles on the Buttons: A Black Infantry Regiment in the Civil War.* Columbia: University of Missouri Press, 1999.

Watson, Harry L. *Liberty and Power: The Politics of Jacksonian America.* New York: Hill and Wang, 1990.

Weber, Gustavus A., and Laurence F. Schmeckebier. *The Veterans' Administration: Its History, Activities and Organization.* Washington, D.C.: Brookings Institution, 1934.

White, Deborah Gray. *Ar'n't I a Woman: Female Slaves in the Plantation South.* New York: W. W. Norton, 1985.

Wiley, Bell Irvin. *Life of Billy Yank: The Common Soldier of the Union.* Baton Rouge: Louisiana State University Press, 1952.

Williamson, Joel. *After Slavery: The Negro in South Carolina during Reconstruction, 1861–1877.* Chapel Hill: University of North Carolina Press, 1965.

———. *A Rage for Order: Black-White Relations in the American South since Emancipation.* New York: Oxford University Press, 1986.

Wright, George C. *Life behind a Veil: Blacks in Louisville, Kentucky, 1865–1930.* Baton Rouge: Louisiana State University Press, 1985.

Wyatt-Brown, Bertram. *Southern Honor: Ethics and Behavior in the Old South.* New York: Oxford University Press, 1982.

Yacovone, Donald. *A Voice of Thunder: A Black Soldier's Civil War.* Urbana: University of Illinois Press, 1997.

*Articles*

Abrams, Lynn. "Concubinage, Cohabitation and the Law: Class and Gender Relations in Nineteenth Century Germany." *Gender and History* 5 (Spring 1993): 81–100.

Aptheker, Herbert. "The Negro in the Union Navy." *Journal of Negro History* 32 (April 1947): 169–200.

Berlanstein, Lenard R. "Illegitimacy, Concubinage, and Proletarianization in a French Town, 1760–1914." *Journal of Family History* 5 (Winter 1980): 360–74.

Berlin, Ira. "Time, Space, and the Evolution of Afro-American Society on British North America." *American Historical Review* 85 (February 1980): 44–45.

Berlin, Ira, Steven F. Miller, and Leslie S. Rowland. "Afro-American Families in the Transition from Slavery to Freedom." *Radical History Review* 42 (1988): 89–121.

# Bibliography

Black, Andrew K. "In the Service of the United States: Comparative Mortality among African-American and White Troops in the Union Army." *Journal of Negro History* 79 (Fall 1994): 317–33.

Blassingame, John M. "The Union Army as an Educational Institution for Negroes, 1861–1875." *Journal of Negro Education* 34 (Spring 1965): 152–59.

Blight, David W. "'For Something beyond the Battlefield': Frederick Douglass and the Struggle for the Memory of the Civil War." *Journal of American History* 75 (March 1989): 1156–78.

Bunch, Lonnie G. "Allensworth: The Life, Death, and Rebirth of an All-Black Community." *Californian* 5 (November/December 1987): 26–33.

Burgin, William G. "Concubinage: Revolutionary Response or Last Resort? The Attitudes of Town Authorities and of Couples Rejected in Their Marriage Suits in Nineteenth Century Germany." *Consortium on Revolutionary Europe: 1750–1850: Proceedings*. Tallahassee, Fla.: Institute on Napoleon and the French Revolution, 1983.

Burnham, Margaret A. "An Impossible Marriage: Slave Law and Family Law." *Law and Inequality* 5 (July 1987): 187–225.

Christian, Marcus B. 'The Theory of the Poisoning of Oscar J. Dunn." *Phylon* 6 (1945): 254–66.

Clark, James C. "John Wallace and the Writing of Reconstruction History." *Florida Historical Quarterly* 67 (April 1989): 409–27.

Clawson, Mary Ann. "Fraternal Orders and Class Formation in the Nineteenth Century United States." *Comparative Studies in Society and History* 27 (October 1985): 672–95.

Cornelius, Janet. "'We Slipped and Learned to Read': Slave Accounts of the Literacy Process, 1830–1865." *Phylon* 44 (September 1983): 171–86.

Davies, Wallace E. "The Problem of Race Segregation in the Grand Army of the Republic." *Journal of Southern History* 13 (August 1947): 354–72.

Dillard, Tom W. "Isaac T. Gillam: Black Pulaski Countian." *Pulaski County Historical Review* 24 (1976): 6–11.

Drago, Edmund L. "The Black Household in Dougherty County, Georgia, 1870–1900." *Prologue* 14 (Summer 1982): 81–88.

Edwards, Laura F. "'The Marriage Covenant Is at the Foundation of All Our Rights': The Politics of Slave Marriage in North Carolina after Emancipation." *Law and History Review* 14 (Spring 1996): 81–124.

Fishel, Leslie H. "Northern Prejudice and Negro Suffrage, 1865–1870." *Journal of Negro History* 39 (January 1954): 8–26.

Furstenberg, Frank F., Jr., Theodore Hershberg, and John Modell. "The Origins of the Female-Headed Black Family: The Impact of the Urban Experience." *Journal of Interdisciplinary History* 6 (Autumn 1975): 211–33.

Grosz, Agnes Smith. "The Political Career of Pinckney Benton Stewart Pinchback." *Louisiana Historical Quarterly* 27 (1944): 527–612.

Gutman, Herbert G. "Persistent Myths about the Afro-American Family." *Journal of Interdisciplinary History* 6 (Autumn 1972): 181–210.

Hahn, Steven. "'Extravagant Expectations' of Freedom: Rumour, Political Struggle, and the Christmas Insurrection Scare of 1865 in the American South." *Past and Present* 157 (November 1997): 122–58.

Hardwick, Kevin R. "'Your Old Father Abe Lincoln Is Dead and Damned': Black Soldiers and the Memphis Riot of 1866." *Journal of Social History* 27 (Fall 1993): 109–28.

Harley, Sharon. "For the Good of Family and Race: Gender, Work, and Domestic Roles in the Black Community, 1880–1930." *Signs* 15 (Winter 1990): 336–49.

Harris, William. "Work and the Family in Black Atlanta." *Journal of Social History* 9 (Spring 1976): 319–30.

Horton, James Oliver. "Freedom's Yoke: Gender Conventions among Antebellum Free Blacks." *Feminist Studies* 12 (Spring 1986): 51–74.

Lammermeier, Paul. "The Urban Black Family of the Nineteenth Century: A Study of Black Family Structure in the Ohio Valley, 1850–1880." *Journal of Marriage and Family* 35 (August 1973): 440–56.

Langellier, John Phillip. "Chaplain Allen Allensworth and the 24th Infantry, 1886–1906." *Smoke Signal* (Fall 1990): 192–96.

Lempel, Leonard. "African American Settlements in the Daytona Beach Area." *Annual Proceedings of the Florida Conference of Historians* 1 (1993): 108–24.

Levstick, Frank R. "William H. Holland: Black Soldier, Politician, and Educator." *Negro History Bulletin* 36 (May 1973): 110–11.

Lovett, Bobby L. "Memphis Riots: White Reaction to Blacks in Memphis, May 1865–July 1866." *Tennessee Historical Quarterly* 38 (Spring 1979): 9–33.

Manfra, Jo Ann, and Robert R. Dykstra. "Serial Marriage and the Origins of the Black Stepfamily: The Rowanty Evidence." *Journal of American History* 72 (June 1985): 18–44.

McClintock, Megan J. "Civil War Pensions and the Reconstruction of Union Families." *Journal of American History* 83 (September 1996): 456–79.

McConnell, Roland C. "Selected African American Musicians and Bands in the United States Military from Colonial Times through the Civil War." *Journal of the Afro-American Historical and Genealogical Society* 12 (Spring and Summer 1991): 11–15.

Metzer, Jacob. "The Records of the U.S. Colored Troops as a Historical Resource: An Exploratory Examination." *Historical Methods* 14 (Summer 1981): 123–32.

Mitchell, Michelle. "'The Black Man's Burden': African Americans, Imperialism, and Notions of Racial Manhood: 1890–1910." *International Review of Social History* 44 (1999 Supplement): 77–99.

Moore, James T. "Black Militancy in Readjuster Virginia, 1879–1883." *Journal of Southern History* 41 (May 1975): 167–86.

Ng, Kenneth, and Nancy Virts, "The Value of Freedom." *Journal of Economic History* 49 (December 1989): 956–65.

Rankin, David C. "The Origins of Black Leadership in New Orleans during Reconstruction." *Journal of Southern History* 40 (August 1974): 417–40.

Reidy, Joseph P. "Black Men in Navy Blue during the Civil War." *Prologue* 33 (Fall 2001): 154–67.

Ryan, James Gilbert. "The Memphis Riot of 1866: Terror in the Black Community during Reconstruction." *Journal of Negro History* 62 (July 1977): 243–57.

Semonche, John E. "Common-Law Marriage in North Carolina: A Study in Legal History." *American Journal of Legal History* 9 (October 1965): 320–49.

Skocpol, Theda. "America's First Social Security System: The Expansion of Benefits for Civil War Veterans." *Political Science Quarterly* 108 (Spring 1993): 85–116.

Smallwood, James. "Emancipation and the Black Family: A Case Study." *Social Science Quarterly* 57 (March 1977): 849–57.

Stark, William C. "Forgotten Heroes: Black Recipients of the United States Congressional Medal of Honor in the American Civil War, 1863–1865, Parts I–III." *Lincoln Herald* 87 (Winter 1985): 122–30, 88 (Spring 1986): 511, (Summer 1986): 70–80, (Winter 1986): 178–79.

Thurber, Evangeline. "The 1890 Census Records of the Veterans of the Union Army." *National Genealogical Society Quarterly* 34 (March 1946): 7–9.

Tolnay, Stewart E. "Black Family Formation and Tenancy in the Farm South." *American Journal of Sociology* 90 (September 1984): 305–25.

Vandal, Gilles. "The Origins of the New Orleans Riot of 1866, Revisited." *Louisiana History* 22 (Spring 1981): 139–65.

Vinovskis, Maris. "Have Social Historians Lost the Civil War? Some Preliminary Demographic Speculations." *Journal of American History* 76 (June 1989): 34–58.

Walker, Altina L. "Community, Class and Race in the Memphis Riot of 1866." *Journal of Social History* 18 (Winter 1984): 233–46.

Wallace, Maurice. "'Are We Men? Prince Hall, Martin Delany, and the Masculine Ideal in Black Freemasonry, 1775–1865." *American Literary History* 9 (Fall 1997): 396–424.

*Theses and Dissertations*

Cooke, Michael Anthony. "The Health of Blacks during Reconstruction, 1862–1879." Ph.D. diss., University of Maryland, College Park, 1983.

Lee, Changsin. "Beyond Sorrowful Pride: Civil War Pensions and War Widowhood." Ph.D. diss., Ohio University, 1997.

Silver, David Mark. "In the Eye of the Storm: Isaiah T. Montgomery and the Plight of Black Mississippians, 1847–1924." Honor's thesis, Amherst College, 1993.

Skarstedt, Vance Robert. "The Confederate Veteran Movement and National Reunification." Ph.D. diss., Florida State University, 1993.

Suliman, Sirag Eldin Hassan. "Estimation of Levels and Trends of the U.S. Adult Black Mortality during the Period 1870–1900." Ph.D. diss., University of Pennsylvania, 1983.

# Index

South, African-American soldiers in, 24, 46

Southern Branch Home, 139, 140

Southern Democrats, Reconstruction and, 85

*Southern History of the War* (Pollard), 174

*Southern Rebellion, The* (Crafts), 178

Spanish-American War, 94, 233n5

Special examinations, 128, 130

Spencer, John, 156

Spiers, W. W., 168

Spight, Tuck, 176–77

Spikes, James, 133

"Spirit of Freedom" sculpture, 200

Springsteen, Diannah, 116

Stacke, Henry, 179

Stampp, Kenneth, 1–2

Stanton, Cathy, 199

Stanton, Edwin M., 28

State Colored Men's Convention, 68

State Convention of Colored Men in Kentucky, 91

State University of Kentucky, 91

Steele, Elmo, 20

Stephens, Peter, 112

Stephens, Thomasine, 112

Stephenson, John H. A., 117

Stereotypes, racist, 178

Stevens, Thaddeus, 171, 172

"Still Marching to the Grave," 61

Subordination, 32, 34, 60, 145, 159, 176, 241n23

Suffrage, 152, 225n34

  African-American, 70, 76, 188

  African-American male, 5, 49, 50, 67, 68, 69, 71, 72, 73, 78

  battle for, 67, 68, 73, 74–75, 77

  cartoon supporting, 70

  citizenship and, 3

  claiming, 68, 173

  equality and, 159

  interest in, 69–70

  manhood and, 5, 50, 68–69, 159

  military service and, 82–83

  movement, 68, 183

  preserving, 188

  property requirements for, 5

  women's demand for, 3

Summers, Elsie, 106

Sumner, Charles, 171, 172, 173

Surnames, changing, 100, 101, 124

Survival rates, African-American veteran, 206 (table)

Survivors, veterans and, 209 (table)

Sweeny, John, 17

Sweetser, A. H., 131

Tappan, Franklin D., 144, 145

Taylor, Henry, 55, 168

Temperance campaign, 93

Temple, Mary Jane, 117

Tensas Parish, 83

Thibaut, A. L., 71

Thirteenth Amendment, 28, 99

Thomas, L., 101

Thomas, Lorenzo, 19

Thomas, Nancy, 135

Thompson, John Means, 101

Thurston, Lloyd, 131

"Time, the Great Problem Solver," 60

Townsend, Charles G., 107

Townshend, James, 80

Tremont Temple, 161

Trotter, James Monroe, 1, 9, 48

Trotter, William Monroe, 1, 161

Trowbridge, T. W., 30

Truman, Harry S., 197

Tuberculosis, 55, 56

Turner, Henry McNeal, 84, 85, 93

Turner, James Milton, 74, 83, 224n20

Turner, Jerry, 108

Twelfth Baptist Church, 180

Twentieth-Century Baptist Association, 90

Twiggs, H. D., 175

Ullman, Daniel, 97–98

Uncle Army Jack, 176–77

Unemployment, 38, 140

Union army

  African-Americans in, 11, 13, 21

  equality in, 143

  transition out of, 23

  white Southerners in, 237n25